SunWatch

SunWatch

Fort Ancient Development in the Mississippian World

ROBERT A. COOK

THE UNIVERSITY OF ALABAMA PRESS
Tuscaloosa

Manufactured in the United States of America

Typeface: AGaramond

∞

The paper on which this book is printed meets the minimum requirements of American National Standard for Information Sciences-Permanence of Paper for Printed Library Materials, ANSI Z39.48-1984.

Library of Congress Cataloging-in-Publication Data

Cook, Robert A. (Robert Allen), 1970–
Sunwatch : Fort Ancient development in the Mississippian world / Robert A. Cook.
p. cm.
Includes bibliographical references and index.
ISBN-13: 978-0-8173-1590-0 (cloth : alk. paper)
ISBN-10: 0-8173-1590-X
ISBN-13: 978-0-8173-5458-9 (pbk. : alk. paper)
ISBN-10: 0-8173-5458-1
1. Sunwatch Site (Dayton, Ohio) 2. Fort Ancient culture—Ohio River Valley. 3. Mississippian culture—Ohio River Valley. 4. Social archaeology—Ohio River Valley. 5. Ohio River Valley—Antiquities. I. Title.
E99.F67C66 2008
973.1′73—dc22

2007016106

For Andrea

Contents

Illustrations

Figures

Tables

Acknowledgments

This project would not have been possible without financial support from the Dayton Society of Natural History (DSNH) (Anthropology Department), Michigan State University (Department of Anthropology, College of Social Science, and Graduate School), the Ohio Archaeological Council, and Ohio State University (Anthropology Department, Newark campus).

Two individuals were instrumental in very different ways in the genesis and development of this project. I became deeply interested in the SunWatch site a decade ago while working as the site anthropologist under the direction of J. Heilman, whose passion for the site is truly infectious. I was struck by J's vivid interpretation of the SunWatch villagers—and Fort Ancient peoples more generally—as "country cousins" of Mississippian peoples. After intense study in Mississippian archaeology under the tutelage of Lynne Goldstein, I developed a way to examine such a claim. Lynne and J. have provided just the right balance of criticism and praise over the years. Their support of my research efforts is greatly appreciated.

Several people associated with the Dayton Society of Natural History and SunWatch were invaluable to the completion of this project. Lynn Simonelli offered complete support from beginning to end in too many ways to list. William Kennedy has also been very supportive, particularly with GIS questions and the improvement of several figures. Andrew Sawyer assisted with mapping a stockade line and provided access to artifacts currently on exhibit at SunWatch. Mark Meister allowed access to DSNH collections and kindly encouraged development of the project. The DSNH American Indian Advisory Committee provided access to burials for AMS dating of two very important individuals. Mike Shaw reorganized the entire artifact assemblage, ensuring accuracy of distributional data.

Many people shared primary data: Sarah Evans-Eargle (mortuary data), Theodore Sunderhaus (pottery), James Roberston (chipped stone from features excavated between 1971 and 1977), Lynn Simonelli and William Kennedy (bone and shell artifacts), John Nass (types and volumes for most features), and Orrin Shane (seasonality data).

Several individuals helped improve earlier versions of the manuscript. Two anonymous reviewers for the University of Alabama Press helped considerably in shaping the final product. The first reviewer provided very detailed and constructive comments on two versions of the manuscript. This individual expended a tremendous effort, greatly improving many details of the book. The second reviewer also made very useful comments and was particularly helpful in streamlining my graphic presentations. In addition, discussions with Lynne Goldstein, J. Heilman, William Lovis, Penelope Drooker, Gwynn Henderson, David Pollack, Cheryl Munson, Lynne Sullivan, Lynn Simonelli, William Kennedy, and Kevin Nolan have improved various aspects of my arguments. Small portions of chapters 3 and 4 have appeared previously and are reprinted by permission from *American Antiquity* 72(3):439–460.

Several individuals affiliated with or recommended by The University of Alabama Press were instrumental. Robin DuBlanch improved much of my prose and greatly improved the layout of the tables. Bonnie McLaughlin did an excellent job preparing the index.

Most important has been the unending support of Andrea Cook, my wife and closest friend, to whom I dedicate this work, which has been as much a part of her life as it has been of mine.

SunWatch

1

To Be Mississippian or Not to Be Mississippian?

This study examines whether or not Mississippians influenced the development of Fort Ancient societies (ca. A.D. 1000–1650), the last prehistoric "culture" to inhabit the Middle Ohio valley (Figure 1.1, Figure 1.2). It has long been known that Fort Ancient assemblages contain a variety of Mississippian characteristics (Griffin 1943:257–260). The increase over time in the occurrence of Mississippian-style artifacts at Fort Ancient sites has also been recognized (Pollack and Henderson 1992:289, 293). However, the social processes associated with the adoption of these items have not been specifically investigated. Despite earlier suggestions that Mississippian migrations contributed heavily to the development of Fort Ancient societies (Griffin 1943:257–260; Prufer and Shane 1970:258–262), more recent studies have downplayed this issue (Pollack and Henderson 1992:282, 2000; Henderson 1998:566). The key point of recent conclusions hinges on whether Fort Ancient societies were ranked in terms of clearly identifiable elites and settlement hierarchies akin to many Mississippian cases. The finding that ranking is absent among Fort Ancient societies has been used to conclude that Mississippians did not significantly influence Fort Ancient development (Pollack and Henderson 1992, 2000).

I follow a different approach to assessing the development of Fort Ancient in relation to its Mississippian neighbors, one oriented away from typological models and spatial-temporal frameworks designed for other purposes (e.g., phases) (Dunnell 1971; Essenpreis 1978; Hart and Brumbach 2003). I suggest that classifying Fort Ancient and Mississippian societies into social types and overemphasizing regional differences limits examination of the evolutionary consequences of the interactions between them. The problem of the usual approach is that it establishes that Fort Ancient societies are different from Mississippian before examining ways in which they are similar. While social typologies can be useful for other ends, they are not useful for examining culture change, particularly with respect to interregional interaction. Alternatively, a nontypological or processual approach is better suited for this purpose as it breaks down this rigid distinction to facilitate the examination of a broader spectrum of possibilities situated between social types.

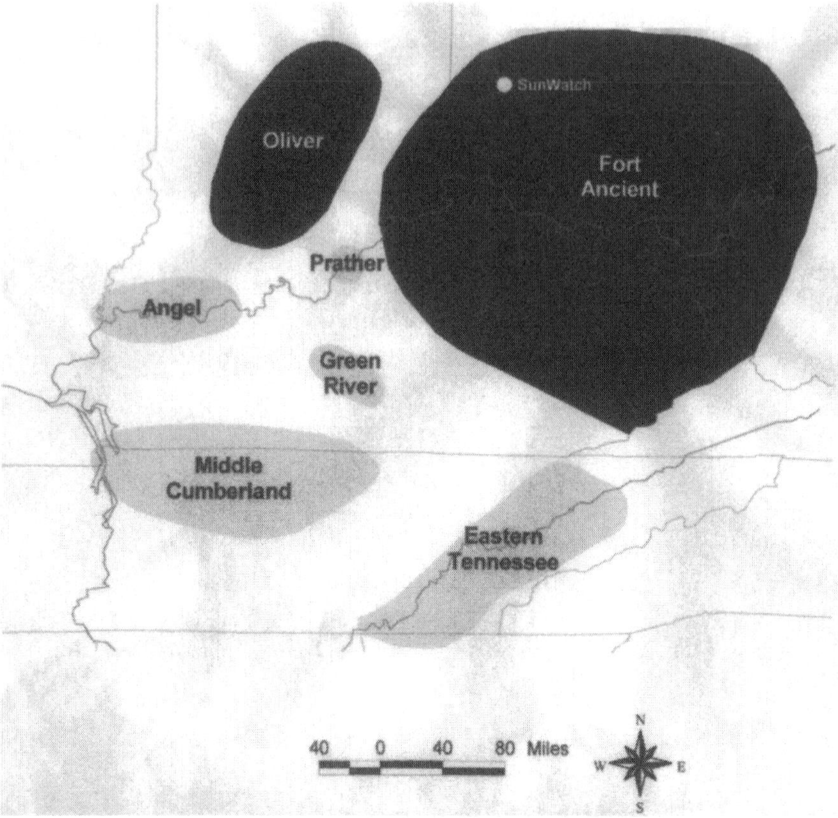

Figure 1.1. Location of Fort Ancient and neighboring Upper Mississippian (black) and Middle Mississippian (gray) cultures (ca. A.D. 1200–1400). (Sources: Drooker 1997:Figure 4.2; Green and Munson 1978; Henderson 1992b:Figure 1.1; Munson and McCullough 2004:Figure 6; Pollack 2004:Figure 1.2; Redmond and McCullough 2000:Figure 24.20; Schroedl 1998: Figure 4.1.)

This investigation of the development of Fort Ancient social structure with respect to Mississippian interaction utilizes a theoretical framework that accommodates broader and narrower scales than have been previously examined. Key influence was drawn from the work of Chang (1958:324), who stated: "[O]ne must look at archeological sites as local social groups instead of as cultures or phases. Cultures are fluctuant, but social groups are clear-cut. Therefore, I suggest that it should be the archaeologist's first duty to delimit local social groups such as households, communities, and aggregates, rather than to identify archeological regions and areas by time-spacing material traits, since cultural traits are meaningless unless described in their social context." Follow-

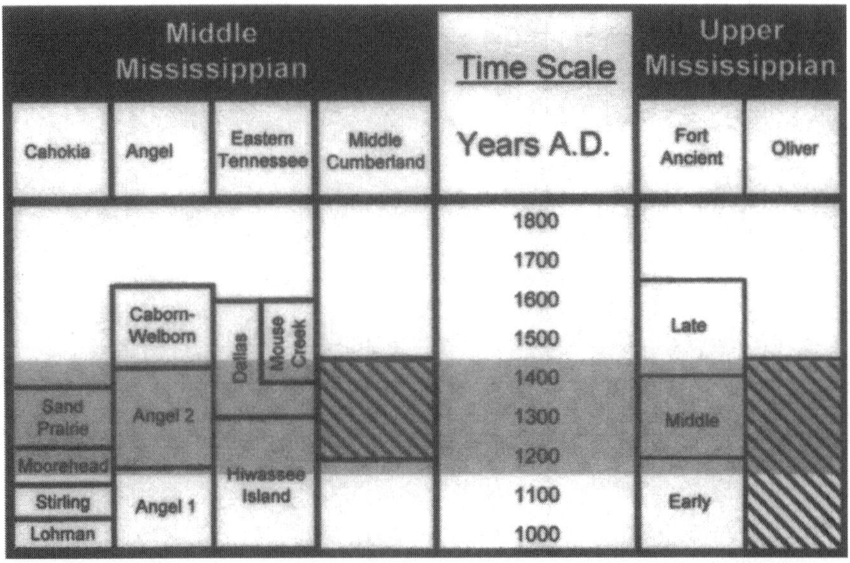

Figure 1.2. Established chronologies for culture historical units located within the study area. The shaded area represents the general time range for the SunWatch occupation(s) (see Figure 4.1.) (Sources: Ferguson 1972:38–40; Henderson et al. 1992: 255–278; Hilgeman 2000:324–332; Milner 1998:Figure 1.7; Sullivan 1995:100).

ing this lead, the study focuses on small social units as a starting point for examining the importance of Mississippian characteristics present in Fort Ancient societies, considering in particular leadership development. This introductory chapter sets the stage for reconsidering the Mississippian dimensions of Fort Ancient societies, beginning with a description of the theoretical orientation and an introduction to the SunWatch site, the main case study used to investigate the problem.

Broadening the Perspective

Early approaches attempting to identify culture process focused on delineating the internal workings of social systems, with later endeavors moving toward inclusion of external influences (Crumley 1979). Peripheries are now seen as particularly active loci of social change (Lightfoot and Martinez 1995; Rice 1998; Schortman and Urban 1987, 1998; Stein 2002). In contrast to core/periphery frameworks, which have been applied to nonstate societies, with questionable conclusions (Lightfoot and Martinez 1995), peer polity interaction models are more appropriate for investigating the development of less complex societies (Brown et al. 1990; Renfrew 1986). This growing body of theory is rooted in concepts of interregional symbiosis (Flannery 1968; Sanders 1956). Studies utilizing this framework have examined societies ranging from state to tribal levels of social organization and have included both Mississippian (Brown et al. 1990) and Fort Ancient (Drooker 1997) groups. In general, the approach was developed to address interregional interaction and has often been so applied (Renfrew 1986).

The basic tenet common to peer polity or coevolving interaction models is that one cannot look to the development of a given polity in isolation; separate polities develop simultaneously (Renfrew 1986; Schortman and Urban 1998). A "polity" is defined as "the highest order sociopolitical unit in the region in question" (Renfrew 1986:2). Key components of this theory are drawn largely from the work of Renfrew.

Several expectations can be derived regarding the outcome of peer polity interactions and sociopolitical change. Fundamentally, the expectation is that groups change together, and that innovations cannot be attributed to a single locus. Competition, including warfare and emulation, is common, as is increased social complexity of the less complex partner. Social interaction between neighboring polities should result in similarities at highly visible levels (Renfrew 1986). The causal role of peer polity interaction can be hypothesized if there is evidence of contact prior to the changes in question as well as some idea why interaction can be seen to have had a role in facilitating the observed change (7).

Peer polity interaction specifically focuses on the development of social structures such as political institutions, systems of specialized ritual and nonverbal communication, and ethnic groups and language (Renfrew 1986:1). Peer polities should share many structural homologies, including similarities in site layout, indicative of similarities in social organization (4–5). New institutional features form to increase production, and societies become more complex. "In a region with peer polities which are not highly organized internally, but which show strong interactions both symbolically and materially, we predict transformations in these polities associated with the intensification of production and the further development of hierarchical structures for the exercise of power" (8). Furthermore, emergent elites will often adopt foreign ideologies and associated materials "in an effort to distinguish themselves from those they would rule while proclaiming a link with distant, high-prestige interaction partners" (Schortman and Urban 1998:111).

My use of the peer polity concept is distinct from other applications with respect to what is considered to constitute "peers," requiring an expansion of the original concept. Technically, the most extreme versions of Mississippian and Fort Ancient societies are not peers, as chiefdoms and tribes (general types associated with these respective societies [see Chapter 2]) contain fundamentally different polities. However, this investigation is a study not of types but of variability and interaction at smaller spatial scales. In Chapter 2 we learn that there are exceptions to the ranked Mississippian model. These cases must be considered closely, particularly concerning interactions in "frontier" settings. This raises the question: What types of Middle Mississippian communities are most appropriate to compare with Fort Ancient villages? I suggest the most logical place to begin is with those types of Middle Mississippian sites that would have been in closest proximity to Fort Ancient ones. In the Mississippian settlement system, these would be smaller villages. While admittedly these Mississippian communities were often part of settlement hierarchies, some recent studies support a view of little control over smaller sites in the hierarchy (e.g., Muller 1997:286). This would place them on more equal footing with non-Mississippian neighbors. For these reasons, I refer to my use of the peer polity concept as the "periphery peer" model (Figure 1.3).

Village design characteristics are often highly visible and, hence, would have been a very recognizable part of daily life. They are in effect "written" on the ground and, as a result, would have been routinely seen by village residents and visitors. At the largest scale, the main focus is on examining whether leadership and ritual precincts in Fort Ancient villages are similar to those found in Mississippian villages. The rise and fall of Mississippian elites has been repeatedly defined as a system of status validation best characterized in terms of peer interaction (e.g., Brown et al. 1990), often marked in terms of site structure (Benchley 1970; Hall 1991). Can we include a place in this interaction sphere for Fort Ancient leaders and the general structure of their villages? If a form of leadership exists in Fort Ancient villages that fits within the known range of leadership in Mississippian villages, the key question then becomes: Did Fort Ancient villages and leadership structure form in relation to interactions with Mississippian peoples? In other words, did they coevolve?

Studies of intersocietal interaction have begun addressing the role of material culture. Researchers have commonly noted that highly visible and nonutilitarian items are the most frequent types of objects signifying ethnic affiliation in such instances (e.g., Gibbon 1982, 1995; Wobst 1977). Schortman and Urban (1987) build on these ideas by noting the importance of key artifacts that signal ethnicity in interaction (diacritics), stressing that these items specifically pave the way for interregional interaction. These interactions may be between only a few people in higher-level positions in their respective societies. Despite the few people involved, however, the consequences may be significant, leading to larger social changes. These changes need not be acculturative in the strict sense; rather, they often result in the increased complexity of the less complex

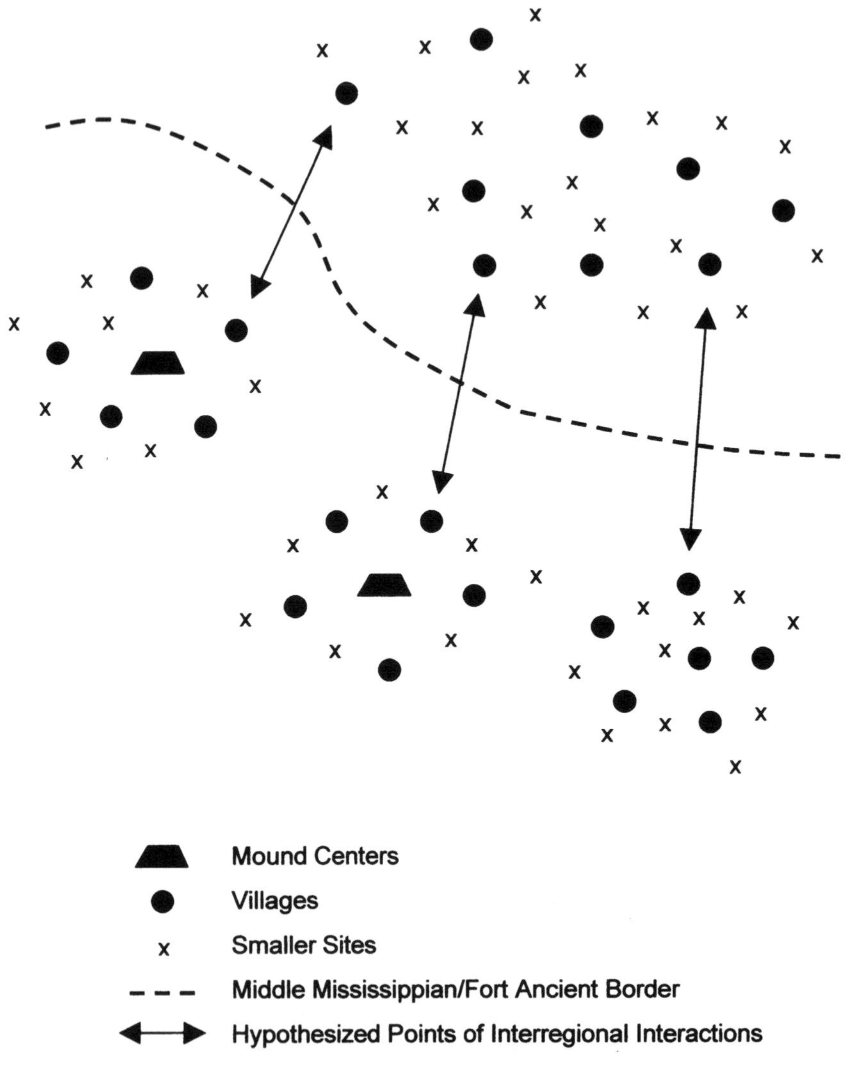

Figure 1.3. Generalized view of the Middle Mississippian/Fort Ancient boundary and the "periphery peer" model of village interaction.

group. A corollary to this finding pertains to the potential significance of a few "exotic" artifacts that may be present in a given archaeological assemblage: "Rather than lamenting the 'noise' commonly found in the material culture at the margins of social units, we should take advantage of this ambiguity in considering the implications of cross-cutting social networks and the creolization of cultural constructs" (Lightfoot and Martinez 1995:488).

Narrowing the Perspective

The smaller scale of the investigation focuses on the dynamics between households and larger social groups in a village setting. The village was selected as the unit of analysis as it is the largest social arena known to exist for Fort Ancient communities. Furthermore, the social structures of autonomous farming villages are well known from ethnographic studies, which provide useful analogues from which to draw behavioral inferences.

Village-Level Kin Groups

A literature review of autonomous villages with particular attention to deriving models for archaeological interpretation revealed three forms: unplanned villages, planned villages, and segmented villages (Chang 1958:306–307). Unplanned villages lack formal structure. Planned villages are usually small groups of a few independent houses arranged according to a preconceived plan. They are often circular in form with a central plaza, which sometimes contain a men's house or chiefly residence. Segmented villages contain lineages arranged in localized groups forming clusters of households within the community. If a village contains more than one lineage, one is usually of greater political importance. Within lineage segments, households may or may not be arranged according to a preconceived plan. Segments sometimes contain their own plaza, men's house, or other special buildings. Ninety-four percent of the ethnographic cases of segmented villages included in the sample contained two or more lineages, each being localized in one segment of the community (Chang 1958:306–307).

Keesing (1975:Figures 16 and 17) differentiates segmented villages into two types: Type III and Type IV. Both of these village patterns consist of several descent groups, usually in distinct "wards," the distinction being whether or not the descent groups have segments in other villages (Type III does not and Type IV does). As a result of this distinction, Type III villages generally lack strong ties to other communities, while Type IV villages have strong kinship ties with other villages (42–43). An example of this pattern would be for similar clans to be located in several communities in the Type IV case but not in the Type III one.

Evolution of Village-Level Political Complexity

Social evolution has been examined from one of two perspectives: typological and processual (Upham 1990). The typological approach assumes that all human groups move through the same basic social stages, each being composed of key social and economic attributes (e.g., Johnson and Earle 2000:32–37; Service 1962). In contrast, processual approaches focus on the development of institutions and covarying sets of behavior, emphasizing that changes may occur at different rates in different subsystems. The processual approach is better able to identify the range of variation present in a given society rather than forcing it into a specific type (Upham 1990; Yoffee 1993, 2005:20–21). This approach is more conducive to examining specific forces of change.

However, societal types serve a useful purpose in much the same way that categories such as "fish," "amphibian," "reptile," and "mammal" aid paleontological investigations of biological evolution. Archaeologists would find it difficult to study social change if all societies were simply lumped into one group. Types are useful for ethnological purposes, and societies throughout the world at points of relative stasis do appear to be quite similar; the periods of transition are the most unique (e.g., Marcus and Flannery 1996:245; Spencer 1997). The usefulness of each approach has led many contemporary researchers to integrate both type and process perspectives, depending on the questions being asked. The present study focuses on process, as it seeks to delimit small-scale social changes and the development of groups that may well fall somewhere between a "tribe" and "chiefdom" on the continuum of social complexity. (See Chapter 2 for definitions of these social types.)

Johnson and Earle's (2000:32–37) typological evolutionary scheme, based on changes in residential unit size and socioeconomic organization, has been applied to several cases of emerging social complexity, including Fort Ancient (Pollack and Henderson 2000). The model posits that scattered lineages of related households (25–35 people) aggregated into local groups (100–200 people) during the Middle Fort Ancient period (A.D. 1200–1400) (Pollack and Henderson 2000). Based on Johnson and Earle's (2000:32–37) model, a number of factors could have precipitated this development, including food storage or defense. Communities often form a politically and ritually integrated group, although many religious and ceremonial functions in multilineage communities continue to center around separate residential units. Several households often share activity areas, and segmentation of social groups is continuous (33). The group usually has a headman, but it typically fragments on a seasonal basis into its constituent kin groupings. Also, internal disputes can often lead to fragmentation, particularly in the context of growing communities. Relationships between communities are often important for security, as warfare is common, and such relationships are contracted on an individual family basis. Ceremonialism is important for publicly defining groups and these interrelationships. Initially, resources are held by each kin group, although the group may become more centralized under a charismatic leader as population increases (33).

Lineages and households that compose them are the key building blocks of human societies, and they are particularly important in middle-range social groups. As a result, they have factored heavily into theories of social evolution. Larger villages contain complex social arrangements whereby lineages are increasingly controlled by an individual authority. Autonomous villages are fundamentally a collection of independent lineages. Differentiating lineages is important in villages containing several independent groups. Land ownership becomes marked when more than one lineage is present and may become more important as social stress increases within expanding villages.

It has long been recognized that societies and communities become more complex as smaller social groups develop into larger ones. Larger groups of people require more formal systems of control, as mobility is not as regular an option (Kelly 1989:58), and these structures change as scalar thresholds are reached (Johnson 1982). A critical change happens when it becomes necessary to integrate formerly separate social units. New integrative institutions often form in villages by promotion from the original autonomous units, and one lineage usually becomes dominant (Flannery 1972:402; Johnson and Earle 2000:35; Knight 1990). Whether this asymmetry evolves into social rank or stratification, however, is another question. Only in some cases were conditions present to foster such a development (Flannery 1972:414; Knight 1990).

Integrating Scales through Practice

Thus far, theoretical expectations regarding basic social divisions in villages have been outlined. However, as the problem is a dynamic one involving the examination of change in one community, relationships between corporate households need to be explored. Practice theory is a useful approach for this purpose as it focuses on the interdigitation of larger and smaller scale contexts, facilitating the analysis of change as a result of individuals interfacing with social structures (Bourdieu 1977; Giddens 1984). To understand larger processes associated with social change, smaller contexts need to be examined, as the relationship between the two is dialectic (Giddens 1984).

Recent archaeological applications of practice theory emphasize social differences between remains of daily, repetitive tasks such as trash disposal and food preparation and larger scales such as site structures. This approach is particularly useful for contact situations (Lightfoot et al. 1998). Larger public contexts such as those exhibited by the overall structure of a site tend to be consistent and controlled by the more dominant group if more than one group is present. Smaller contexts such as households exhibit more variation indicative of histories of these smaller social groups (Lightfoot et al. 1998).

Political power is associated with control of resources or organizational aspects of society. According to Giddens (1984:258), power is generated through two structures of domination: ones involving allocative resources and those using authoritative resources. Allocative resources include materials and means of production, whereas authoritative resources involve organizational aspects of human beings and time. Many evolutionary models emphasize allocative resources when authoritative resources are just as crucial, as they are essential to the successful development of material resources: "allocative resources cannot be developed without the transmutation of authoritative resources" (260). The combination of both is needed.

This framework has been used to examine the emergence of elites in Mississippian society (Smith 1992). The role of solar observatories in Mississippian societies had long been explained as emerging for managerial purposes to facilitate better scheduling of crop planting during times of economic stress (e.g., Peebles and Kus 1977). However, solar observatories (a.k.a. woodhenges) also served as storage containers for the solar calendar, signifying the esoteric knowledge of the elite (Smith 1992). Additionally, they were impressive visual reminders of the elite role in maintaining this important connection with the solar sphere: "They confirmed in monumental fashion the direct link between the sun and the chiefly elite" (28). In doing so, according to Smith, power was legitimized.

Practice theory has been invoked to explain the process associated with differential ranking between lineages and the importance of this in the evolution of human societies. According to Marcus and Flannery (1996:238), population growth was an unintended consequence of sedentism and agriculture. While they utilize data from the Oaxaca valley, they suggest that this is a more general conclusion. Groups could not fission as they had in the past as leaving a village meant losing housing, storage facilities, and land, each of which involved considerable labor investments. Integrative mechanisms were developed to overcome the social problems associated with aggregation. Larger social groups such as clans and moieties were created through the recognition of descent from common mythical ancestors. In many societies, highly respected men drawn from each major descent group in the village were initiated into fraternal sodalities from which less respected men were excluded. Female rituals focused on residential areas where immediate ancestors were invoked, while male ritual activities were performed in a men's house, a ritual structure built by the initiates. This social structure crosscut kin groups, thus serving to integrate the village. Unintended consequences of this system were that egalitarian relations became asymmetrical, which ultimately led to social hierarchy (Knight 1990; Marcus and Flannery 1996:239).

On Choosing SunWatch Village

This investigation focuses on the SunWatch site (a.k.a. Incinerator, 33My57), located on the west bank of the Miami River in Dayton, Ohio (Figure 1.4). The reasons for choosing this site as a case study are simple. This village is the most extensively excavated and analyzed Fort Ancient site, and its occupation occurred between A.D. 1150 and 1450 (see Figures 1.2 and 4.1), which coincides with the "crest" of neighboring Mississippian developments (Griffin 1985:63). While the SunWatch site is not among the Fort Ancient sites located closest to Mississippian settlements (see Figure 1.1), it may in fact be quite useful for investigating interregional interaction between Fort Ancient and Middle Mississippians due to its location far removed from the main avenues of river-based interaction, where sites are complicated by multiple occupations and generally nonextensive and/or poor excavation histories (Drooker 2000). The SunWatch site clearly has all of the key characteristics of Fort Ancient villages, often being used as one of the primary examples of social structure at the village level (Henderson and Pollack 2001).

Excavation History

In 1964 avocational archaeologist John Allman began excavations in the northeastern part of the village (Allman 1968). Allman was later joined by another avocational archaeologist, Charles Smith (n.d.). These investigations revealed numerous burials, pit features, hearths, and a wall trench house. Excavations proceeded until 1969. The team excavated a sizeable portion of the northeastern quadrant of the village, using a 10 x 10–foot coordinate system oriented along West River Road. As far as can be discerned based on field notes and collections, excavation strategy consisted of removing the plowzone, locating features, and sifting feature fill for diagnostics and larger artifacts (sometimes using screens). Inventories were made of individual pit and burial features, although these consist only of tools and diagnostics. Unfortunately, artifacts were not labeled according to pit provenience and the inventories are useful only on the most general level.

In 1969, a week after J. Heilman started as curator of anthropology for the Dayton Society of Natural History, Charles Smith brought the site to his attention. At the time the site's preservation was not an issue, and the museum logged it as a potential research interest. However, in 1970 it became known that the City of Dayton was inadvertently planning to destroy the site in the process of upgrading and expanding a nearby sewage treatment facility. Additional sewage treatment ponds, of which several are located to the west of the site, were going to be constructed over the village. Heilman realized the danger

Figure 1.4. SunWatch site map. (Produced with assistance from William Kennedy.)

to the site. Because the site contained numerous intact features, human burials, and a house and had great potential for further significance, the DSNH began extensive salvage excavations in 1971. The City of Dayton permitted this initial salvage work while continuing to make plans for the sewage treatment expansion.

The DSNH excavated the site each summer from 1971 until 1989. The initial goal of the excavations was to salvage as much of the site as possible before it was destroyed by the City of Dayton. As a result, from 1971 to 1975 DSNH excavations proceeded rapidly as the city continued planning the expansion project. In 1975 the site was placed on the National Register of Historic Places, and the city abandoned plans for expanding the sewage plant in the vicinity (Lileas 1988a, 1988b). By the early 1980s excavation had slowed considerably, due largely to the shift toward reconstruction, planning for an interpretive center, and analysis efforts. The pattern of the village was well established by this time and included the general range of feature forms encountered during avocational excavations. The most notable distinction was the finding that all other houses in the village were of single post construction and there were a series of what I call "ritual-communal" facilities (see Figure 1.3). These are poorly understood thermal features, which have long been interpreted as "sweat lodges." This issue is not directly examined in the present study; however, I do briefly investigate their spatial relationship with the burial pattern (see Chapter 4). Formal excavations ceased in 1989, the year after the site and interpretive center opened to the public.

The excavation method was relatively straightforward. A grid pattern of 10 x 10–foot squares was established to be consistent with avocational excavations, although the grid pattern was oriented toward magnetic north instead of following the orientation of West River Road (see Figure 1.3). Throughout the salvage period, features were excavated as one provenience, and ¼-inch mesh was used regularly for screening feature fill after 1971. Throughout excavations, the plowzone was hand sorted, with the exception of one 10-foot transect that was stripped with a bulldozer. After 1975 excavation strategy shifted to include excavation of all features in 3-inch levels and the flotation of ¼ of most features (Heilman 1988a). All artifacts recovered were collected and curated with the exception of fire-cracked rock, which was noted but not consistently counted or weighed and was generally discarded in the field.

There have been limited excavations since 1989, mostly testing in advance of museum-related construction activities (e.g., picnic shelter, utility lines). However, one research-driven excavation has occurred since formal excavations ceased. In the summer of 2005 a joint field school was conducted by Ohio State University and the DSNH to investigate two critical problems: (1) to assess the integrity of prehistoric deposits beneath West River Road, long thought to have seriously impacted if not completely destroyed the eastern portion of the village; and (2) to locate the wall trench house discovered by avocational archaeologists. The wall trench house was located and a large trash pit was discovered beneath West River Road (Cook and Kennedy 2005). We are now sure that the village was a complete circle and have a precise location of the wall trench house within the community plan.

Previous Social Analyses

Intensive excavations at SunWatch have provided an unmatched database for exploring Fort Ancient village social structure. The site contains clear spatial patterning indicative of an occupation by an integrated social group. There are several discrete clusters of structures and pit features in a well-defined village plan organized around a large central posthole. It has been suggested that the large post was used in part to chart solar alignments (Heilman and Hoefer 1981). Previous research has also presented a series of strong cases for localized households and possibly clans (Evans-Eargle 1998:96–97; Heilman 1988b), a leader's residence (Nass and Yerkes 1995:76–77), a male-oriented sodality (Harold 1985:76–78; Robertson 1980:75–78, 1984), a system of dual social organization (Cook and Sunderhaus 1999), and Green Corn ceremonialism (Harold 1985; Heilman and Hoefer 1981; Robertson 1980). These hypotheses are briefly discussed below.

The central posthole complex has been interpreted as an astronomical calendar, aligning with solar and stellar phenomena and particular houses, pit features, burials, hearths, and posts within the village (Goss 1988; Heilman and Hoefer 1981). The discovery of eastern red cedar in the center posthole (Wagner 1979) is consistent with other well-documented eastern woodland calendrical systems (e.g., the Cahokia "woodhenge" [Wittry 1969]). According to Heilman and Hoefer (1981) and Goss (1988), the central posthole aligns with the rising sun and the hearth inside House 1/71 at two times each year, near the beginning of spring (April 29) and in late summer (August 14). These dates coincide with the planting and harvesting schedule for this locale. The central posthole forms another alignment with the rising sun and the hearth inside House 2/87 on the winter solstice (December 22). Three overlapping pits contain an abundance of broken artifacts and burned corn and are positioned on the solar alignment that occurs at each equinox (Heilman and Hoefer 1981; Goss 1988). Solstices and equinoxes are commonly marked in other early calendrical systems in various regions of the world, lending cross-cultural support to these hypotheses (Aveni 2003) (Figure 1.5). While it has not been specifically investigated, the center pole was likely a significant religious symbol, perhaps similar to the meaning of sacred poles among the Delaware, which are seen as "the emblem of contact between the Great Spirit and man, a symbol of the maintenance of life" (Speck 1931:27).

Heilman (1988b) conducted a cross-feature refit analysis of pottery rim sherds and was the first to recognize that the site contained discrete spatial pat-

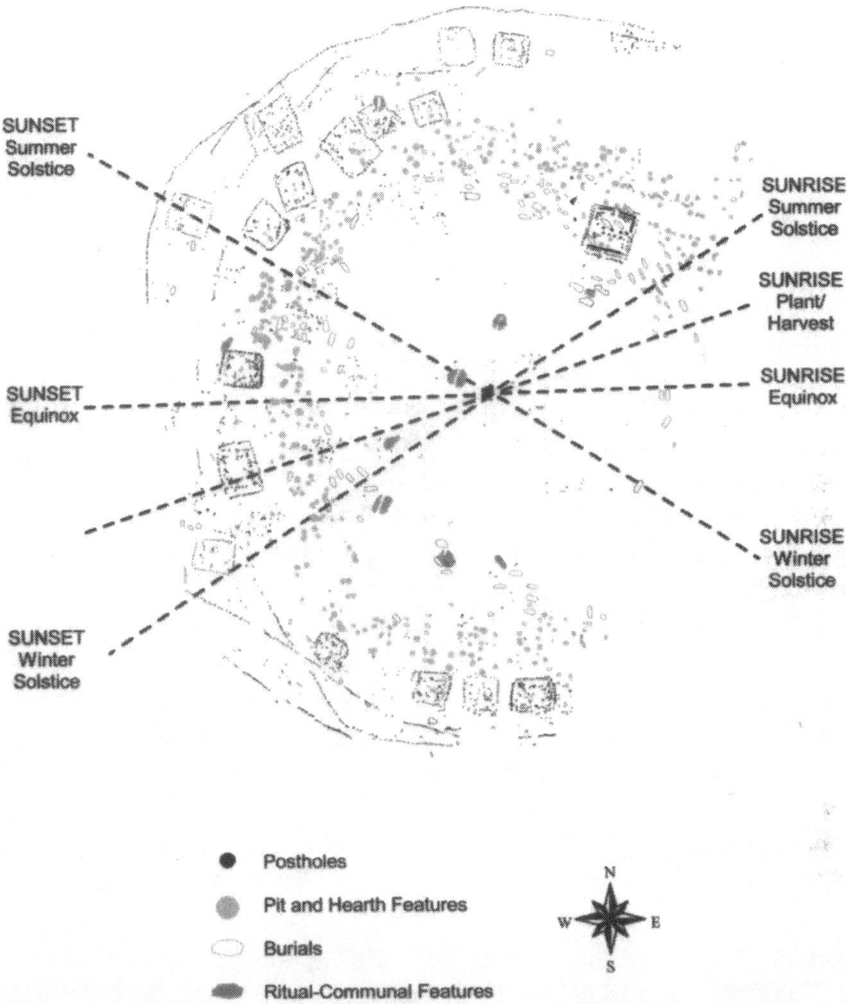

Figure 1.5. Proposed solar alignments. (Adapted from Heilman and Hoefer 1981:Figure 15.7, with updated site map.)

terning, perhaps related to the localization of households. Results suggested that there were three to four spatial units; refits occurred within each area but not between them. Minor differences in temper types and design motifs were also noted between these areas. Heilman (1988b) suggested that these units represent matrilocal groupings on the basis of criteria employed in earlier hypotheses (Deetz 1965; Hill 1968; Longacre 1970; see Stanislawski 1978 for a critique of this approach based on ethnoarchaeological data).

Lithic refits produced a pattern distinct from pottery. The pattern is more focused on linkages between a single house, House 2/78 (the only house constructed from red cedar), and the remainder of the village. Robertson (1980, 1984) utilized spatial divisions based on pottery refits and solar alignments to compare frequencies of lithic tools and debitage. A large percentage of lithic debitage was recovered from the vicinity of House 2/78, while the majority of finished tools were located elsewhere in the village. Based on a series of carefully constructed criteria, it was suggested that House 2/78 was a "men's council house" (Robertson 1980:71–72, 1984).

Several lines of evidence support the hypothesis that Green Corn ceremonialism was practiced at SunWatch. I suggest that the most compelling evidence is related to the concentration of burned corn itself, as ears of corn are offered to a sacred fire during Green Corn ceremonies (Witthoft 1949:32, 56). Burned corn is concentrated in the western portion of the site, defined between the summer and winter solstice alignments, where it was present in more than two-thirds of the pit features, considerably more than the southern and northern parts of the village (Heilman and Hoefer 1981:10). Based on this finding and the presence of a large house (House 1/71) along the planting/harvesting solar alignment, Heilman and Hoefer suggest that the structure was a "big house," a large communal structure often used during the Green Corn ceremony, as noted for several tribes in the southeastern United States (Hudson 1976:365–375; Witthoft 1949:83). However, a later study reached a different conclusion regarding the function of the large structure in the western portion of the village. Nass (1987, 1989) and Nass and Yerkes (1995) utilized the same spatial units but concluded that this locale more likely housed a village leader. They suggest that the area contained more large storage pits than other portions of the site, consistent with a general model for the identification of a leader's residence.

Robertson (1980:55–72), Harold (1985:52–57), and Cook (2004:211–217) have offered additional evidence in support of the Green Corn hypothesis. The most compelling evidence marshaled in these studies is the ethnographically documented use of cedar houses in Green Corn festivals (Witthoft 1949:7) and the location of large concentrations of broken artifacts (including exotics) in the western part of the site, presumably from communal disposal of trash, also commonly associated with renewal activities (Cook 2004:Figure 60; Robertson 1980:57–58). When people of a town celebrated the busk (Green Corn), "[t]hey collected all their old clothing, pots, furniture, grain, and all old things while cleaning their households, and burned them in a common heap, a radical finish to the old year" (Witthoft 1949:59, after Bartram 1853 [1789]). Robertson (1980:63) suggests that the intensive manufacture of hunting implements in the "men's council lodge" area was partially the result of preparations for male hunting expeditions to procure meat to use in the Green Corn ceremony (as noted by Witthoft 1949:42). An extensive review of ethnographic literature added additional support for the Green Corn hypothesis (Harold 1985:52–57).

Evans-Eargle (1998) analyzed the mortuary pattern to assess basic characteristics of the village social structure and demonstrated that the site contains evidence for an egalitarian social organization; different burial treatments can generally be associated with age and gender. Burial areas contain clusters of males, females, and children suggestive of kin groupings (97). Evans-Eargle further suggests that these groupings represent internally ranked clans, as one individual per group appears higher in rank than others. A total of three individuals are unique in status markers, with one being a good candidate for a village leader or shaman. Interestingly, she noted that an area near the "men's council house" contains only adult males and children.

The most recent social analysis involved further investigation of the pottery assemblage. The main goal of this study was to further examine Heilman's (1988b) spatial hypothesis based on a more representative sample of pottery, which included all neck and rim sherds. Pottery refits were nearly doubled in quantity, including several refits that connected previously bounded areas (Figure 1.6). Based largely on this pattern, it was hypothesized that the village contained evidence of a dual division (Cook and Sunderhaus 1999). Importantly, each of the hypotheses briefly discussed above (localized households, clans, men's council house, big house, leader's house) fits with a dual division social system. Dual divisions are common among indigenous southeastern groups and have been noted for several Mississippian sites (Blitz 1999; Hudson 1976:237; Knight 2006; Zeder and Arter 1996).

Previous findings regarding the social structure of SunWatch are impressive. However, there are four basic problems that weaken current interpretations. First, although there are several published maps of museum excavations, none of them are complete. Second, analyses have not integrated avocational findings with those of the museum, with the exception of a biological distance and stress study (Giesen 1992). (It is important to note that Chuck Smith's field notes were not donated to the museum until 1993; therefore, most previous investigations did not have access to them.) While avocational collections and notes lack much provenience data, they are critical for interpreting this village, most notably for addressing the presence of a wall trench house. This is particularly important because some studies have hinted at a Mississippian connection with the development of certain social institutions (e.g., Robertson 1980; also see Chapter 7). Although there are problems with the avocational records,

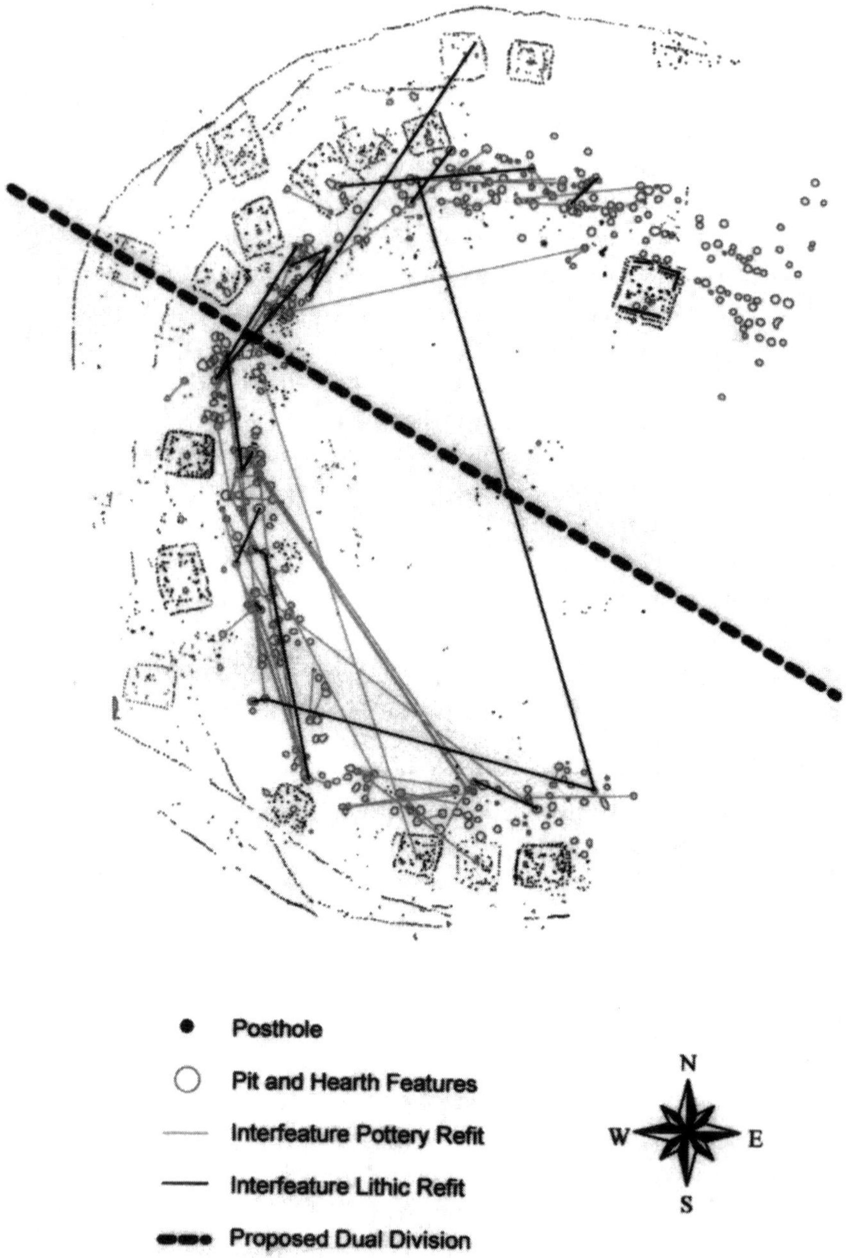

Figure 1.6. Interfeature pottery and lithic refits and proposed dual division. (Dual division based on Cook and Sunderhaus 1999.)

detailed mortuary data are included in feature descriptions and profiles were completed for all excavated features, from which basic form and volume can be derived. Third, most previous investigations of artifact or feature sets were completed before excavations ceased; hence, data sets were incomplete. Fourth, previous investigations have assumed the site did not contain spatially discernible time depth. However, two studies specifically investigating this issue have demonstrated that the site contains potential in this respect (Cook and Merz 2000; Turnbow 1989). By remedying these issues, the present study furthers several of the hypotheses that have been forwarded regarding the social structure of SunWatch.

Conclusion

This study asks the question: Did the social structure of SunWatch form independently of Mississippian influence, as current models suggest? Or, alternatively, is the village social structure itself partially relatable to Mississippian cases, forming as a result of periphery peer interactions with those societies? In addressing this question, this study has the potential to contribute to our understanding of Mississippian evolution and, on a more general level, add to our understanding of regional processes of social interaction and change. This study moves beyond the missing Mississippian characteristics that have been used to downplay involvement in Fort Ancient development, namely, the low occurrence of diagnostic trade items and the lack of clear settlement and social hierarchies. Are Fort Ancient villages, particularly some of the social structures they housed, similar to Mississippian communities in other ways? If so, what are the implications for competing models of Fort Ancient development?

To investigate the problem, a theoretical approach was developed that both broadens and narrows the perspective. On a broader scale, particular attention is placed on investigating the potential significance of low occurrences of Mississippian items in Fort Ancient villages within a periphery peer framework. At the narrow end of the spectrum, the focus is on small-scale social units (e.g., households, lineages, village leadership). The evolution of autonomous villages was chosen as the focus of the investigation, as this is the predominant Fort Ancient site type. Therefore, defining the formation and social structures associated with this site form is a critical step in refining our models of Fort Ancient evolution.

The remainder of the volume begins with a summary of the ways in which Mississippian societies have been differentiated. After describing variability in Mississippian social structure and settlement layout, the methodology is presented. The focus is on outlining a multidimensional approach for discerning temporal patterning, corporate behavior, and leadership development in relation to intraregional and interregional interaction. After investigating in detail the SunWatch case, other Fort Ancient villages are examined to begin the task of investigating the regional extent of the pattern.

2
Fort Ancient and the Range of Mississippian Social Complexity

In this chapter, the basic range of Mississippian and Fort Ancient site and social structures and mortuary patterns are outlined, along with evolutionary models that have been previously formulated regarding the development of Fort Ancient with respect to Mississippian interactions.

Defining Mississippian

Differentiating the Mississippian continuum began with Holmes's (1886) geographical differentiation of late prehistoric pottery in the midwestern United States into Upper, Middle, and Lower Mississippian types. Middle Mississippian was based largely on the presence of shell-tempered pottery (Holmes 1903). Middle and Upper Mississippian terms were in common usage by 1930 (Griffin 1985) and would later contribute to the development of the Midwestern Taxonomic System (McKern 1939; Phillips et al. 1951), which continues to form the basis for differentiation of late prehistoric societies located in the Midwest. The Midwestern Taxonomic System consists of four archaeological constructs based on nested sets of shared material attributes (mostly pottery): components (single sites), foci (sets of closely related sites), aspects (series of foci), and phases (many aspects). Middle Mississippian and Upper Mississippian were defined as phases (Griffin 1943). Holmes's (1886) Middle Mississippi area included large portions of Alabama, Arkansas, Illinois, Indiana, Iowa, Kentucky, Louisiana, Mississippi, Tennessee, and Texas.

Middle and Upper Mississippian phases are generally located in distinct environmental zones. Middle Mississippian mound centers are typically located along major rivers, with the more complex ones being situated in broad aggraded valleys with developed backwater areas containing abundant wetland resources and soils most suitable for intensive agriculture (Smith 1978, 1985; Ward 1965). Upper Mississippians are generally located in areas within the prairie peninsula (Stuckey 1981; Transeau 1935). This is particularly clear for the Oneota (Brown 1982), although I would extend this to include Oliver phase and Fort Ancient societies that inhabited the fragmented eastern portion of this ecoregion dotting parts of central Indiana and southwest Ohio (SunWatch is located in such a prairie opening [Cooper 1800]). This environmental distinction appears to have had consequences in terms of maize dependency, which was lower for Fort Ancient groups than for neighboring Middle Mississippian societies (Schurr and Schoeninger 1995). In contrast, deer were more intensively utilized in the Fort Ancient region (Smith 1986).

This well-known pattern of the general boundaries between Middle and Upper Mississippian groups in the study area may be obscuring reality a bit. A recent examination of Middle and Upper Mississippian site distributions included all recorded sites in state inventories (including many in the vast "gray" literature) for Ohio, Kentucky, Indiana, Wisconsin, Minnesota, Michigan, and Illinois (Schroeder 2004). Results of this effort differ from the generalized depiction in two respects (Figure 2.1; compare with Figure 1.1). First, it is clear that there is inconsistency regarding what is deemed to be the distinction between Middle and Upper Mississippian sites, particularly in central Indiana, as sites referred to as Middle Mississippian are attributable to the Oliver phase, which are equivalent in social structure to Fort Ancient and other Upper Mississippian sites (Redmond and McCullough 2000). Second, and more germane to the present study, was the finding that both Middle and Upper Mississippian sites are commonly represented in counties situated at the interface of Middle and Upper Mississippian site concentrations; this is particularly evident in the tri-state area (Kentucky, Indiana, Ohio) and northern Illinois (see Figure 2.1). This depicts more of a gradation of one group into another, from those attributed to Middle Mississippian into those defined as Upper Mississippian, rather than rigid boundaries, which may be more an artifact of our own creation than "on the ground" reality, a fact that will become apparent in the present investigation.

Following Service's (1962, 1975) model of social evolution and the general fit with archaeological correlates (see Creamer and Haas 1985:742–743), most researchers have categorized Middle Mississippians as "chiefdoms" and Upper Mississippians as "tribes." Chiefdoms consist of clearly defined social hierarchies with significant differences between groups of higher and lower status. These differences are maintained by the restricted and conspicuous use of sumptuary goods by elite kinship groups. Chiefdoms are also socially and politically centralized, consisting of economically interdependent communities (Adams 1975; Fried 1967; Sahlins 1968; Service 1962, 1975). In contrast, tribes consist of economically independent villages. Production is usually for subsistence purposes; limited surpluses are produced but are not centralized. Surpluses are usually

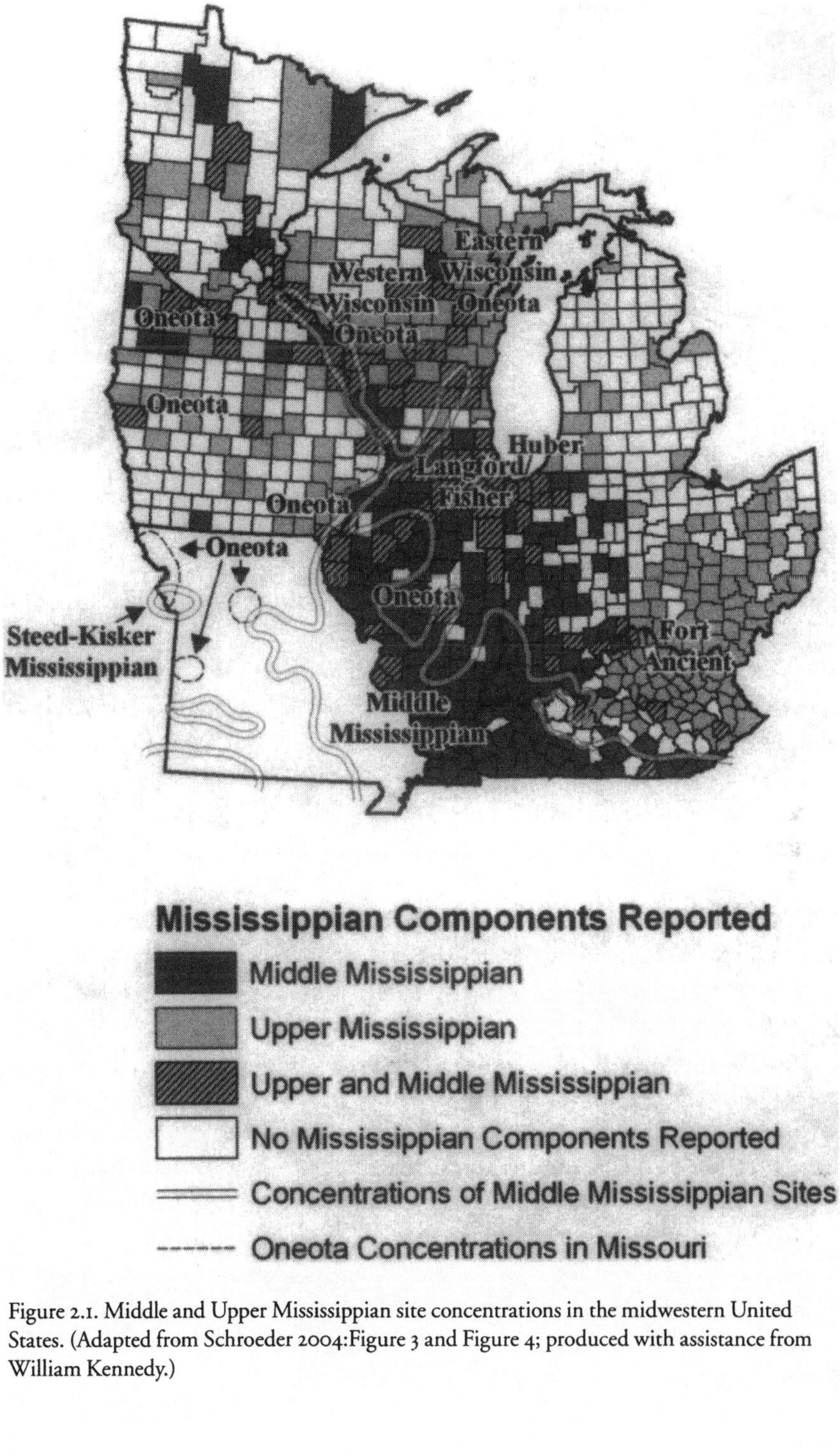

Figure 2.1. Middle and Upper Mississippian site concentrations in the midwestern United States. (Adapted from Schroeder 2004:Figure 3 and Figure 4; produced with assistance from William Kennedy.)

stored at the household, extended kinship, or community level and are used for insurance in bad years or in times of nonproduction or for cementing exchange relationships (Sahlins 1968; Service 1962). Tribes are nonhierarchical in terms of village autonomy and mortuary ranking, although some kinship units may have higher status than others and some individuals may have higher status due to positioning in their respective kin or ceremonial systems or as a consequence of specialized skills (Service 1962:121–123). However, the positions held by such individuals are not inheritable, nor are these leaders able to make decisions for the whole group (Creamer and Haas 1985:739). Importantly, tribes often form in relation to more complex societies (Fried 1983).

Middle Mississippian chiefdoms range in size and complexity, and there have been two major ways of understanding this complexity. A long-favored view is that Middle Mississippian chiefdoms cycled between "complex" and "simple" types based on the numbers of vertical differentiations in respective settlement hierarchies (Anderson 1994:Figure 1, using terms coined by Wright 1984:42–43). Complex chiefdoms contain two or more tiers of political administration, while simple chiefdoms contain only one. Recently a horizontal alternative to this model has been presented, suggesting that paired mound sites may represent two simple chiefdoms that fused together instead of "complex" chiefdoms. As these settlements grew they fissioned into "mother-daughter" chiefdoms (Blitz 1999; Blitz and Lorenz 2006:17–21, 140). Similar systems of dual organization have been hypothesized for several Middle Mississippian sites (Blitz 1999; Hudson 1976:237; Knight 2006; Zeder and Arter 1996). This model presents an alternative commensurate with archaeological and ethnographic data without utilizing more complex political models. Other recent studies have also failed to locate evidence supporting high levels of complexity among Middle Mississippian chiefdoms. The most notable conclusion is that there are few cases for full-time craft specialization and that even the largest mounds could have been built by relatively few individuals over extended periods of time (Milner 1998:148; Muller 1997:390).

Within the original Mississippian classification scheme, supplemented by evolutionary terms developed in the 1960s, Fort Ancient tribes were considered to be an Upper Mississippian variant bordering the larger Mississippian world of chiefdoms, alternate evolutionary outcomes resulting from adaptations to less agriculturally productive environments. However, more recent definitions have restricted what we call "Mississippian" by emphasizing hierarchical relations, leaving only Middle Mississippians to be included. For example, a widely regarded definition presented by Griffin (1985:63) suggests that Mississippians:

(1) developed many cultural innovations over much of the southeast between A.D. 700 and 900,
(2) added these innovations to local cultural inventories by contact between neighboring and distant groups,
(3) increased in population as a result of a more effective agronomy,
(4) constructed planned permanent towns and ceremonial centers, villages and subsidiary support hamlets, farmsteads, and extractive camps,
(5) had regional and temporal variations of a hierarchical social, political, and religious structure,
(6) participated in an area-wide belief system, with an elaborate symbolic iconography encoded on marine shells, copper, ceramics, and stone,
(7) had an extensive trade network between neighboring and distant societies over rivers and trails involving exchange of symbolic and mundane items and raw materials, and
(8) reached an area-wide cultural crest between A.D. 1200 and 1500, slowly receding to less formally organized and controlled groups encountered in the post-A.D. 1700 colonial period.

The fourth and fifth criteria isolate most (but not all) Middle Mississippians as being "Mississippian" when in fact there is a continuum of social complexity even among Middle Mississippians themselves (see below).

While not part of Griffin's (1985:63) definition, key material traits in earlier Middle Mississippian definitions included the presence of wall trench houses, shell-tempered pottery, and substructure mounds. The problem with these criteria is that they are not associated with all Mississippian communities and have occasionally been found as early as Middle Woodland times. However, they remain key criteria in many regions and do in fact occur in many Middle Mississippian contexts.

Middle Mississippian Mound Centers and Villages

Middle Mississippian sites are often situated in hierarchical settlement patterns typical of chiefdoms (Fowler 1974), which leads to the prevailing Mississippian definition outlined above. Ranging from largest to smallest, Middle Mississippian site types include mound centers, villages, and small sites such as hamlets, farmsteads, and limited-activity sites (e.g., resource procurement). Because this study focuses on village (Middle Mississippian) to village (Fort Ancient) interactions, the following section summarizes key dimensions associated with this site type.

Site Layout and Housing

Middle Mississippian mound centers contain an architectural grammar consisting of three elements—mounds, plazas, and stockades—arranged in a variety of configurations (Lewis et al. 1998). The clearest use of flat-topped mounds was to support public buildings, including religious structures and leader residences. The largest mound at a site, often positioned closer to the site center, was likely the residence of a chief or ruling lineage, while smaller mounds supported various functionaries associated with the nobility (Knight 1997:240). The general pattern is that higher-ranked people lived near the chiefs on the edge of the plaza, and lower-ranked people lived on the perimeter of the town (Varner and Varner 1951:171). Large structures often predate construction of these mounds (e.g., Mistovich 1995:174; Schroedl 1998:67).

In Mississippian settlements, plazas are defined by mounds and often contain "marker posts." The use of mounds and marker posts to chart solar alignments has been proposed for many mound centers (e.g., Cahokia [Fowler 1974; Wittry 1969], Toqua [Polhemus 1990:135]) and at least one village (Wolforth and Munson 1994). The Cahokia site provides the clearest example of the connection between a solar alignment and leadership. On the equinoxes, the sun rises from behind the leader's residence situated atop Monk's Mound in direct alignment with the central red cedar posthole of the wood henge monument. This is perhaps the ultimate connection between leadership and solar power! These posts were also used for other purposes, such as displaying town emblems and the scalps of enemies, or to play various games (Smith 2000:88). Some of these posts undoubtedly had deeper meanings as well, as was suggested earlier (see Chapter 1).

Spatial patterning of houses and the occurrence of plaza posts in Middle Mississippian villages were examined at seven sites. These sites were chosen on the basis of being complete enough in excavation extent to have exposed the bulk of the architectural features of interest and in the general time frame in which SunWatch was occupied (see Figure 1.2). The sample sites are: Averbuch (Middle Cumberland, ca. A.D. 1275–1400 [Eisenberg 1991:72]), Bridges (central Illinois, ca. A.D. 1100–1300 [Oetalaar 1993:672]), Annis (Green River, ca. A.D. 1265–1405 [Hammerstedt 2005:17]), Southwind (Angel, ca. A.D. 1000–1300 [Hilgeman 2000:Figure 6.6]), King (Coosa, ca. A.D. 1500–1600 [Hally 1988], although earlier [A.D. 1410] and later [A.D. 1670, 1830] radiocarbon dates are also associated with the site [Hally 1975]), Carden Farm II (Hiwassee Island, ca. A.D. 1000–1300 [Schroedl 1998:67]), and Ledford Island (Mouse Creek, ca. A.D. 1400–1600 [Schroedl 1998:83]) (Figure 2.2).

There are two things to note with respect to the sample. The one obvious absence is the lack of a village from the Prather Complex (Griffin 1978), the only Middle Mississippian region in the study area missing from the comparison (see Figure 1.1). While this region is critical to consider given the close proximity to Fort Ancient, it is poorly known (Munson and McCullough 2004:1). No village plans have been documented, although the Prather site mound center is clearly circular in structure with a well-defined plaza (82). Two site plans were included that are technically outside of the region proper (King and Bridges). The King site was included in this comparison because it represents a village related to the Mouse Creek but in a more complex chiefdom that some have argued includes Mouse Creek sites (Hally et al. 1990). The Bridges site was included because it is a completely exposed Middle Mississippian village reasonably close to the area of interest.

Generally, the housing pattern of each village is circular, although stockades and ditches enclosing some of the sites are rectangular in form. More than half of the sample (57%) contains central postholes within a plaza area. Plazas range in diameter from approximately 90 to 280 feet. There is a tendency for plazas to be either on the small or large end of the spectrum, although this observation requires a larger data set to further ascertain its validity. One or two houses (often larger ones) are positioned in closer proximity to the village center in most cases (71%). Larger Mississippian structures have been related to communal or chiefly functions (e.g., Polhemus 1987:258). A relationship between larger structures and centralized food storage has led some researchers to conclude that local leaders were present in Middle Mississippian villages (e.g., Nass and Yerkes 1995:77–79). Larger structures have also been likened to communally used "big houses" or "council lodges" (Anderson 1994; Munson 1994; Sullivan 1995:107).

Middle Mississippian houses were often (but not always) constructed using wall trenches. Houses were often rebuilt multiple times in one location (Conrad 1991:133; Hally and Kelly 1998:Figure 3.3; Munson 1994; Oetelaar 1993:Figure 3; Schroedl 1998:82). However, three villages in the sample contain both single post and wall trench house types (see Figure 2.2). In at least one case, structures associated with earlier stages of Middle Mississippian mound construction shift from those consisting only of single post construction to ones containing both single posts and wall trenches to a final stage containing only a wall trench structure (e.g., Annis [Hammerstedt 2005:13–15]).

Several investigators have noted that Middle Mississippian houses are often clustered into groups, each distributed around a small courtyard (Collins 1997; Mehrer 1995; Mehrer and Collins 1995; Muller 1997:221; Polhemus 1987:1240; Rogers 1995). The general understanding of Middle Mississippian residential units is that they consist of multiple households, representing either functional

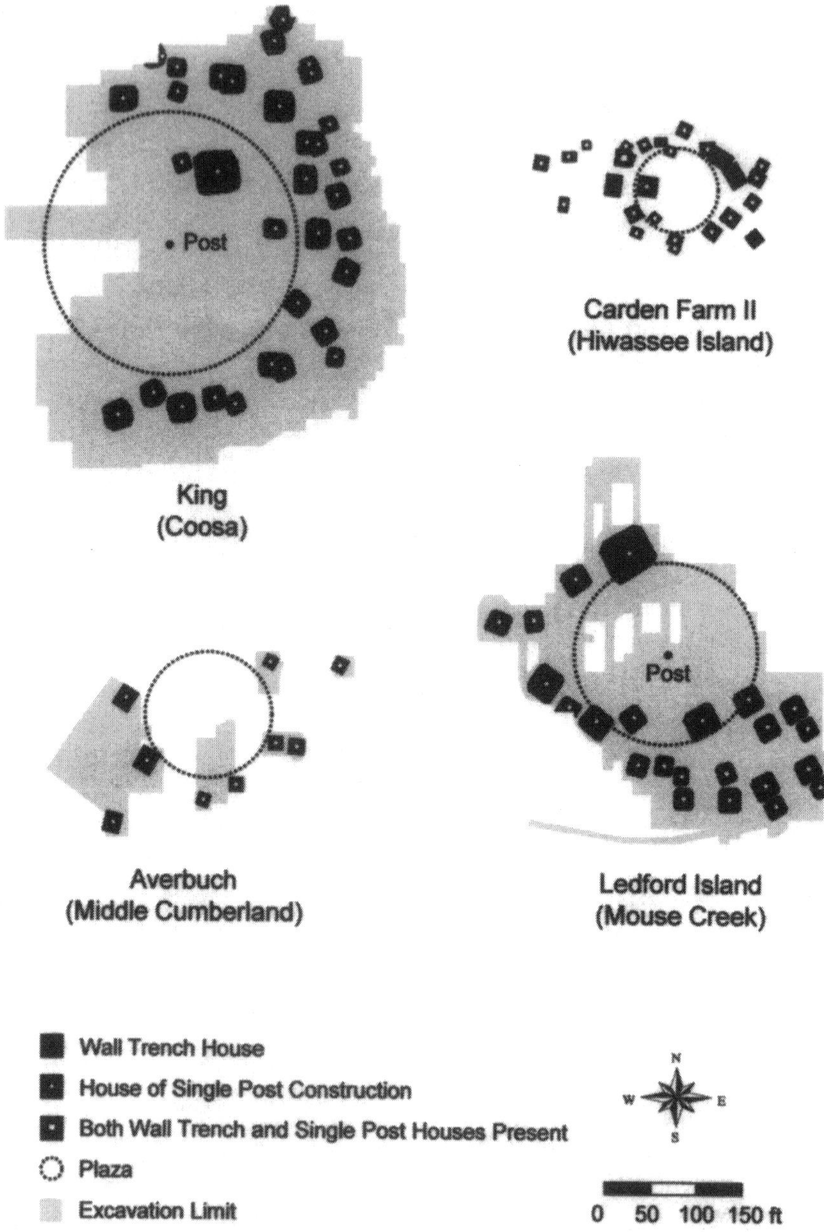

Figure 2.2. Selection of Middle Mississippian village plans. Excavation limits not shown for villages where the complete architectural plan of houses was exposed. (Adapted from Berryman 1981:9 [Averbuch]; Hally and Kelly 1998:Figure 5.5 [King]; Hammerstedt 2005:Figure 2 [Annis]; Munson 1994 [Southwind]; Oetelaar 1993:Figure 3 [Bridges]; Schroedl 1998:Figure 4.2 [Carden Farm II]; Sullivan 1995:Figure 5.5 [Ledford Island].)

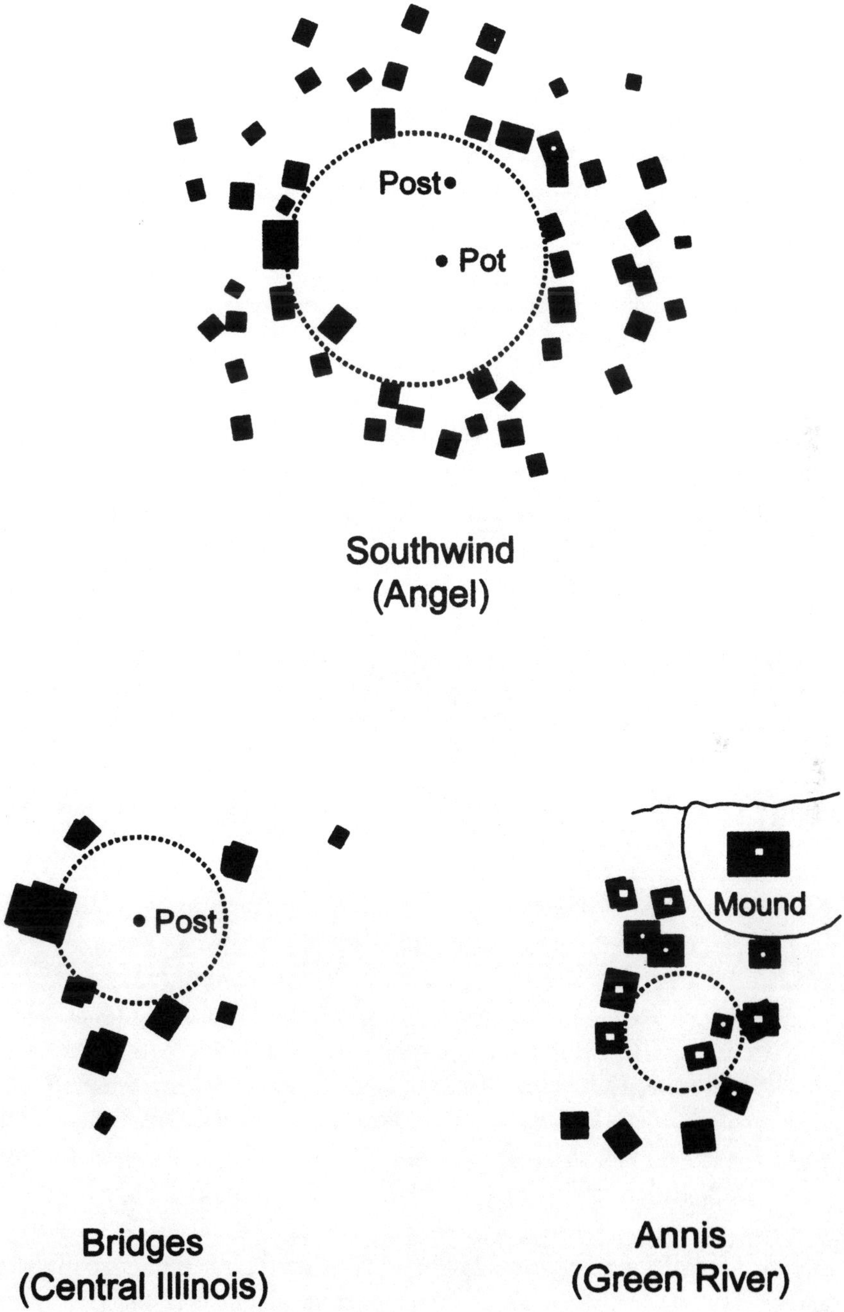

Figure 2.2. *Continued*

differentiation for one family or different stages in the growth cycle of domestic units (Muller 1997:190; Hally and Kelly 1998:58–63). This conclusion is largely derived from early accounts of native peoples living in the Southeast: "The dwellings of the Upper Creeks consist of little squares, or rather four dwelling-houses inclosing a square area. . . . Every family, however, has not four of these houses; some have but three, others not more than two, and some but one, according to the circumstances of the individual, or the number of his family" (Bartram 1853:54 [1789]).

Mortuary Practices

While there is considerable variation in Middle Mississippian burial patterns over time and space, one of the most commonly mentioned aspects of Middle Mississippian mortuary domains is that they were hierarchically structured, with evidence for social ranking being restricted to mound centers where a particular segment of the population was interred in mounds accompanied by exotic artifacts (Brown 1971). In a comparison of Moundville, Etowah, and Spiro, two points of commonality were noted: (1) "high status is associated with interments in, on, or near platform mounds"; and (2) "high status individuals are often buried with preserved status accoutrements, exhibiting symbols of the 'supra-local' type" (2; also see Chapter 3). A mound center (Bell Field) in the emerging Coosa chiefdom but dating to the time period of interest (ca. A.D 1200–1350) and associated with pottery similar to examples from eastern Tennessee (Smith 2000:25) contained a fairly typical assemblage associated with elites interred in a mound summit: "The tombs contained the remains of adult males buried with elaborate grave goods, probably symbolic of their chiefly status. Such material as finely crafted, negative-painted dog and human effigy pots . . . copper headdresses and earspools, a shell cup for the black drink ceremony, a large flint knife or sword, shell beads, and such exotic materials as a sawfish bill, are evidence of long-distance trade connections" (26).

In contrast to the mound center pattern, villages and smaller sites have produced mortuary assemblages more consistent with egalitarian societies, although they were most often still part of hierarchical settlement systems (Goldstein 1980:135–136; Hally 2004; Milner 1984). A general "rule" for Middle Mississippian burials—at sites of all sizes—is that many were placed in row patterns (Goldstein 1980:127–133). The mortuary pattern of Middle Mississippian villages is similar to the pattern noted for "outlying" cemeteries, located on the American Bottom periphery (Milner 1984:470–477). Milner's peripheral elite of the Cahokia system are often accompanied by marine shell cups (475). Coosa mound centers contain evidence of elite behavior, but not in smaller sites such as the King village (Hally 2004).

There are few detailed studies of mortuary patterns located within Middle

Mississippian villages. To construct a model to apply to the SunWatch case, I reviewed the findings from four sites: Arnold and Ganier (Middle Cumberland), Ledford Island (Mouse Creek), and King (Coosa). Each site contains burial groups and often rows, and higher statuses are associated with adult males whose leg positions are usually extended. At Ledford Island the row patterns are often oriented toward the village center pole. There adults in general and males in particular were buried closer to the plaza and with more artifacts, whereas this same segment of the population tended to be interred in mounds in Dallas phase sites (Sullivan 1995:117–119). Prestige goods present in elite burials at Dallas phase sites such as negative-painted pottery, copper ornaments, and marine shell cups (Scott and Polhemus 1987:391) are lacking in Mouse Creek settlements (Boyd and Boyd 1991:83; Lewis and Kneberg 1946; Sullivan 1995:118–120). At Ledford Island the northeastern burial plot contained all males with many artifacts, while the southwestern group contained few artifacts. Whelk shells and triangular projectile points were noted as status markers for the Arnold site (Ferguson 1972). Flint blades, triangular projectile points, and bone pins were noted as status symbols for the Ganier site (Broster 1972). Celts (greenstone, spatulate), elbow pipes, flint blades, triangular projectile points, chisels, and quartz crystals were noted as status markers for the Ledford Island site (Sullivan 1987). Marine shell cups, discoidals, a "new fire" bowl (used in the Green Corn ceremony), flint blades, celts (spatulate, iron), and triangular copper "badges" have been noted as status symbols for the King site (Hally 2004).

Burials do not appear to be present in Angel phase villages (based on the Southwind site [Munson 1994]) and may be restricted to the mound center (Angel site), where they are common. In contrast, burials are present within eastern Tennessee (both Dallas and Mouse Creek), Coosa, and Middle Cumberland sites of various types. The Middle Cumberland region is also "home" to stone box graves (I. Brown 1981:Figure 3).

It has been noted that Middle Mississippian burials tend to be aligned along summer and winter solstices, for both mound centers and villages. This includes sites in central Illinois (Orendorf phase, ca. A.D. 1150–1250 [Conrad 1991:136], Dickson Mounds [Harn 1971]), eastern Tennessee (Toqua site [Polhemus 1990:Figure 19]), and northwestern Alabama (Koger's Island [Peebles 1971:73–74]). The widespread geographical distribution of these sites suggests this phenomenon was common throughout much of the Middle Mississippian world.

Accounting for Settlement System Variability

This brief overview of Middle Mississippian settlement systems has identified variability that complicates a clean division between Middle and Upper Mississippians in terms of social organization. In returning to Griffin's (1985:63) definition that stresses hierarchy as being an important component in what we call "Mississippian," we must closely consider the exceptions. There are at least three reasons for the occurrence of nonhierarchical settlement systems within the Middle Mississippian world: developmental process, timing, and inherent variability.

Clay (1976) has proposed a typology of Middle Mississippian development, ranging from single villages to hierarchical settlements, based on the relationship between cultural systems and their environments (139–140, employing terms developed by Emery and Trist 1965). Clay suggests that the Middle Mississippian site form was a function of environmental variation and the perceived shift in the importance of immediate subsistence concerns relative to the regional coordination of activities. The first type of site (tactical) results when a group emphasizes environmental variables. Generally, the members of such a group do not cooperate with people at other sites and they are scattered in areas of maximum economic productivity. Settlements represent considerable change through time, as they adapt to their local environment. Intrasite patterning reflects egalitarian relations as there are few status distinctions, artifact assemblages are relatively homogenous, and few trade items are present. The second type of site (strategic) depicts greater regional interaction. This site type contains evidence of greater planning and more labor is expended, most markedly in mound construction. There is less temporal change as site size remains stable and structures are rebuilt, often in the same locations. Greater regional cooperation appears as surrounding sites are established of various sizes, complexity, and functions. The third type of site (operations) is often associated with environments containing clustered resources with social groups reaching carrying capacities. Competition often increases in these communities, including the appearance of fortifications (Clay 1976:139–140).

The timing problem pertains to developments after A.D. 1400 in much, but not all, of the southeastern United States—namely, the collapse of chiefdoms. The general trend in many parts of the Southeast is a shift from more complex chiefdoms to less complex tribal forms of social organization before European contact (Emerson 1988; Green and Munson 1978; Milner et al. 1984; Morse and Morse 1983; Peebles 1978; Steponaitis 1983:168–169; but see Knight 1986).

The third option is that there were a variety of responses by local populations to the spread of Mississippian ideas, resulting in nonhierarchical arrangements in some cases. These do not necessarily have to be cases of arrested development or a post-A.D. 1400 return to simpler times. In the study region, the best example of the complexity of the problem is how the distinction between the Dallas and Mouse Creek phases has been viewed. Dallas settlements are arranged in simple chiefdoms, but Mouse Creek settlements lack mounds or any other evidence for social ranking, either in terms of settlement hierarchies or mortuary behavior (Schroedl 1998; Sullivan 1995). Mouse Creek appears to be typified by villages with central poles, larger structures positioned closer to the plaza, and burials within the community. Schroedl (1998:83) considers Mouse Creek to have formed after the collapse of Dallas chiefdoms (but see Hally et al. 1990; the authors consider Mouse Creek and some of the Dallas settlements as part of the paramount Coosa chiefdom). Sullivan (1995:122) argues that Mouse Creek and Dallas were contemporary and distinct variations of Mississippian culture: "each of the cultural entities or polities subsumed within the Dallas phase, as well as the one represented by the Mouse Creek phase, may have had differing developmental trajectories." The Aztalan site in Wisconsin represents another example of a Mississippian site lacking a settlement hierarchy. This could be a case of a tactical site that did not further develop or a different evolutionary trajectory altogether, the general view favored by Goldstein (1991) and Goldstein and Richards (1991).

The above scenarios for explaining why we find some nonhierarchical cases of Middle Mississippian settlement systems are not mutually exclusive. They each likely apply to certain cases for various reasons. The point of presenting them is to offer a more dynamic landscape in which to examine what it means to be Mississippian. We need to abandon the notion that Mississippian societies had a unitary origin and single developmental history (Milner and Schroeder 1999; Muller and Stephens 1991:297; Smith 1984). Observation of variability in Middle Mississippian settlements is important for many reasons, but for present purposes it considerably shapes the way in which we model interaction between regions. This is particularly important to consider as we shift the focus to Fort Ancient developments.

Fort Ancient

The Fort Ancient concept can be traced back to the late nineteenth century when it was used to define the remains of an extensive village-dwelling culture inhabiting southwestern Ohio (Moorehead 1892; Putnam 1886). Mills (1906: 135–136) coined the term "Fort Ancient Culture," which he defined as a pre-Columbian way of life represented by established homes, developed agriculture, stored food, and intertribal trade. The Fort Ancient archaeological construct included sites located in central Ohio (Mills 1904), northern Kentucky (Smith 1910), southeast Ohio (Griffin 1943), and adjacent parts of West Virginia and eastern Kentucky (Dunnell 1961; Mayer-Oakes 1955). Griffin (1943) was the first researcher to provide a comprehensive analysis of sites in the Fort Ancient region.

Culture History

Griffin's (1943) original definition of the Fort Ancient aspect recognized four foci: Anderson, Baum, Feurt, and Madisonville; related sites in Indiana have since been designated "Oliver," and related sites in West Virginia have also been pulled into the definition of the Fort Ancient region (Figure 2.3; compare with Figure 1.1). These foci were based largely on pottery attributes, as has also been the case with subsequent additions to the region (Griffin 1978; see Drooker 1997:64–70 and Henderson and Turnbow 1992 for detailed discussions of Fort Ancient subgroups and updated maps of subsequently located sites). The following overview focuses on changes in settlement structures, housing, and mortuary practices; changes in Fort Ancient material culture are summarized in Chapter 3 and Chapter 6.

Our understanding of the Fort Ancient region has improved dramatically in the last 20 years, due largely to research projects aimed at establishing major changes over time in central Ohio (Church 1987; Dancey 1992, 1998), southwest Ohio (Cowan 1986, 1987; Drooker 1997; Riggs 1986, 1998), and northern and central Kentucky (Henderson, ed. 1992). Most researchers recognize a three-part division in Fort Ancient society: Early Fort Ancient (A.D. 1000/1050 to 1200/1250), Middle Fort Ancient (A.D. 1200/1250 to 1400/1450), and Late Fort Ancient (A.D. 1400/1450 to 1650/1670). Several regional sequences have been assigned specific names that adhere to this temporal scheme (see Drooker 1997:Figure 4.3).

The Early Fort Ancient period is the most poorly defined, and site structure appears to differ between subregions. Small, scattered hamlets of five or six structures lacking a distinct plan may be typical for Fort Ancient sites in Kentucky that date to this period (Pollack and Henderson 1992:283–284; Sharp and Turnbow 1987:150), although there are few sites presently known. Features often consist of small basins, and pottery is undecorated and generally similar to Late Woodland vessels. In Kentucky, Middle Fort Ancient villages developed as several kin-based social groups aggregated under a variety of situational types of leadership (Henderson 1998; Pollack and Henderson 1992:284, 2000). In contrast, villages appear in the Early Fort Ancient period in central and southwest Ohio (Church 1987; Cowan 1987:12).

Distinct changes in Fort Ancient settlement and interaction occur after the restructuring of Angel, Middle Cumberland, and Green River Mississippians and the development of Mouse Creek settlements (see Figure 1.1). The clearest pattern is that Late Fort Ancient (A.D. 1400/1450–1650/1670) settlements are fewer in number and tend to be concentrated nearer the Ohio River (Drooker 1997:Figure 4.5; also see Chapter 6). Some artifact styles become more ho-

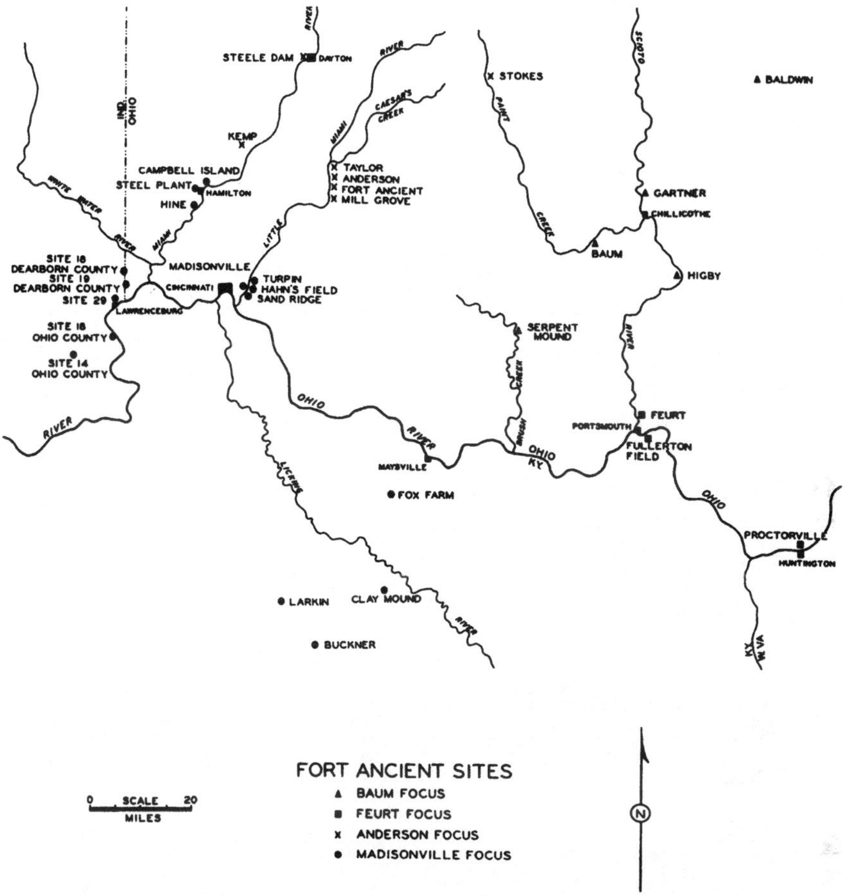

Figure 2.3. The original definition of the Fort Ancient region, including four foci that remain in use by many archaeologists today. (After Griffin 1943:Map 1.)

mogenous across the Fort Ancient region (e.g., pottery), reflecting increased internal interaction and the establishment of broader exchange networks (283–337; Henderson et al. 1992:267, 270). It has been suggested that Late Fort Ancient villages are larger and less formally organized (Cowan 1988, 1992; Pollack and Henderson 1992, 2000) and that stockades occur more regularly (Graybill 1981:169), although these ideas are not statistically substantiated (Drooker 2000). Residences do appear to generally increase in size over time, and storage pits are more frequently located inside houses (Drooker and Cowan 2001:91–92; Pollack and Henderson 1992:286). As is the case in surrounding regions, this trend is perhaps indicative of subsistence pressure due to overcrowding (Hart 1993).

There are no clear indications that the settlement system changed over time, although there have been speculations that the Late Fort Ancient time period witnessed increases in uses of special-purpose sites (Purtill 1999; Turnbow and Jobe 1984; Turnbow et al. 1983) and the development of settlement hierarchies. The problem with the first conclusion is that it has been proposed that Middle Fort Ancient villages were abandoned seasonally (Shane and Wagner 1993), and there are now several small, seasonally used sites dating to this period (see Chapter 6). The settlement hierarchy possibility was first championed by Essenpreis (1978), who proposed that the Late Fort Ancient Madisonville system contained a ranked series of site types as a result of direct affiliations with Middle Mississippian groups. However, Essenpreis (1988) subsequently altered this model, and the Marietta mound (which was initially interpreted as a higher-order site) has been shown to be Middle Woodland in age (Pickard 1996). While many consider the case to be closed, recent research has identified several smaller Fort Ancient sites in the upper portions of the Miami valleys that could be lower-order farmsteads, but the evidence is inconclusive (Riordan 2000). Additionally, there are still some candidates for higher-order Fort Ancient sites that deserve more careful consideration in this respect (Vickery et al. 2000; also see Chapter 6).

A final consideration of the Fort Ancient settlement pattern involves village reuse. A general pattern of site reoccupation has been suggested on the basis of the bimodal clustering of radiocarbon dates. This has been specifically postulated at four Fort Ancient sites: Madisonville (Drooker 1997:137–141), Schomaker (Cowan et al. 1990), South Fort (Harper 2000), and SunWatch (see Chapter 4) and is warranted for many others on the basis of radiocarbon dates and diagnostic artifacts. This may also be a more widespread pattern, based on an extensive survey of radiocarbon assays at Late Woodland and Fort Ancient sites in southern Ohio (Carr and Haas 1996). Harper (2000:362) noted that this is suggestive of a swidden agricultural system, in that groups would revisit villages after the field had lain fallow for a period of time.

Single post houses were the norm for Fort Ancient populations, although a few sites do contain wall trench structures, usually as a solitary occurrence (see Chapter 6). As is also the case with Middle Mississippian sites, groups of related houses have been proposed for Fort Ancient sites (Heilman 1988b; Mills 1904; Nass 1987, 1989). The clearest cases have come from less intensively occupied villages, such as the Capitol View (Henderson 1992) and Horseshoe Johnson sites (Hawkins 1998). Each site contains two clear house groups. Nass (1987:178–180, 255) and Nass and Yerkes (1995:76–78) suggest that SunWatch contains evidence for a leader's house based on one larger house with increased storage potential, a phenomenon they argue is similar to that which occurs in

Middle Mississippian villages. Larger houses have also been interpreted as communally used "big houses" (Hawkins 1998; Lileas 1988b:45–46; also see Chapter 1).

Fort Ancient mortuary remains appear to generally reflect egalitarian social structures in that differences in mortuary treatment can be explained largely as a function of sex and age (Griffin 1992). The Fort Ancient mortuary program did become more structured over time, including a higher incidence of multiple burials, and more burials were associated with artifacts in general and pottery in particular (Drooker and Cowan 2001; Henderson and Pollack 2001). There is evidence that some degree of social differentiation existed within Middle Fort Ancient communities, and this tendency became more pronounced in Late Fort Ancient social groups (Drooker 1997:272–282, 2000:256–257). During the Late Fort Ancient period, mounds are no longer present, and burials may be more often arranged in rows or inside houses. Children and young adults are more frequently buried with status items. Limited evidence exists in parts of the Fort Ancient area for a mortuary program involving defleshing, manipulation, curation of selected bones before burial, and the use of corn and bean offerings (Drooker 1997:Tables 4.6, 4.7, 4.12, 4.13). At the Larkin site, ritual killing of pottery vessels was noted (Henderson and Pollack 2001:178). Ossuary-like deposits, with as many as 14 individuals represented in one feature, have also been reported (Henderson and Pollack 2001).

Origins

Models formulated to address interactions between Middle and Upper Mississippian societies have been directly influenced by differing conceptions of Middle Mississippian social complexity (Pauketat and Emerson 1997:18–21). Those who favor greater complexity for Middle Mississippian groups often view material patterning in the archaeological record within a core/periphery perspective, arguing that Upper Mississippian peripheries were under the control of paramount chiefdoms or states like Cahokia (e.g., Dincauze and Hasenstab 1989; Peregrine 1992; but see Griffin 1993 and Kelly 1990a, which find little evidence for sustained exchanges between Cahokia and Fort Ancient societies). In contrast, those who conceive of smaller, less complex Middle Mississippian centers maintain that peripheries were likely to have been politically autonomous (e.g., Muller 1997:286). The less complex view places smaller Middle Mississippian villages and their neighbors on a relatively equal footing.

Three scenarios—migration, interaction, and independent development—have been used to interpret the origins of Fort Ancient and other Upper Mississippian groups. One of the key questions has been: How much if any of the content of the social structure of these societies can be associated with Middle

Mississippian influence, and how much is related to local Late Woodland populations? Answers to this question have changed considerably over the years as a result of increased data and shifting theoretical viewpoints, and it could well be that multiple answers are in fact correct (Gibbon 1982).

Early studies relied heavily on migration scenarios to account for the origin of Fort Ancient and other Upper Mississippian societies.

> The Fort Ancient Aspect appears to have been strongly influenced by Middle Mississippi, both by actual migration of peoples bearing a "Mississippi" culture into the southwestern part of the Fort Ancient territory and by diffusion of traits. . . . Fort Ancient could hardly have appeared as a cultural entity until after the Middle Mississippi peoples had formed a strong group. . . . The Oneota Aspect and the Fisher Focus also were strongly influenced by Middle Mississippi, so that, to some extent, the Oneota and Fort Ancient aspects can be linked together on the basis of their marginal relationship to what is thought of as "pure" Middle Mississippi [Griffin 1943:257–258].

Prufer and Shane (1970:258–262) shifted the geographical focus from the southwestern part of the Fort Ancient region to central Ohio as the point of origin for Mississippian migrants who developed into Fort Ancient peoples. Subsequent radiocarbon dates have revealed that the timing of these putative migrations would have been earlier, as the first Upper Mississippian sites are coeval with the earliest Middle Mississippian sites (Gibbon 1982).

Subsequent research considered the development of Fort Ancient as stemming from local groups interacting with Middle Mississippian societies, downplaying migrations in the development of interpretive models (Essenpreis 1978; Robertson 1980:77–78). Robertson specifically focused on the emergence of social institutions as a response to interaction with Middle Mississippian groups, a process that created the need for social solidarity, particularly among male members. Essenpreis argued that distinctions in Fort Ancient assemblages and settlement systems reflect different levels of interaction between local groups and Middle Mississippians. Groups located closer to Middle Mississippians became more "Mississippianized." Nass and Yerkes (1995) specifically compared Fort Ancient and Middle Mississippian village structures, suggesting that they were similar, the key distinction between them being that they were part of very different settlement systems. While the purpose of their study was not to address relationships between Middle Mississippian and Fort Ancient groups, they were the first to suggest structural similarities at the village level, which are the focus of the present study.

More recent syntheses have de-emphasized Middle Mississippian involvement in the formation of Fort Ancient societies, focusing instead on continuity with Late Woodland predecessors (e.g., Pollack and Henderson 1992:283). Late Woodland continuities with Fort Ancient are supported in terms of pottery vessel forms and the lack of social ranking and settlement hierarchies in Late Woodland and Fort Ancient societies. In this perspective, Middle Mississippian characteristics of Fort Ancient assemblages have been largely depicted as inconsequential to the development of Fort Ancient societies (Pollack and Henderson 1992, 2000; but see Drooker 1997:89–95, 301–302, Figure 8.23). Significant interactions are noted only for the Late Fort Ancient period and are mainly interpreted as having led to changes in foodways (Pollack et al. 2002; but see Drooker 1997:283–337; Drooker and Cowan 2001: 96–98, 103–104).

While I do not present an overview of the Oneota, a brief consideration of how their origins have most recently been examined is useful for comparative purposes. Emerson (1999) has described Oneota development as a result of a "tribalization," a process that emphasizes Middle Mississippian involvement in the formation of peripheral societies. This model is distinct from earlier interaction and migration models for three reasons. First, it situates influence specifically in simpler (non-Cahokia) chiefdoms nearer to Oneota developments. Second, it relies primarily on social reasons for Oneota developments. Third, it provides a specific example of chiefdom/tribe expectations based on ethnographic support. Expectations for tribes influenced by asymmetrical relationships with more complex chiefly societies include: (1) population aggregation into larger groups; (2) increased leadership centralization; (3) increased evidence of warfare (also see Hollinger 2005); and (4) the presence of a buffer zone and territorial boundedness (Emerson 1999:12). These expectations are supported with archaeological evidence from Langford Tradition sites. The main conclusion is that Langford originated in direct relation to more complex Middle Mississippians: "complexly organized, warlike societies 'create' neighbors who must, for the sake of survival, emulate them and socially, politically, and even spatially coalesce to defend themselves" (40). The main conclusion is that resulting changes were a way of creating an ethnic identity distinct from Middle Mississippian chiefdoms.

Conclusion

Several characteristics of Middle Mississippian village layout and mortuary practices were reviewed, resulting in the identification of several common characteristics. Plaza postholes are present in Middle Mississippian sites located to the south (eastern Tennessee) and west (Angel) of the Fort Ancient region. Solar alignments have been noted for several Middle Mississippian mound centers and at least one Angel phase village (Southwind), although I suspect they may also be present in other cases. Burials orientated to solstice alignments have been reported in several regions. Stone box graves are concentrated in the Middle Cumberland region. Burial rows are a general Middle Mississippian pattern, present in sites of various sizes and complexity. There are few ascribed status distinctions in lower-order Middle Mississippian villages. While the burials are generally egalitarian, males are the most likely to reflect higher statuses, which are often marked by supralocal symbols. One or two houses in villages are often positioned in closer proximity to the center (I suggest that this pattern mirrors the more centralized large mounds in mound centers); sometimes this is obvious (King) and sometimes it is subtle (Ledford Island, Southwind). These houses are often quite large and have been interpreted as council houses or leader residences.

The current view that Middle Mississippian influences on Fort Ancient development were minimal stems largely from the lack of clear burial ranking and settlement hierarchies. The problem with this conclusion is that it focuses on the most complex types of Middle Mississippian sites for comparisons when we have known for some time that Middle Mississippian villages and rural sites (and at least one entire Middle Mississippian system bordering the Fort Ancient [Mouse Creek]) exhibit an egalitarian structure similar to that expressed in Fort Ancient settlements. Many current models of Middle Mississippian social complexity present a relatively decentralized view. By extension, this renders smaller Middle Mississippian villages as being more autonomous than previously thought. However, the less complex Middle Mississippian model has not been integrated into studies of peripheral developments, nor has the broader range of Middle Mississippian settlement patterns been considered when drafting Fort Ancient evolutionary frameworks.

Models of Fort Ancient origins have shifted from migration-based explanations (e.g., Griffin 1943:257–260; Prufer and Shane 1970:258–262) to those downplaying significant interactions between Middle Mississippian and Fort Ancient groups (e.g., Pollack and Henderson 1992, 2000). Earlier models argued that Middle Mississippian migrants were solely responsible for initiating the development of Upper Mississippian groups, while more recent explanations have relied exclusively on Late Woodland contributions to the development of Fort Ancient societies. There have been few attempts to bridge the gap between these extreme views, although a few have made strong suggestions along these lines (Brose 1982:63; Cowan 1987; Drooker 1997; Essenpreis 1978; Robertson 1980).

3
An Approach to the Problem

Multiple spatial scales of analysis are considered in this examination of Fort Ancient village development, including household remains, mortuary domains, and overall site structure. Assessing the structure and growth of households is the focus at the residential level. The identification of leadership and assessing its development in relation to interactions with Middle Mississippians is the focus at the village level. As behavior is a multivariate phenomenon, data sets were developed from all key features and artifact classes, seeking concordance between them for the most robust conclusions (Carr 1985). This basic approach of concordance was used for the entire study, including the assessment of temporal change, defining household and leadership groups, and the examination of regional processes.

Several elements commonly associated with Middle Mississippian villages are used for exploring the fit between Fort Ancient and Middle Mississippian social structures. The goal is to develop a comprehensive understanding of the similarities and differences between these groups. However, the reader should not infer that existence of any one element in non–Middle Mississippian contexts weakens the observed relationships. One-to-one connections are not the goal of this analysis. The attempt is to demonstrate a "package deal": that if elements are common among Middle Mississippians *and* coupled with more diagnostic Middle Mississippian–style attributes in a Fort Ancient context, they are unlikely to have originated independently.

Temporal and Functional Indicators

Radiocarbon dates are compared with archaeological data indicative of temporal distinctions. Evidence embedded in the architectural patterns composed of postholes that form houses and stockades is considered, along with feature and artifact attributes that have been recognized as temporal indicators in regional studies. Temporally affiliated pit feature and artifact attributes were also compared with the sequence of architectural construction, the expectation being that houses that were rebuilt should be concentrated near earlier feature and artifact forms and, conversely, single-use structures should be located near more recent artifact and pit feature attributes.

In addition to radiocarbon dates, multiple lines of evidence were used to examine the temporal affiliation of pit features, including the relationship between feature form and diagnostic artifact attributes, refits, and seasonal associations of individual features. I suggest here that the problem of assigning relative contemporaneity to a series of disparate feature forms and addressing their relationship to a long radiocarbon sequence in a single-occupation site requires such an approach.

The most secure temporal indicators associated with Fort Ancient feature and artifact attributes are architectural reconstruction and the form of triangular projectile points. Other lines of evidence are somewhat problematic, although general trends for Fort Ancient do support higher occurrences of shell-tempered pottery over time and more cases of straight-sided storage features; the temporality of these attributes is examined by radiocarbon dating associated materials and by examining relationships with other diagnostic attributes. In other words, while certain attributes such as shell-tempered pottery and straight-sided storage pits are problematic as a temporal indicator (see below), they become secure if linked with later radiocarbon dates and/or more secure diagnostics. The following sections describe the temporal aspects of feature and artifact attributes.

Artifacts

Artifact analysis focused on developing a comprehensive data set, including basic artifact forms and frequencies from all pit features (with the exception of a recently excavated pit [Feature 2/05] located under West River Road [see Figure 1.4]). Specific attention was placed on temporal and functional differences.

Lithics. Lithic artifacts include chipped-stone projectile points, tools, debitage, and a variety of ground-stone implements and adornment. Chipped-stone tools and debitage data from excavations between 1971 and 1977 are based on Robertson (1980), supplemented with data from other excavations gathered by the author utilizing comparable categories. Ground stone data are based on Cook (2004).

Throughout the Fort Ancient region, significant temporal variation has been proposed for changes in the shape of triangular point sides and bases (Bradbury and Richmond 2004; Litfin et al. 1993; Railey 1992). The general finding has been that Early Fort Ancient assemblages are typified by incurvate sides and convex bases, Middle Fort Ancient assemblages often depict straight or serrated

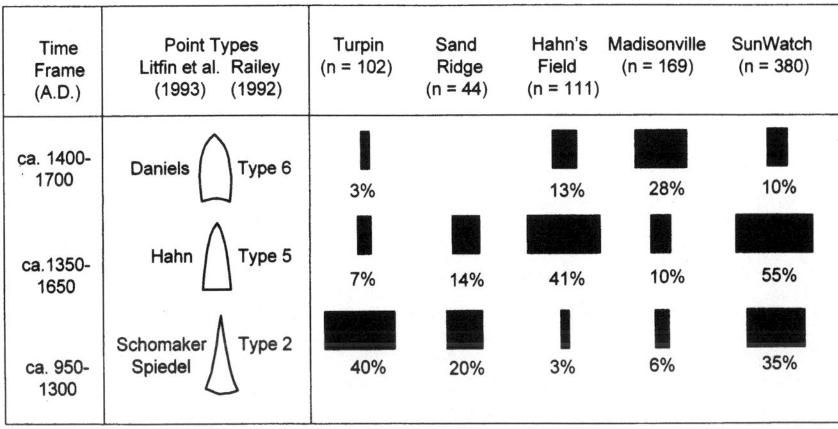

Figure 3.1. Seriation of triangular projectile point attributes at selected Fort Ancient sites with counterparts in the SunWatch assemblage. The SunWatch sample includes all triangular projectile points with intact bases, and percentages are based only on base form. (Adapted from Drooker 1997:Figure 6.63.)

sides and flat bases, while Late Fort Ancient assemblages are dominated by excurvate sides and concave bases (Figure 3.1).

Knives, drills, scrapers, preforms, spokeshaves, wedges, and burins constitute the formal chipped-stone tools. Knives were of two basic forms: Fort Ancient and large triangular. The distinguishing characteristic of Fort Ancient knives is the presence of a weak shoulder approximately 15–25 millimeters above the base. Drills were triangular, bipointed, or corner notched, the latter of which are possibly reworked projectile points. Scrapers include two forms: endscrapers and sidescrapers. Endscrapers were manufactured by removing small flakes from the distal margin of a large flake; sidescrapers were manufactured by working a lateral flake margin. Preforms were divided into triangular and nontriangular forms. Spokeshaves contain a broad concavity and are often referred to as "shaft straighteners," as their form suggests use for scraping and smoothing spear or arrow shafts or similarly shaped implements. Wedges are tools that were either the intentional end product of the bipolar technique (Tixier 1963) or the result of uses indicative of battering or pounding hard, dense materials such as bone, antler, or wood. They are generally rectangular in shape and exhibit bifacial flaking and battering on two or more edges. Burins are pointed piercing tools. Retouched flakes are casual tools that contain sporadically located flake scars limited to small areas of consecutive retouch that are too ambiguous for assignment to a specific tool type.

Chipped-stone debitage is the debris that results from the manufacture of tools and consists of cores, shatter, and flakes. Cores include any block of raw material from which flakes were removed during the manufacture of chipped-stone tools. Shatter denotes angular pieces of chert lacking attributes of controlled flaking (e.g., striking platform, bulb of percussion). Shatter is often the result of flaws in raw material and can occur at any point in the reduction sequence, though most are from core interiors. Flakes are usually the smallest form of debitage, consisting of waste material from the reduction of larger flakes or cores into distinct tool forms. The flake assemblage was divided into "primary thinning" and "secondary thinning" categories (Callahan 1979). Primary thinning flakes are removed early in the reduction sequence and are relatively thick in cross-section. In contrast, secondary flakes are removed later in the reduction sequence and are relatively thin in cross-section (Callahan 1979; see also Odell 2003:100, 127).

A variety of artifacts were fashioned by grinding or utilizing granite, limestone, or slate. These include tools, gaming pieces, pipes, and adornment. Tools consist of hammerstones, pitted stones, abraders, celts, choppers, manos, and metates. Gaming pieces include discoidals and presumably small circular discs and limestone or slate discs. Ground-stone pipes were elbow-shaped, effigy-shaped, or contained a platform. Ground-stone adornment included one slate pendant.

Pottery. Pottery has been the most intensively examined artifact class in Fort Ancient artifact assemblages, producing a variety of temporal and functional associations. Data from museum excavations used in this study were collected by Sunderhaus and include all rim and neck sherds (Cook and Sunderhaus 1999). Rim and neck sherd data from Allman's excavations were based on Shepherd (1992). Smith's pottery assemblage was not included because it could not always be reliably provenienced to the site level.

Pottery characteristics sensitive to change over time in the Fort Ancient region include temper type, vessel form, and decoration. Shell-tempered pottery appears to have been differentially adopted by Fort Ancient societies but by A.D. 1400 became the dominant tempering agent throughout the region (Prufer and Shane 1970:241; Riggs 1998; Turnbow and Henderson 1992). Early and Middle Fort Ancient assemblages in much of the Fort Ancient region have small percentages of shell-tempered pottery (Carskadden and Morton 2000; Prufer and Shane 1970:232–245; Turnbow and Henderson 1992). Generally, Early Fort Ancient sites nearer the Ohio River contain pottery that is more often shell tempered than sites farther up the drainages, which generally contain more pottery that is more often tempered with crushed rock.

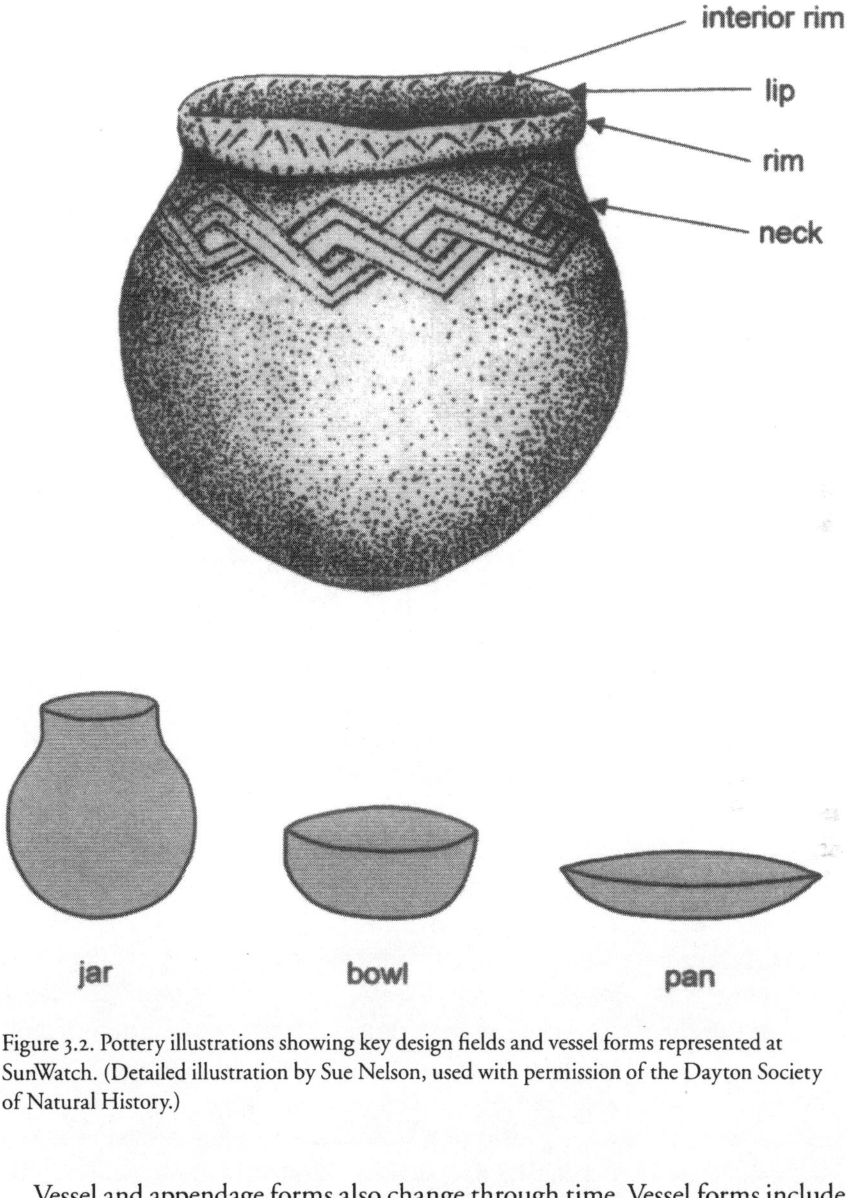

Figure 3.2. Pottery illustrations showing key design fields and vessel forms represented at SunWatch. (Detailed illustration by Sue Nelson, used with permission of the Dayton Society of Natural History.)

Vessel and appendage forms also change through time. Vessel forms include jars, bowls, and pans. Appendages include lugs, straps, and a variety of effigies. Assemblages from before A.D. 1400 are almost exclusively composed of jar forms and lug handles, while later sites have the full range of vessel types and appendages. SunWatch contains jars, bowls, and a pan (Figure 3.2). This diversification in morphology occurs as Madisonville ceramics develop, which are shell tempered with strap handles and few decorative motifs (Turnbow and Henderson 1992). Effigy adornos (a.k.a. "rim riders") also become more common at this time (Pollack et al. 2002).

Pottery design characteristics also change over time in the Fort Ancient region, and a variety of Middle Mississippian–style designs have been observed. Plain bodies and necks are more common in the Early and Late periods, whereas the Middle Fort Ancient period is marked by the most intensive neck, rim, and appendage decorations. The most common types of Middle Mississippian pottery designs in Fort Ancient assemblages are Ramey Incised–like and negative-painted designs, which Pauketat and Emerson (1991) and Hilgeman (1991: 11–13) argue on the basis of design motifs and breakage and discard patterns are elite symbols that were distributed within the context of elite-orchestrated renewal ceremonies (e.g., Green Corn [Witthoft 1949]). SunWatch contains several negative-painted sherds and a complete jar; interestingly, the jar contains both characteristic Fort Ancient (rectilinear guilloche, grit temper) and Middle Mississippian (negative paint, shell temper) attributes (Figure 3.3). The SunWatch examples appear to be similar to the Angel negative-painted unslipped "black-on-buff" variety (Black 1967; Hilgeman 1991:5). However, most sherds of this type recovered at the Angel site were from plates (86%), and negative painting accounts for a small minority of the total sherd assemblage (<1%) (Hilgeman 1991:5). There are several examples of Ramey Incised–like designs and negative-painted designs at Early to Middle Fort Ancient sites in southwest Ohio (see Chapter 6). Several other examples of Middle Mississippian pottery styles are present in Late Fort Ancient assemblages, including a vessel in the shape of a human head at Madisonville (similar to vessels from southeast Missouri [Drooker 1997:322]).

Pottery data utilized in this study included several morphological and design characteristics. Morphological data included vessel form (bowls, jars, pans), appendage form (strap and lug appendages), and temper type (grit, shell, grit/shell, sand, micaceous schist, quartz, gritty grog [crushed pottery]). The only pottery designs included are from vessel necks (see Figure 3.2), as this design field is the most variable. Specific neck decorations were grouped into six categories: guilloche, line-filled triangles, scrolls, crosshatching, single slash, and herringbone motifs (Figure 3.4).

Bone and shell. A wide variety of artifacts was manufactured from animal bone, antler, shell, and teeth. Lynn Simonelli and William Kennedy gathered these data.

Artifacts were grouped into two functional categories, tools and adornment. Tools were made from bone, antler, and shell. A variety of awls was manufactured from deer bones, although several elk and turkey bones were also used.

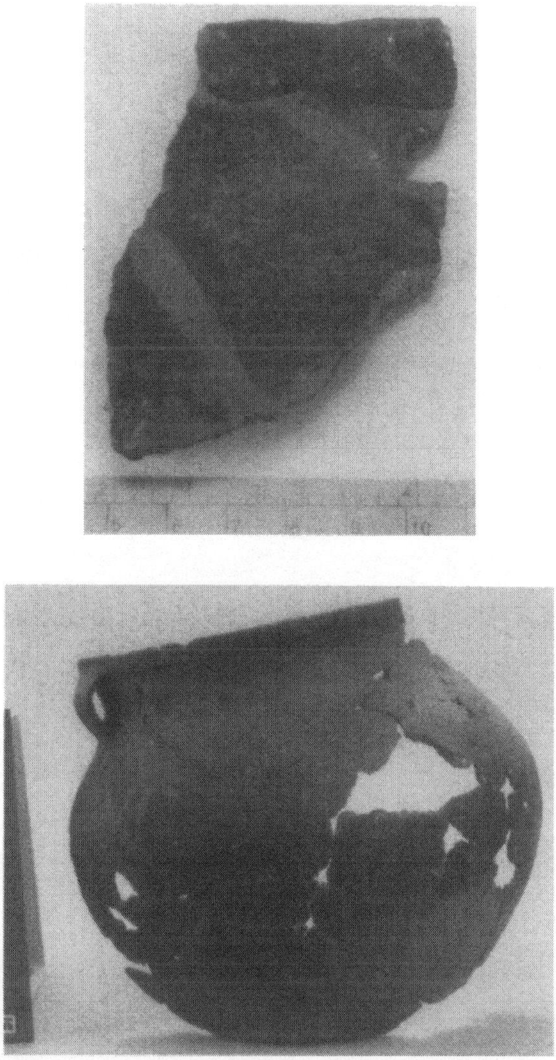

Figure 3.3. Selections of Middle Mississippian–style negative-painted pottery from SunWatch. (Photographs by Thomas Patterson.)

Pins, fishing hooks, beamers, knives, combs, turtle shell bowls and spoons, and needles comprise the remainder of the bone tool assemblage. Antler tools include flakers, projectile points, awls, and scrapers. Mussel shell was also used for the manufacture of hoes and spoons.

Adornment includes beads and pendants. Pendants were usually manufac-

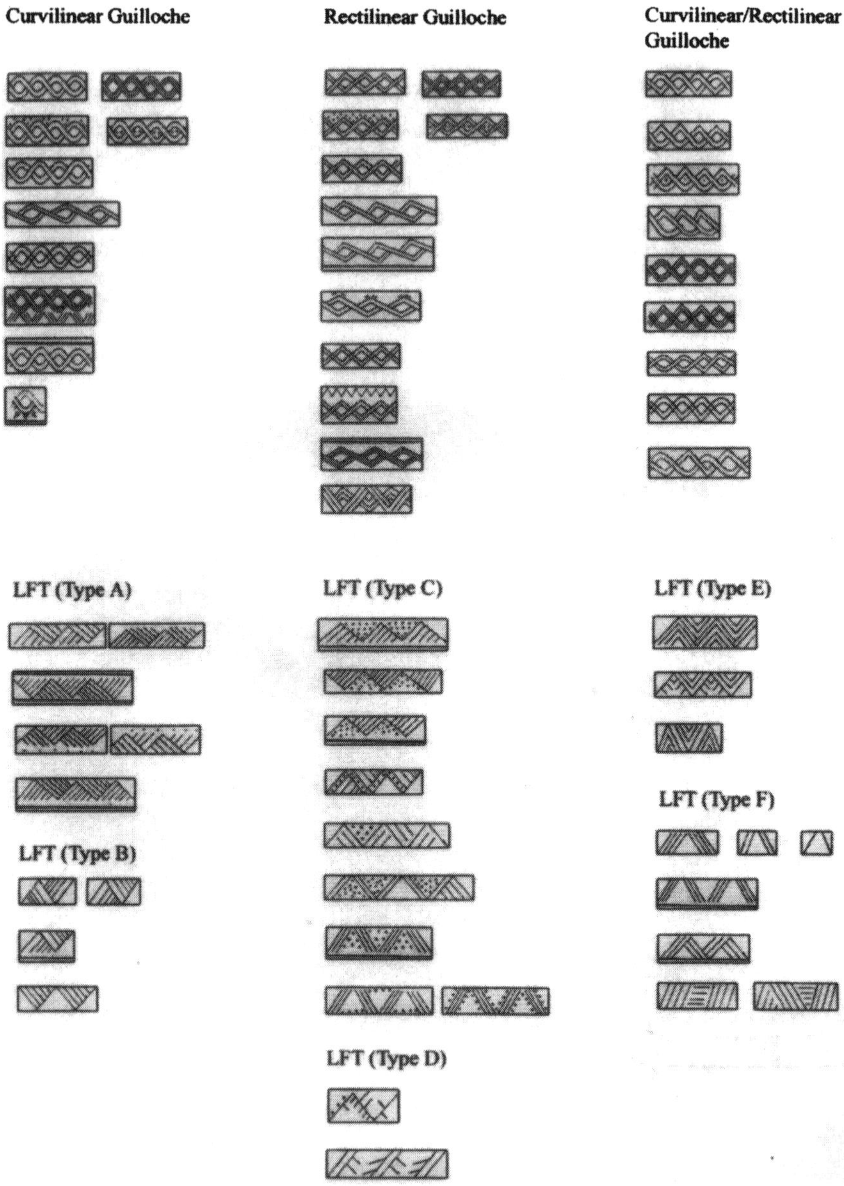

Figure 3.4. Incised designs on SunWatch pottery necks. (Drawings by Robert Cook and Thomas Grooms.)

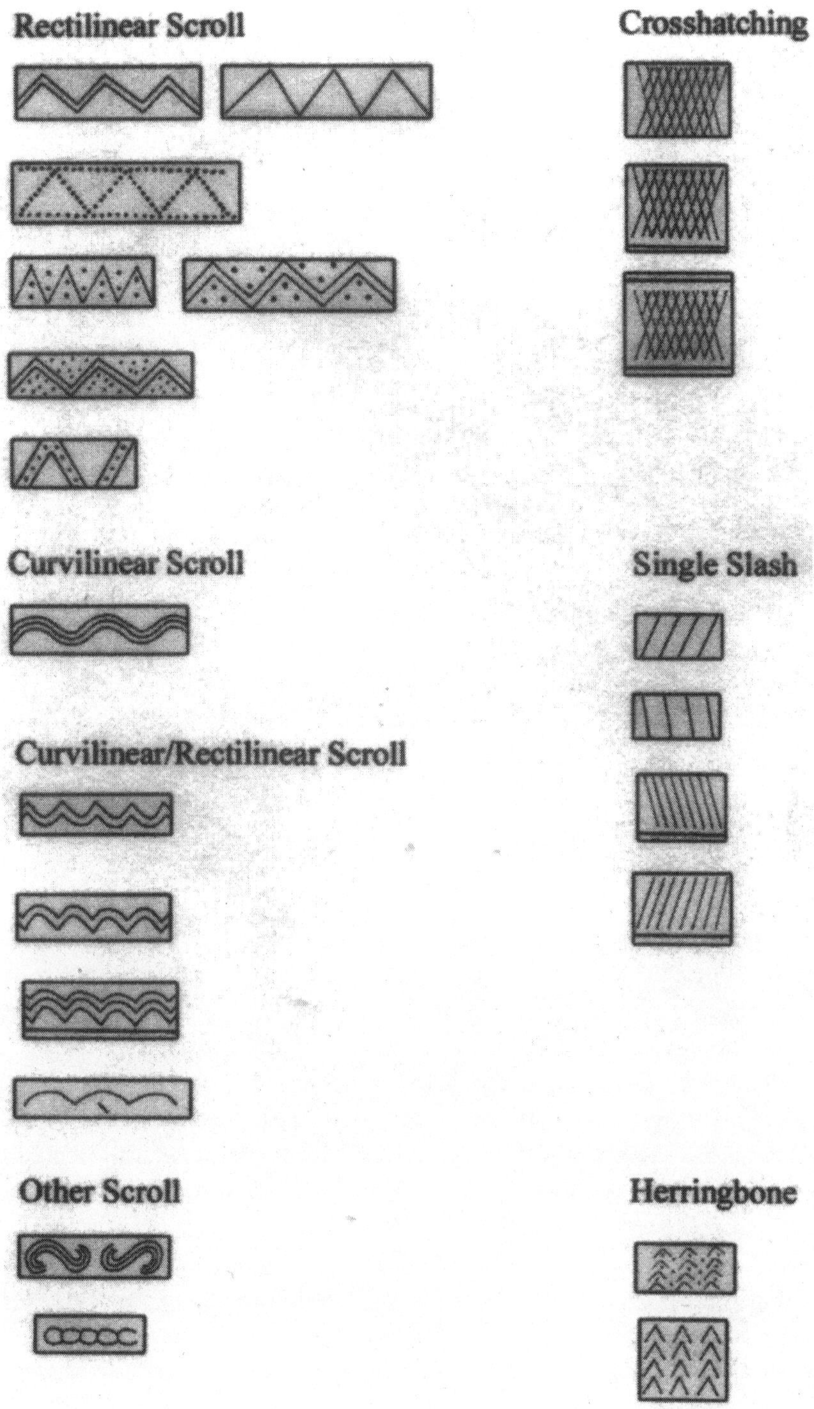

Figure 3.4. *Continued*

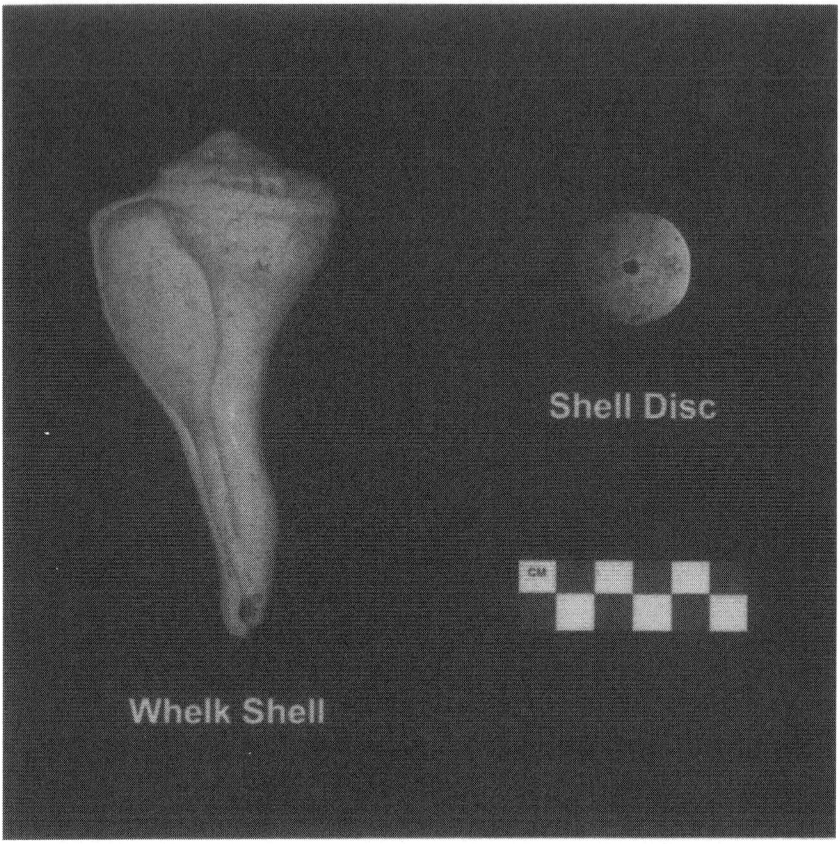

Figure 3.5. Photographs of the whelk shell and a shell disc from SunWatch. (Photograph of whelk shell courtesy of Andrew Sawyer.)

tured by drilling a single hole in elk, bear, fish, or wolf teeth. Single drill holes were also present on fragments of bone or shell, suggesting their use as pendants. Pendants were generally carved from local shells into triangular, circular, or amorphous forms. Beads were primarily fashioned from shell, although bone beads were also present. Bone and shell discs were also present (Figure 3.5), which were primarily used as ear, wrist, and chest adornment, based on the locations of these items in burials.

One complete lightning whelk shell was present (see Figure 3.5). It appears to have been worn as part of a headdress, as it was drilled and positioned with a bone pin on top of the head of a burial near a fish teeth "mosaic." The specimen is similar to whelk shell pendants on Spiro and other Middle Mississippian shells (Phillips and Brown 1978:Figure 176, Figure 179). While the SunWatch specimen is not engraved, the placement of a drill hole near the basal tip of the shell is similar to locations of drill holes on Middle Mississippian examples (28 and Figure 10).

Faunal remains were also used to assess seasonality in relation to site chronology. Seasonality data were examined in relation to occupation, assessing whether the same parts of the year are represented equally at different times during the occupation of the site (i.e., was there a change in seasonal use of the site over time?). Seasonality was based on dental eruption, tooth wear, and bone absorption of the alveolus of deciduous teeth of juvenile deer. Data were sorted into three seasons: spring (April–June), summer (late May–September), and winter (October–April) (Shane 1988; Shane and Wagner 1993).

Artifact refits. A final consideration to assist in temporal affiliations of pit features is the locations of artifact refits, commonly used to establish contemporaneity (Orton et al. 1993: 210). As attractive as artifact refits are in terms of their direct association with a single artifact, their interpretation is rarely given critical thought. They are in fact a limited data set in at least two ways. First, not only do we know them to be incomplete, but it is also very difficult to estimate the percentage of the assemblage that has actually been refitted which renders it a qualitative data set (Orton et al. 1993:210); this is particularly true for large assemblages. Second, artifacts refitted from secondary deposits (e.g., trash pits) are particularly problematic because it is not certain how long the discarded artifacts were in provisional refuse areas before regular or ad hoc maintenance activities relocated them into "permanent" subterranean storage (Schiffer 1987:67).

Due to these limitations, refits are used to examine whether pit types associated with different points in the village occupation are contemporary only *after* more complete temporal criteria have been utilized. I also limit my consideration of artifact refits to pottery, as this is the only artifact class that has been completely examined; lithic artifacts excavated after 1977 have not been comprehensively subjected to refit analysis. I also consider distance to be an important variable in the analysis of artifact refits and examine the relationship between three distance categories and other data sets, based on natural breaks in the distribution (<25 feet, 25–100 feet, >100 feet). Pottery refits were completed by Heilman (1988b) and Sunderhaus (Cook and Sunderhaus 1999).

Pit Features

There are four basic pit feature forms at SunWatch: bell-shaped storage pits, straight-sided storage pits, shallow straight-sided features, and shallow basin-shaped features (modified from a typology developed by Nass 1987:151–152). This feature typology was utilized in the present study, adding subsequently excavated features (museum and avocational). Nass (161–166) also determined feature volumes for most features; I followed his methodology for adding this measure for the additional features. Depth was added to the present study in order to numerically divide deep and shallow pit features. Storage pits were limited to deep straight-sided and bell-shaped pits as these meet the requirements of depth and volume presented by several researchers (see below) (Hatch and Stevenson 1980; Schroedl 1980:33; Siegel 1982; Webb 1992:94). Pit features generally increase in volume throughout the Fort Ancient period (Cowan 1987:13). It is also generally thought that pit features changed from bell-shaped to straight-sided through time (see Cook 2007). (Note that this approach is distinct from that followed in Cook 2004, which utilized Nass's types directly.)

Architecture

Two lines of evidence were used to assess architectural construction episodes: stockade/house relationships and in situ house rebuilding. Posthole densities and daub concentrations were used to examine the rebuilding of SunWatch houses. In an examination of Iroquois houses—also of single post construction—posthole density proved to be the best indicator of occupation duration (Warrick 1988:34). Single-use houses were considered to be those with the fewest postholes per square foot of structure area; houses containing twice this ratio were used for a minimum of two use-lives (not accounting for rebuilding episodes that utilized the same postholes). Ethnographically documented structures similar to those at SunWatch (i.e., earth and wood) most often have use-life ranges between 5 and 15 years (McIntosh 1976:96–97), although there are a few instances of longer uses (Cameron 1991:160–161). The low end of this range is consistent with wood decay rates for oak (6 years) and hickory (4 years) (Warrick 1988:Table 4 and Table 5); these are the primary wood types used in house construction at the site (Wagner 1979). However, experimental observations of reconstructed houses at SunWatch suggest that 15 years is not an unreasonable estimate (Cook 2005:383). Based on these lines of evidence, 5 to 15 years is the narrowest estimate for the use of a single use-life of a SunWatch house.

The occurrence of wall daub was examined as an independent test of architectural rebuilding. If houses with higher posthole densities were rebuilt, they should be spatially associated with a higher incidence of wall daub, as houses that were not renovated would lack wall material in household garbage. The assumption was that some daub from the initial structure would have been discarded in trash pits in preparation for house rebuilding episodes.

Examining Corporate Behavior

Examination of corporate behavior was based on data from residential and mortuary domains. The combination of approaches, if in general agreement with each other, was reasoned to provide a robust identification of this form of social organization. Several studies of Middle Mississippian communities have assumed that houses grouped together constitute extended kin groupings (see Chapter 2), but this assumption has not been explicitly tested (Muller 1997:190). Furthermore, the examination of temporal change at a single site is a critical aspect of mortuary investigations, though often neglected, largely due to methodological difficulties (O'Shea 1984:14). In this study, household activity areas provide a critical link between burial groups and house structures with which to test a general ethnographic model of residential development. Burial data are based on Evans-Eargle (1998) and Smith (n.d.).

Household Clusters

I assumed that household units should consist of houses, pit features, and burials in spatially segregated areas. An important part of spatial analysis in the mortuary domain is observability. If the use of mortuary space was patterned in such a way as to be obvious to those using the site, then its structure should be obvious through visual inspection, not always distinguishable on the basis of quantitative methods (Goldstein 1980:136). I extended this logic to the spatial analysis of household composition. "House clusters" were defined on the basis of discernible breaks between house, pit, and burial groups (Winter 1976:25). A poster-sized site map was visually inspected for discernible breaks between closely spaced houses, pits, and burials.

Assessing the formation of house clusters began by delimiting their internal spatial units. Pit features were also grouped on the basis of visually discernible breaks in their distribution on a poster-sized site map. Features in closer proximity to each other than to other features were considered to be distinct activity areas. Interfeature pottery refits in the shortest distance class (<25 feet) were used to refine these groupings. These activity areas were considered to be household-specific if they were located in close proximity to particular houses. Each resulting household activity area—consisting of a house, a pit feature group, and burials—formed the basis of the smallest spatial comparisons in this study. Diagnostic feature and artifact attributes were compared between pit feature groups to identify a sequence of use. Medium-distance pottery refits (25–100 feet) were examined to assess how residential units of differing ages were related to each other. The expectation was that older areas would be linked with more recently established neighbors, which would support a general ethnographic model of localized family development. In other words, household areas would grow over time (see below).

Linking Residential and Mortuary Spaces

An ethnographic model of residential development was employed to examine the fit between observed formation of house clusters and expectations regarding lineal descent (Goodenough 1956; Goody 1958:79–87, 1972). Specific expectations of this model are that certain structures were occupied first (founders) and formed the nucleus of localized extended family developments consisting of structures linked to the parent (Figure 3.6). The residential component of this model was derived from the work of Fortes (1949:63) among the Tallensi: "The domestic group grows, changes, and dissolves with the growth cycle of (the effective minimal) lineage, and a particular elementary family is only an episode in this cycle. The structure of the Tale family cannot be divorced from its existence in time. We have to examine it as a process: At any given time we find domestic families at every stage of development in a Tale community." While this model has been applied most notably in archaeological contexts to examine the establishment and growth of Mayan households (Haviland 1988; Tourtellot 1988), it is appropriate for examining localized corporate group development more generally (Goody 1972).

The mortuary assemblage was used as an independent line of evidence to examine whether lineal descent groups were present in the village. The ubiquitous nature of lineages and the fact that they often form smaller parts of villages make them an attractive candidate for archaeological investigations of social structure (see Chapter 1). However, as lineages imply a particular system of descent and are notoriously difficult to reconstruct even in ethnographic settings, it is not the most useful starting point for archaeological investigations (Allen and Richardson 1971). The term *corporate group* is preferred in this investigation as it is more neutral in its social implications while maintaining a rule of lineal inheritance (Goldstein 1980:7–8).

The examination of corporate groups further investigates a series of hypotheses derived from ethnographic data (Saxe 1970), which were confirmed and modified using rural Middle Mississippian populations (Goldstein 1980). "To the degree that corporate group rights to use and/or control crucial but restricted resources are attained and/or legitimized by means of lineal descent from the dead (i.e., lineal ties to ancestors), such groups will maintain formal disposal areas for the exclusive disposal of their dead, and conversely" (Saxe 1970:119). Based on this straightforward description, the first step was simply to partition burials into groups based on visual inspection. Three or more buri-

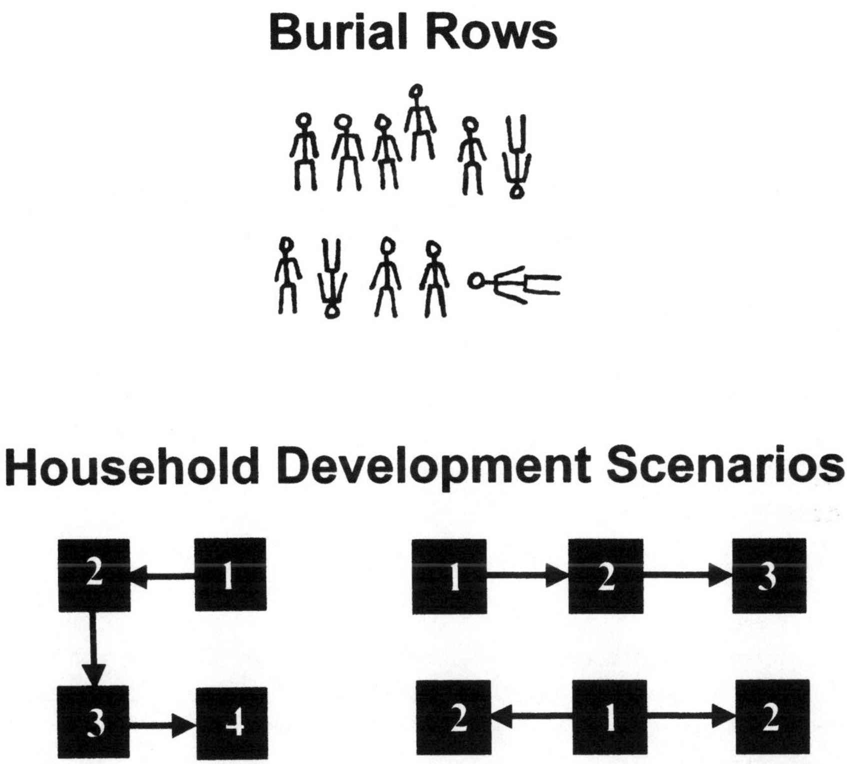

Figure 3.6. Generalized model for lineal descent in mortuary and residential patterning. (Mortuary pattern after Goldstein 1980:104; residential model on left is based on descriptions in Haviland 1988 and Haviland et al. 2005:Figure 9.2.)

als located in closer proximity to each other than to other burials were considered to be a "group," along with arc-row patterns (below).

In applying this model to two rural Middle Mississippian cemeteries, Goldstein (1980:124) determined that the placement of burials in visually distinguishable rows was a key component to their structure and are in other rural Middle Mississippian sites as well. The formal definition of a row followed Goldstein (103): "A row is the set of all burials falling between a pair of parallel lines 1½ body lengths apart, subject to the conditions: (1) that the set includes at least five complete burials, (2) that at least five burials have parallel axes of orientation, and (3) that the rules of inclusion for burials, specified below, are satisfied." The specified rules of inclusion focus on proximity and orientation. Proximity identifies that the burials must be closer to each other than to any other burials, the exception being for a burial in a row but not near others in that row, in which case it should be included so long as it is has the same orientation as the others and is not located near any other row. Orientation specifies that body axes only need to be parallel (i.e., head to toe is acceptable), the only exception being if a perpendicular body is closer to a given row than to any other burials and if it also falls within one body length of the others (103–104; see Figure 3.6).

The Saxe/Goldstein model could not be employed at SunWatch without considering the circular nature of the village structure. This required the addition of a circular dimension to the rules presented above. Exploration of the burial pattern proceeded in the following fashion: (1) circles radiating from the central posthole were drawn in 5-foot increments using ArcGIS; and (2) lines were drawn through burial rows adhering to rules discussed above. This resulted in the identification of a series of arc and row patterns forming spatially distinct groups.

Temporal affiliations for burials were assigned on the basis of interment frequency, types of artifact inclusions, leg positions, and radiocarbon dating of bone collagen of identified "leaders" (see below). It was expected that portions of a corporate group containing more burials and earlier artifacts would be located near activity areas and houses established earlier in the village occupation. Body positions were categorized as fully flexed, semiflexed, extended, secondary, or disarticulated. Flexed burials may be more strongly associated with Late Woodland populations in the region than with Fort Ancient groups (Drooker 1997:87, 143). The best example is from the Turpin site, where a sizeable Fort Ancient village is superimposed over a Late Woodland site. With respect to the mortuary pattern, the following was noted: "All the complete Woodland burials were flexed or partly flexed; all the Fort Ancient burials were intrusive and in an extended position" (Oehler 1973:5).

Correspondence Analysis

Correspondence analysis was used to statistically examine distinctions in the frequency of selected attributes between house clusters, between pit feature groups, and between burial groups. Correspondence analysis is a multivariate technique that plots multiple variables in terms of a measurable Euclidean distance. This technique is similar to principal components analysis, although more useful on the basis of the number of relationships that can be simultaneously examined. Using principal components analysis, component scores can be plotted to see which cases are similar, and relationships between variables and between variables and components can also be plotted. However, in correspondence analysis, the relationship between cases, between variables, and between variables and cases can all be analyzed together and represented in the same scattergram, greatly facilitating interpretation. The result of this test visually reveals which items are most associated with a given spatial unit in relation to all other items in the matrix (Shennan 1988:284). XLSTAT 7.0 was used for completing correspondence analyses.

Village Leadership and Intervillage Interaction

Leadership within a village and intervillage interaction are often interconnected phenomena, as a local leader often uses long-distance exchange relationships to gain status and power within the home village (e.g., Blanton et al. 1996; Chagnon 1968; Cochrane 1970; Douglas 1967; Hayden 1995; Helms 1988, 1993; Leach and Leach 1983; Peregrine 1992; Renfrew 1986). There are also linkages between local population size and the types of sociopolitical institutions needed to administer that group. When a local group exceeds a certain population threshold, leadership institutions develop at a level above the local household (Johnson 1982). With these issues in mind, the basic questions asked in this portion of the study are: (1) Did village-level leadership develop later in the occupation? (2) Was this development concurrent with the growth of other residential zones? (3) Was this a time of demonstrable contact with Middle Mississippians? (4) Is this leadership style similar to that expressed in Middle Mississippian villages?

Identifying Village Leaders

Status can be ascribed or achieved and is often discernible in the archaeological record. The most commonly used method is the analysis of mortuary patterning (Binford 1971; Brown 1971). It is generally assumed that the more varied mortuary treatments an individual possesses, the more statuses that person had achieved in life: "patterning in the variability of mortuary remains will reflect a consciously selected set of distinctions that will be congruent with the social positions held by the deceased in life" (O'Shea 1984:10; see also Goodenough 1965; Linton 1936; Saxe 1970). It has also been observed in some settings that artifact diversity increases with older individuals (e.g., O'Shea 1984:93–94), presumably marking the acquisition of more social statuses.

Sociotechnic artifact types, defined as "material elements having their primary functional context in the social sub-systems of the total cultural system," often accompany leadership positions within a society (Binford 1962:219). This artifact type is contrasted with "technomic" ones, or "those artifacts having their primary functional context in coping directly with the physical environment" (Binford 1962:219). As societies become more complex and hierarchical (i.e., ranked), sociotechnic markers become more common. "Supralocal" symbols, defined as sociotechnic artifacts recognized over a wide geographical area, are often important for identifying the highest-ranking members of a polity (Peebles and Kus 1977). Most notable is the restriction of these types of items to members of a predominantly male ruling group (J. Brown 1981:29–30). Middle Mississippians exchanged a variety of materials over long distances, including fluorite, coal, lithics, copper, and marine shell (Muller 1997:365). Seashells, especially lightning whelk, were one of the most important (248), and it has been suggested that these materials and items fashioned from them served to define ranks of leaders within chiefdoms (Brown 1971).

Mortuary ranking was statistically examined using cluster analysis, a technique that has proven to be well suited for this purpose (Goldstein 1980; O'Shea 1984; Peebles and Kus 1977; Rothschild 1979). Ward's method, an agglomerative type of cluster analysis that combines cases most similar to one another, was employed in this analysis. A variety of cluster solutions was explored, recognizing the heuristic nature of the analysis for a particular data set and understanding that the interpretation of clusters is somewhat subjective (O'Shea 1984:69). A particular artifact type was included in the analysis only if it was present in more than one burial. As my goal was to identify general levels of social distinction, incidence analysis was followed, meaning that artifacts were coded only on a presence/absence basis; artifact abundance was not examined, although this could prove useful in future more fine-grained analyses (after O'Shea 1984:62–63). SPSS 11.0 was used to complete this statistical procedure.

Storage distinctions and unique houses are also commonly used to delimit higher social statuses. In particular, large houses are generally associated with leaders in a variety of settings (Coupland and Banning 1996:3–4). Lightfoot and Feinman (1982) have developed the following set of criteria for identifying "leader" households within sites: leaders' houses should be the largest domestic structures, contain the largest storage facilities, possess intensified subsistence techniques, and contain more exotic artifacts than other households. Wilk and Netting (1984) also suggest that storage volumes may be larger relative to house size, and it has also been noted that leaders may control access to storage facilities (Hendon 2000; Wesson 1999). Households of leaders are often positioned in central locations within settlements and may exhibit unusual construction styles and/or materials.

Plazas contain central postholes in 57% of the cases in my Middle Mississippian village sample. A majority of these same villages (87%) contain one or two houses (sometimes larger ones) positioned in closer proximity to the site center than other residential units (see Chapter 2). To assess whether portions of SunWatch were closer to the central posthole, circles drawn for the burial analysis were employed (see above). Locations of houses, burials, and pit features were examined to determine if a proximity rule could be applied to these domains. Examination of other potential status markers built on previous SunWatch research. Solar alignments were previously identified by Heilman and Hoefer (1981) and Goss (1988) and were used in the present study to examine their relationship to other lines of evidence including burial placement, as Middle Mississippian burial orientations have been linked with solstice alignments in several cases (see Chapter 2). Architectural uniqueness was examined by examining wood species used in construction (identified by Wagner 1979), and house sizes were measured in terms of floor area and average posthole depth and diameter (Cook 2005). Storage was assessed by examining the volume of pit features greater than 1.6 feet in depth (see Chapter 4) and determining if there were any structures that may have been used in limiting access to storage.

Each of the above areas of leadership indicators was examined separately. However, I suggest that one of the strengths of this investigation is the comparison between mortuary and nonmortuary domains in the examination of village leadership. For example, individuals who are singled out on the basis of mortuary data are compared against other attributes (e.g., concentrations of particular artifacts in nonmortuary contexts, locations of unique architecture) to further understand dynamic social issues. Moreover, artifacts that are associated with later burials are compared against other contexts to further evaluate those conclusions. In this sense, this study employs what should be one of the goals of mortuary analysis: to use it in tandem with other lines of evidence to "confront the more complex issues of culture process in the past" (O'Shea 1984:303).

Investigating Interregional and Intraregional Interaction

The investigation of interactions within the Fort Ancient region and with Middle Mississippian neighbors involved applying a modified form of the peer polity interaction model, what I refer to as the "periphery peer" model (see Chapter 1). Middle Mississippian characteristics were examined at SunWatch and other Fort Ancient sites in southwest Ohio to assess whether interactions were primarily between SunWatch and Middle Mississippians or whether they were common throughout the surrounding Fort Ancient subregion. Characteristics include architectural features and Middle Mississippian–style artifacts. Specific theoretical expectations drawn from peer polity interaction (Chapter 1) include:

Highly visible structural homologies. There should be marked similarities between the architectural layout of SunWatch and contemporary Fort Ancient villages and neighboring Middle Mississippian villages. Criteria specifically include use of center poles, closer proximity of large or uniquely constructed houses, and burial rows (many of which are visible through the use of limestone grave covers).

Previous contact. There should be evidence of Middle Mississippian contacts at Fort Ancient sites earlier than SunWatch.

Prestige goods. Artifacts associated with Middle Mississippian "leaders" should be present in Fort Ancient villages.

Increase in social complexity. The social structure of SunWatch should become more complex after interactions with Middle Mississippians. Identified leaders should be associated with later points in the site occupation and in close connection with Middle Mississippian–style features and artifacts.

Peers and polities. The presence of a peer in one community should also be identifiable in others. Also, Fort Ancient villages containing the highest occurrences of Middle Mississippian–style characteristics should generally be evenly spaced from one another.

Conclusion

This chapter has presented a methodology for discerning temporal patterning within a Fort Ancient village, drawing on regional studies that have documented chronological changes of key artifact and feature attributes. Implementation of this approach sets the stage for examination of dynamic models associated with the growth of corporate groups, which includes both residential and mortuary dimensions. These two lines of evidence serve as independent tests of this phenomenon. Determining temporal affiliations of site areas also sets up the examination of the emergence of political power within the village from a periphery peer polity theoretical perspective. I suggest that this approach greatly facilitates examination of Middle Mississippian influence on Fort Ancient village formation and vice versa. After the SunWatch case is presented (Chapter 4 and Chapter 5), a regional analysis examines the extent to which the pattern can be extended to other Fort Ancient villages (Chapter 6).

4
Corporate Behavior in Space and Time

This chapter identifies corporate groups at SunWatch by spatially and diachronically linking residential and mortuary domains. A chronological framework is first established on the basis of relations between temporally diagnostic artifact and feature attributes. The interrelated growth of household clusters and burial groups is then examined.

Chronological Framework

This section establishes a chronological framework to provide the foundation against which to examine the development of corporate groups. Several parts of the village produced evidence for architectural growth (see Figure 1.4). The bimodal temporal pattern of radiocarbon dates is investigated against their spatial distribution in relation to the location of stockades and structures and evidence for their rebuilding, along with the relationship between temporally diagnostic artifact and feature attributes.

Radiocarbon Dates

Calendar ranges for radiocarbon ages were calibrated with CALIB REV5.0.2 using intca104.14c (Reimer et al. 2004). Seventeen of the radiocarbon dates for SunWatch were produced from carbonized wood from house and pit feature contexts, one date was produced from a charred corn kernel recovered from a pit feature, and one date resulted from testing carbonized wood recovered from the large posthole in the center of the village plaza. One of these dates is problematic (CWR-156 [House 1/73]); the size of this sample was too small to obtain a reliable measure and, as a result, will not be considered in making temporal associations.

The temporal distribution of radiocarbon assays suggests two episodes of occupation, particularly when the median dates are considered. However, at the two-sigma level there is overlap between most of the dates, indicating that it is statistically most likely that the majority of dates resulted from a similar temporal event (Figure 4.1). The remainder of this section explores the extent

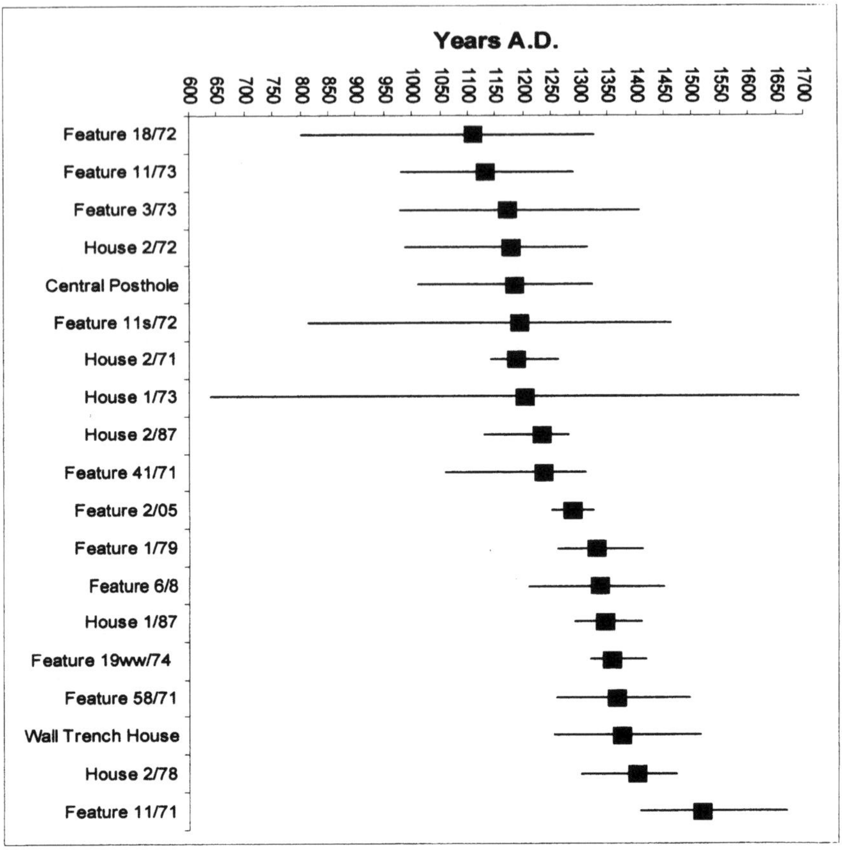

Figure 4.1. Radiocarbon dates associated with houses, pit features, and postholes at SunWatch. Squares indicate median dates and lines indicate two-sigma ranges. (See Cook 2007: table 1.)

to which these dates are indicating a temporal distinction based on their relationship to other lines of evidence.

Architectural Rebuilding

Spatial relationships between stockades, houses, and radiocarbon dates suggest that the village grew outward over time. This growth pattern appears to be restricted to the north and west parts of the site (see Figure 1.4). A stockade segment overlaps House 1/72, and several stockade portions are obscured in areas of subsequent construction (e.g., near Houses 2/87, 2/72, and 3/72); stockade fragments are also located near House 1/72 and House 2/74.

I postulate that the outer stockade lines are more recent; the village grew outward over time. The relationship between stockades and radiocarbon dates for houses is consistent; houses producing later radiocarbon dates are generally located in the outer ring of houses (Figure 4.2). A later radiocarbon date (median = A.D. 1348) for House 1/87 fits its location in the outer ring of houses. The intermediate radiocarbon date (median = A.D. 1233) for House 2/87 is also consistent with reconstruction evidence. Based on the location of stockades, this house appears to have been built after House 2/71 and House 2/72. House 2/71 is a large structure located in the northern part of the site that was commingled with several pit features. An earlier date (median = A.D. 1189) was produced for this structure, which is consistent with its location in the inner ring of houses. House 2/72 also produced an earlier radiocarbon date (median = A.D. 1178). Initially, this seems to be unusual as this house is in the outer ring of structures. However, based on stockade patterning there is good reason to conclude that House 2/72 was constructed before House 2/87, which is consistent with the radiocarbon dates.

Variation in posthole density relative to house size and the distribution of wall daub was used to ascertain temporal differences. Houses were grouped into three rebuilding classes based on natural breaks in the distribution of posthole to area ratios: (1) low = 0.16–0.21 postholes per square foot; (2) medium = 0.21–0.28 postholes per square foot; and (3) high = 0.28–0.38 postholes per square foot. The majority of houses in the high rebuilding class are located in the southern part of the village. In contrast, houses in the low rebuilding class are predominantly located in other portions of the site (see Figure 4.2). The distribution of daub corresponds well to the locations of rebuilt structures. House 1/71 is the only structure situated near a heavy daub concentration lacking a higher proportion of postholes relative to area; this house was possibly rebuilt, which could explain this discrepancy (Cook 2005:361–364).

The relationship between house rebuilding and radiocarbon dates is not as clear, although all rebuilt houses are in the inner ring, which fits the general expectation of the village expanding outward over time (see Figure 4.2). In two cases (1/87, 2/87) nonrebuilt houses were associated with later radiocarbon dates (medians = AD. 1348 and A.D. 1233, respectively). These findings are consistent with expectations. However, there are several exceptions to this pattern. Houses 2/71 and 2/72 produced early dates and were not rebuilt, suggesting that they were not used a second time. House 2/78 produced a late date and appears to have been rebuilt, based on posthole density and daub distribution. However, this structure is unusual in that it contains significantly larger and more closely spaced postholes than all other houses, which likely produced the larger ratio in the absence of apparent rebuilding. Based solely on its location in the inner ring of structures and evidence for rebuilding, House 2/78 seems to date early in the occupational sequence of the village. However, it produced one of the latest dates at the site (median = A.D. 1404). While these lines of evidence

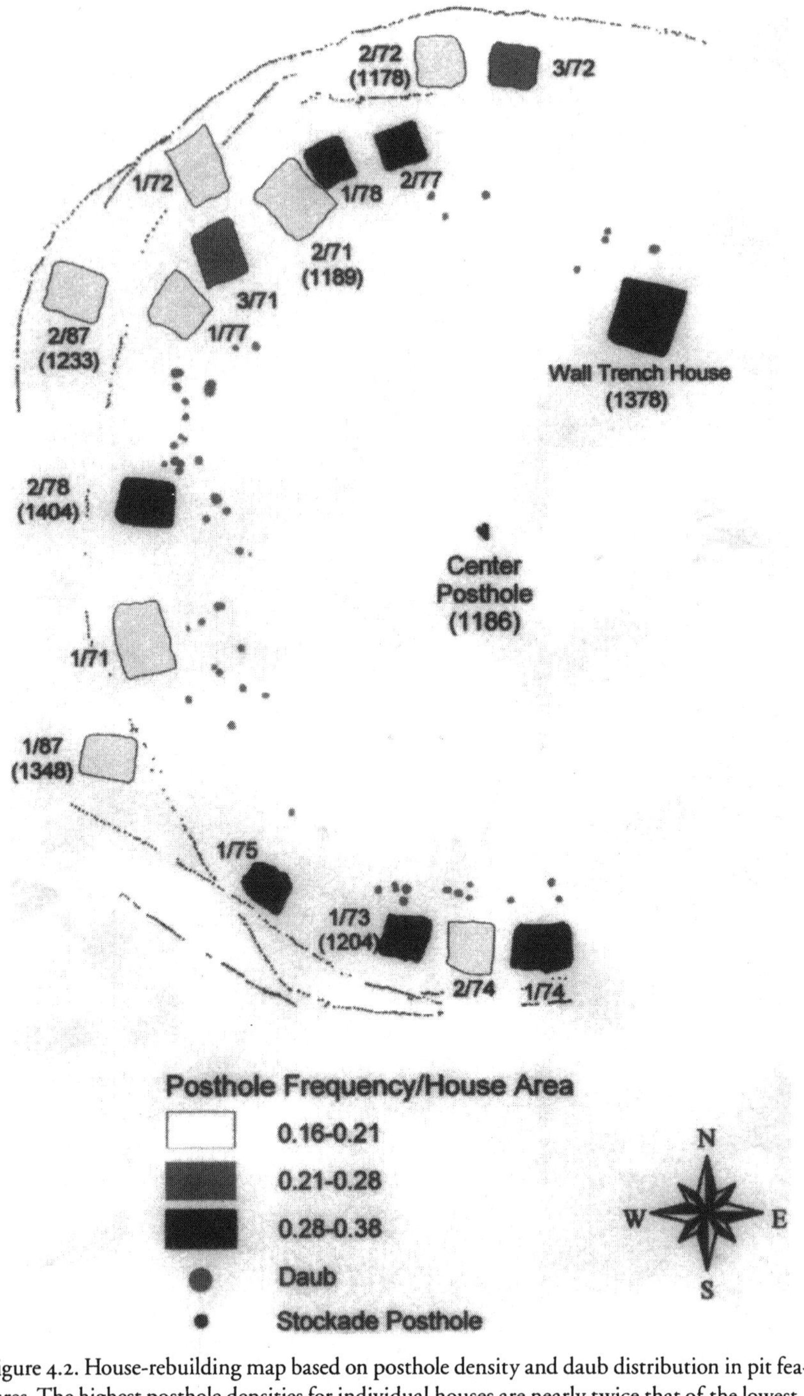

Figure 4.2. House-rebuilding map based on posthole density and daub distribution in pit features. The highest posthole densities for individual houses are nearly twice that of the lowest group, strongly suggesting that these houses were rebuilt one time during the site occupation. Median radiocarbon dates for houses are indicated in parentheses in years A.D.

are contradictory, we know that this structure is unique in many ways and likely served as a ritual house or leader residence (Cook 2004; Robertson 1980, 1984), which typically develop as villages increase in size (Johnson 1982).

Based on rebuilding ratios, it is clear that the village was occupied for a minimum of two periods of house use-life, as houses indicating repair at SunWatch contain twice as many postholes per area than those lacking such evidence. Furthermore, the central posthole contains two distinct lobes, indicating that it was replaced once (Heilman and Hoefer 1981), coinciding with residential growth. Using the estimate of 5 to 15 years for the use-life of houses constructed from wood and clay (see above), the total time the site was used is between 10 and 30 years.

The only house to possibly exhibit stratification was the wall trench structure excavated by avocational archaeologists. Initial impressions were that this area consisted of two houses separated by alluvial deposits (Smith n.d.). The first house was located after uncovering a series of postholes below two burials. Subsequently, several interior postholes and hearth features were located. After documenting these features, excavation continued 6–8 inches below the house floor. More postholes and several wall trenches were located on this level. The first house was located approximately 2.5 feet (75 centimeters) below the ground surface and utilized both single post and wall trench construction.

Current understanding of the evidence, based on a reexcavation of part of this house basin by the author in 2005, is that it was not located below substantial alluvium (Cook and Kennedy 2005). Rather, it is more likely that it was constructed in a relatively deep semisubterranean basin, as has been carefully observed for a wall trench house at a contemporaneous Fort Ancient village—the Schomaker site. The Schomaker wall trench house was rebuilt, but the two structures were separated only by several centimeters of deposits and the basin was set into the ground between 67 and 74 centimeters (Cowan et al. 1990:14). Radiocarbon dates from Schomaker are also bimodal, with thirteenth- and fifteenth-century occupations postulated, each with an associated wall trench feature. Both of these characteristics closely match the SunWatch case and are consistent with the radiocarbon date from this house (i.e., the house is not likely to have originated earlier than the main occupation of the village [Cook and Kennedy 2005]).

Pit Features, Artifacts, and Time

Most pits are bell-shaped storage pits (n = 156 [46%]), with much lower proportions of straight-sided storage pits (n = 65 [19%]), shallow straight-sided pits (n = 55 [16%]), and basin-shaped features (n = 33 [9.5%]) (a total of 33 pit features [9.5%] were of an indeterminate form). As discussed above, the distinction between storage and other pit features was based on depth. Two breaks

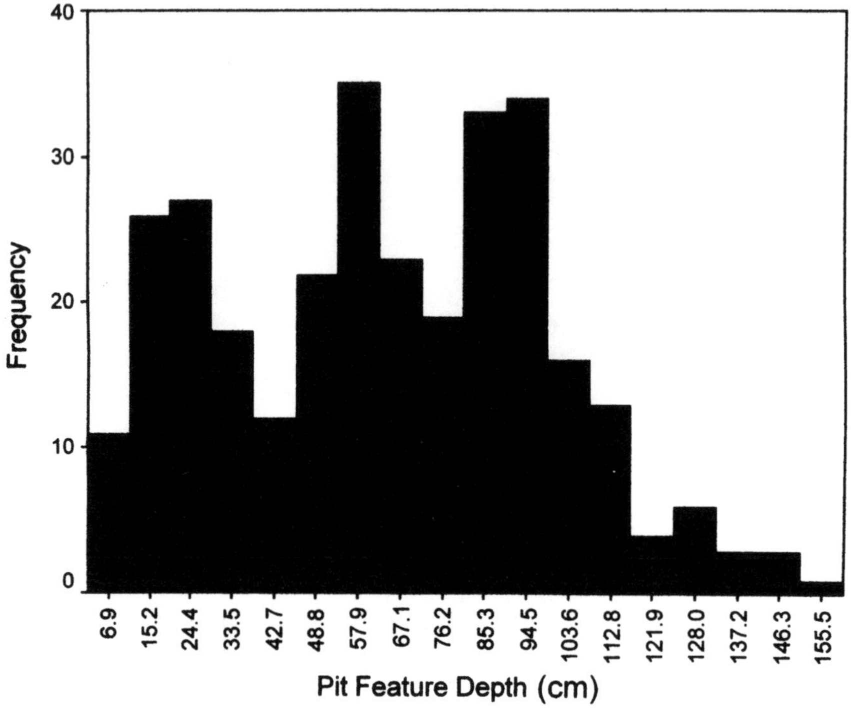

Figure 4.3. Histogram of pit feature depths.

are apparent in a histogram of pit feature depth (Figure 4.3). Based on the first break, deep pits were considered to be ≥ 1.6 feet (48.8 centimeters) in depth; shallow pits were ≤ 1.5 feet (45.7 centimeters) in depth. This finding fits reasonably well with the determination that storage pits should be >1.2 feet (36.6 centimeters) deep (Webb 1992:94). There is also a noticeable break in the distribution of feature volume at 800 liters, with relatively few larger ones (Figure 4.4).

All size measurements for pit features were strongly and significantly correlated: depth and maximum width ($r = 0.71$ [$p = 0.01$]), depth and surface width ($r = 0.48$ [$p = 0.01$]), depth and volume ($r = 0.84$ [$p = 0.01$]), and maximum width and volume ($r = 0.77$ [$p = 0.01$]). In terms of average volume, bell-shaped pits (mean = 656 liters) are larger than straight-sided storage features (mean = 473 liters). Bell-shaped pits are also considerably deeper (mean = 2.9 feet [84.4 centimeters]) than straight-sided storage features (mean = 2.2 feet [67.1 centimeters]).

Eleven radiocarbon dates have been produced from carbon samples in features. These were compared to feature volume and form and shell-tempered

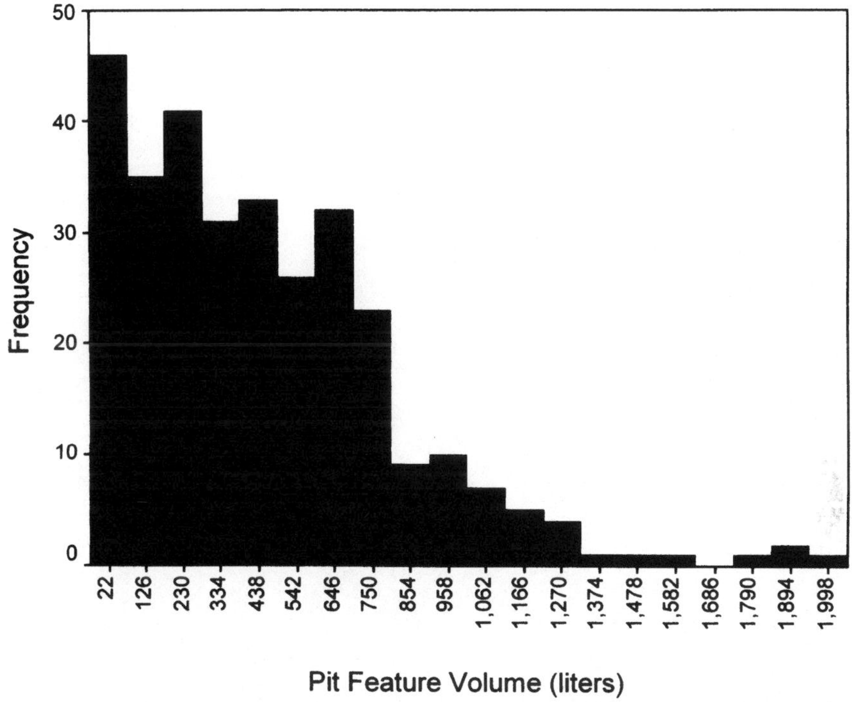

Figure 4.4. Histogram of pit feature volumes.

pottery to assess chronological distinctions. Results indicate that feature volume increased through time. The relationship between radiocarbon dates and pit volumes is significant. A chi-square test with Yates's correction resulted in the following: x^2 [observed] = 4.5, x^2 [critical] = 3.8, DF = 1, p = 0.03. A scatterplot implies that larger pits were a later occurrence, although smaller pits were used throughout the occupation (Figure 4.5). Radiocarbon dates show that bell-shaped features were used throughout the occupation (10 of the 11 dated pits are bell-shaped). Feature 6/8, a straight-sided storage pit excavated by the avocational archaeologists, produced a relatively late date (median = A.D. 1336) (see Figure 4.1). The timing of shell-tempered pottery was assessed by obtaining a radiocarbon date from Feature 19ww/74, where this pottery was most concentrated (this pit contained 12% [n = 14 sherds] of the shell-tempered pottery in the sample, whereas other pits with shell had only 1–3% [n = 1–6 sherds] of the assemblage). The median date for this sample (A.D. 1359) is within the later of the two sets of radiocarbon assays (see Figure 4.1).

The relationship between selected diagnostic artifacts and feature form was examined using correspondence analysis (see Chapter 3). The artifact sample

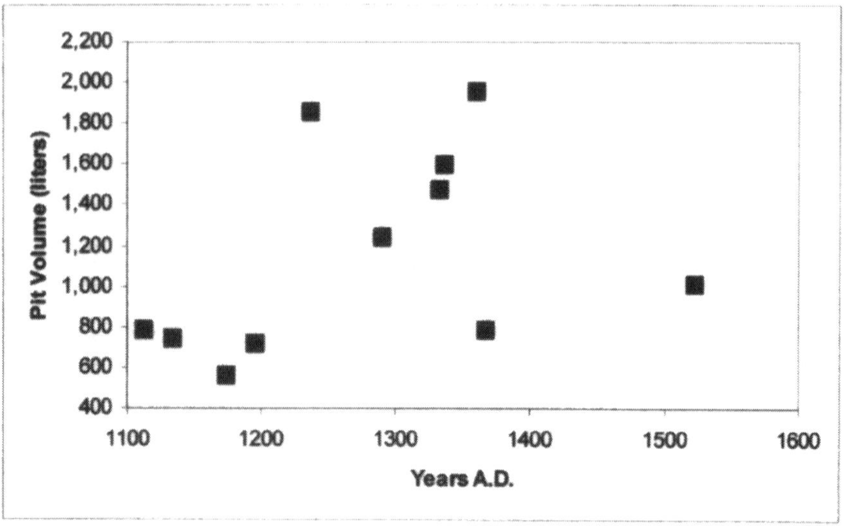

Figure 4.5. Scatterplot of pit feature volumes and associated radiocarbon dates.

included base forms for all complete triangular projectile points and proximal fragments (to maximize the sample size, projectile point sides were not included) and all pottery rim and neck sherds. Results support an association between bell-shaped pits and all forms of triangular projectile point bases, which is expected given the linkage with widely differing radiocarbon dates and this feature form. Straight-sided storage pits correspond with shell-tempered pottery, also suggestive of a later affiliation (Figure 4.6). Negative-painted pottery was recovered only from straight-sided storage pits, indicative of a later association, as this feature form was associated with a later radiocarbon date.

Seasonal indicators were present in 37 features of discernible form and volume. The majority (78%) were bell-shaped storage pits. Winter (41%) associations were most common, although summer (35%) and spring (22%) were well represented. There was no significant relationship between seasonality and feature form or volume, although winter is the only season with all feature types represented. Bell-shaped storage pits were used in all seasons, but usage of straight-sided storage pits, shallow straight-sided pits, and basins was limited to the winter and summer months.

Four general conclusions can be drawn from the examination of the relationship between radiocarbon dates and feature and artifact attributes. First, larger pits are attributable to later stages in site occupation. Second, straight-sided storage pits are attributable to a later point in the village occupation. The

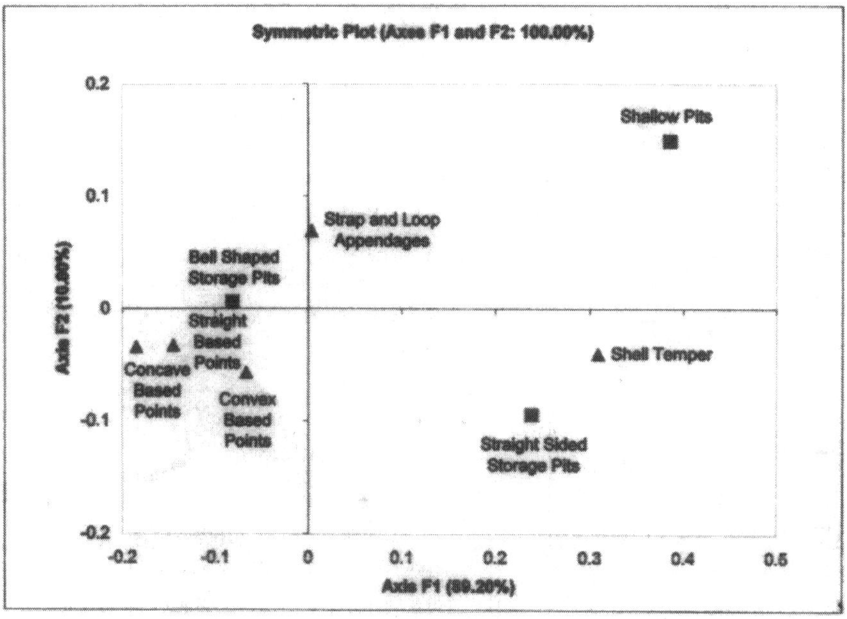

Figure 4.6. Correspondence analysis biplot comparing feature forms and selected diagnostic artifact attributes.

linkage between straight-sided storage pits, a late radiocarbon date, and correspondence with shell-tempered pottery supports this conclusion. Third, shell temper is a relatively late occurrence at the site (based on the highest concentration occurring in a feature producing a late radiocarbon date). Fourth, the linkage between all forms of triangular projectile points and bell-shaped storage pits supports the conclusion that this feature form was used during the entire site occupation. Pottery refits consistently link straight-sided and bell-shaped storage pits, suggesting that both were in use simultaneously. In other words, while straight-sided storage pits were a more recent addition at SunWatch, bell-shaped storage pits continued to be used.

Growth of Residential Units

Features were grouped into spatial units that could be compared with household architecture. First, the site was divided into four analytical units consistent with "household clusters" (see Chapter 3). Second, these units were internally partitioned into house-specific areas, which were then examined in terms of their temporal order.

Household Clusters

Four household clusters were recognized (Figure 4.7). The division between Areas 1 and 2 and between Areas 3 and 4 is clear in terms of gaps in the distribution of pit features and burials. (While there is no gap between houses in Areas 3 and 4, the superposition of pits over House 2/71 led to the conclusion that it was used earlier than others in the area.) There is not a clear division between Areas 2 and 3 in terms of the distribution of pit features. The division between these areas was made due to the location of a distinct burial row located just north of House 2/78, as a similar type of burial group is located near the division between Areas 1 and 2.

There are many distinctions between these four areas (Table 4.1). Area 4 contains more pit features than Area 1, Area 2, and Area 3. Features are considerably larger in average volume for Areas 2 (496 liters) and 3 (506 liters) than for Areas 1 (431 liters) and 4 (405 liters). While similar numbers of houses are associated with each area, they vary considerably in size. Average house size is considerably larger in Area 2 (mean = 452 square feet) and Area 3 (mean = 428 square feet) than in Area 1 (mean = 335 square feet) and Area 4 (mean = 303 square feet), which fits well with the larger average feature volumes in these areas (also see Chapter 5). A correspondence analysis reveals that bell-shaped storage pits are most common in Areas 2 and 3 (in particular), and straight-sided and basin-shaped features are more common in Area 4 (Figure 4.8).

Each area contains similar proportions of artifact classes. However, artifact density is markedly higher in Areas 1 and 2. In particular, there is a higher concentration of chipped-stone debitage in these areas. The low density of debitage in Area 4 is partially related to excavation strategy in that screens were not generally used in the excavation of most features in this part of the site (Cook 2004:123–127), although this does not explain the low density of debitage in Area 3. Pottery is slightly more concentrated in Area 2, while bone, shell, and ground-stone artifacts occur in relatively even proportions throughout the site. (Note that the avocational portion of Area 4 is not included, as data were not comparable [see Chapter 1].)

Temporal and functional differentiation. Numerous artifact forms were related to specific household clusters. Correspondence analyses comparing numerous artifact attributes revealed several clear relationships (Figure 4.9), many of which can be interpreted in terms of temporal affiliations. Frequencies of artifact occurrences were also considered to be associated if they occurred either exclusively or in higher frequency in one or two specific areas (Cook 2004:117–137). The following synthesizes these findings.

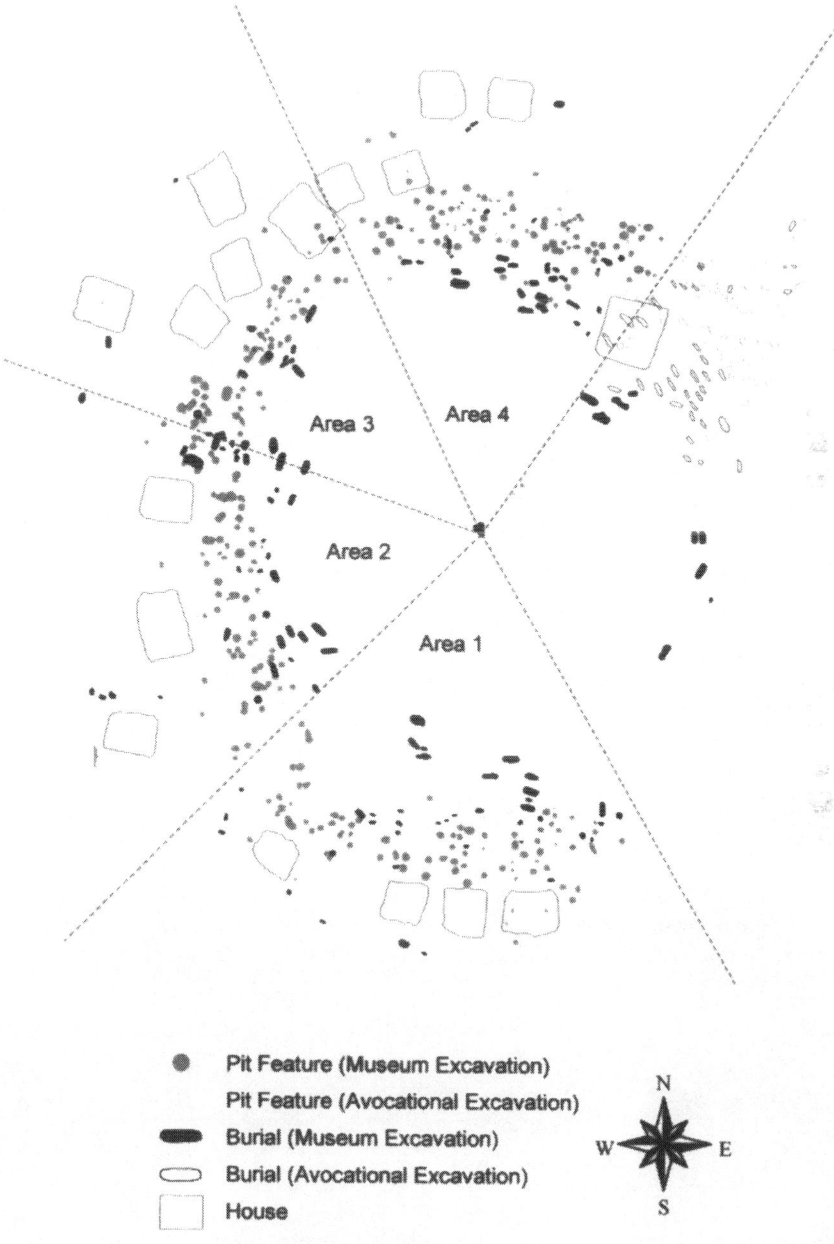

Figure 4.7. Map showing division of site into four house clusters and associated feature areas. Avocational excavations are not included in Area 4 due to lack of associated artifact data.

Table 4.1. General Feature and Artifact Class Characteristics for Four House Clusters

	Area 1		Area 2		Area 3		Area 4	
Characteristic	N	%	N	%	N	%	N	%
Artifact Type								
Chipped stone	8,907	73.8	12,202	73.9	6,548	71.9	5,822	70.1
Pottery rims and necks	2,430	20.1	3,610	21.9	2,080	22.8	1,882	22.7
Bone and shell artifacts	589	4.9	558	3.4	371	4.1	471	5.7
Ground stone	138	1.1	147	0.9	115	1.3	131	1.6
Total	12,064	99.9	16,517	100.1	9,114	100.1	8,306	100.1
Pit Feature Form								
Straight-sided storage	16	17.8	14	17.5	14	21.9	20	18.9
Shallow straight-sided	18	20	7	8.8	7	10.9	22	20.8
Bell-shaped storage	40	44.4	48	60	33	51.6	35	33
Basins	5	5.6	9	11.3	5	7.8	14	13.2
Indeterminate	11	12.2	2	2.5	5	7.8	15	14.2
Total	90	100	80	100.1	64	100	106	100.1
Pit Feature Volume								
Liters	34,060	N/A	38,650	N/A	29,828	N/A	36,841	N/A
Cubic Feet	1,203	N/A	1,365	N/A	1,053	N/A	1,301	N/A
House Size								
Square meters (mean)	31	N/A	42	N/A	40	N/A	28	N/A
Square feet (mean)	335	N/A	452	N/A	428	N/A	303	N/A

Note: Area 4 does not include features in the avocational area and that the total number of features excludes one straight-sided storage pit and one shallow straight-sided feature that are near the middle of the plaza (i.e., they could not be directly linked with one of the four areas).

Area 1
Correspondences include convex-based triangular projectile points (earliest temporal affiliation in the village), grit/shell-tempered pottery fishing hooks, triangular preforms, and miscellaneous broken bifaces. Associations include circular stones, bone pendants, and a turtle shell gorget.

Area 2
Correspondences include straight-based triangular projectile points and shell-tempered pottery (implying a temporal affiliation in the middle to later portion of the occupational sequence). Associations include celts, bannerstones, turtle

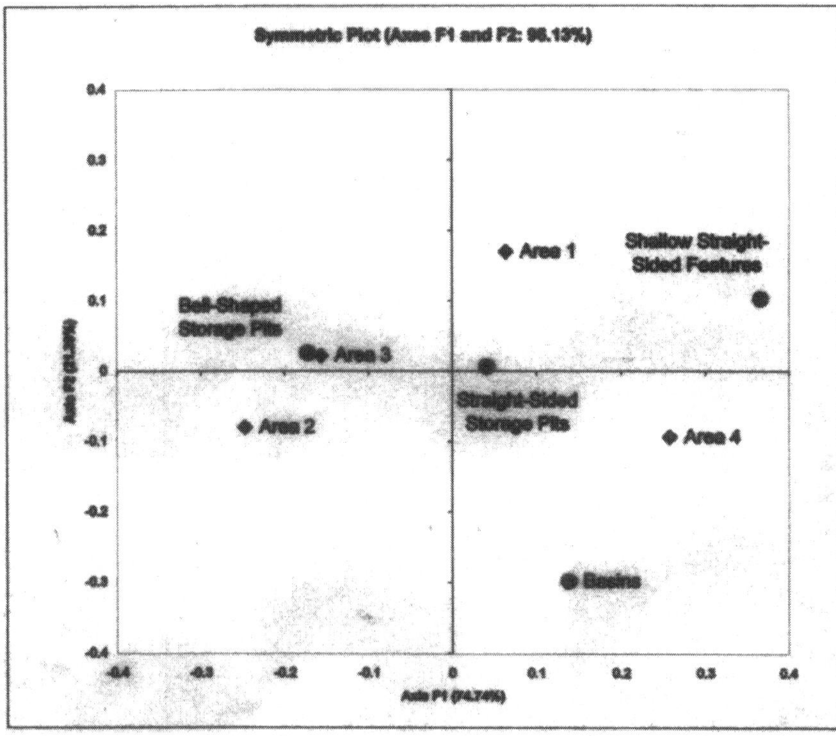

Figure 4.8. Correspondence analysis biplot comparing feature forms and four house clusters.

shell bowls, olivella shell, line-filled triangle (Types C and D) pottery designs, and crosshatched pottery designs.

Area 3
Correspondences include knives, shatter, and micaceous schist-tempered pottery. Associations include metates, an antler awl, an elk tooth effigy (of an owl), quartzite-tempered pottery, limestone/grit-tempered pottery, and grit/grog-tempered pottery.

Area 4
Correspondences include concave-based triangular projectile points and strap and loop appendages (implying a relatively late affiliation), wedges, and drills. Associations include wolf mandibles, a bone disc, a salt pan, and rectilinear scroll pottery designs.

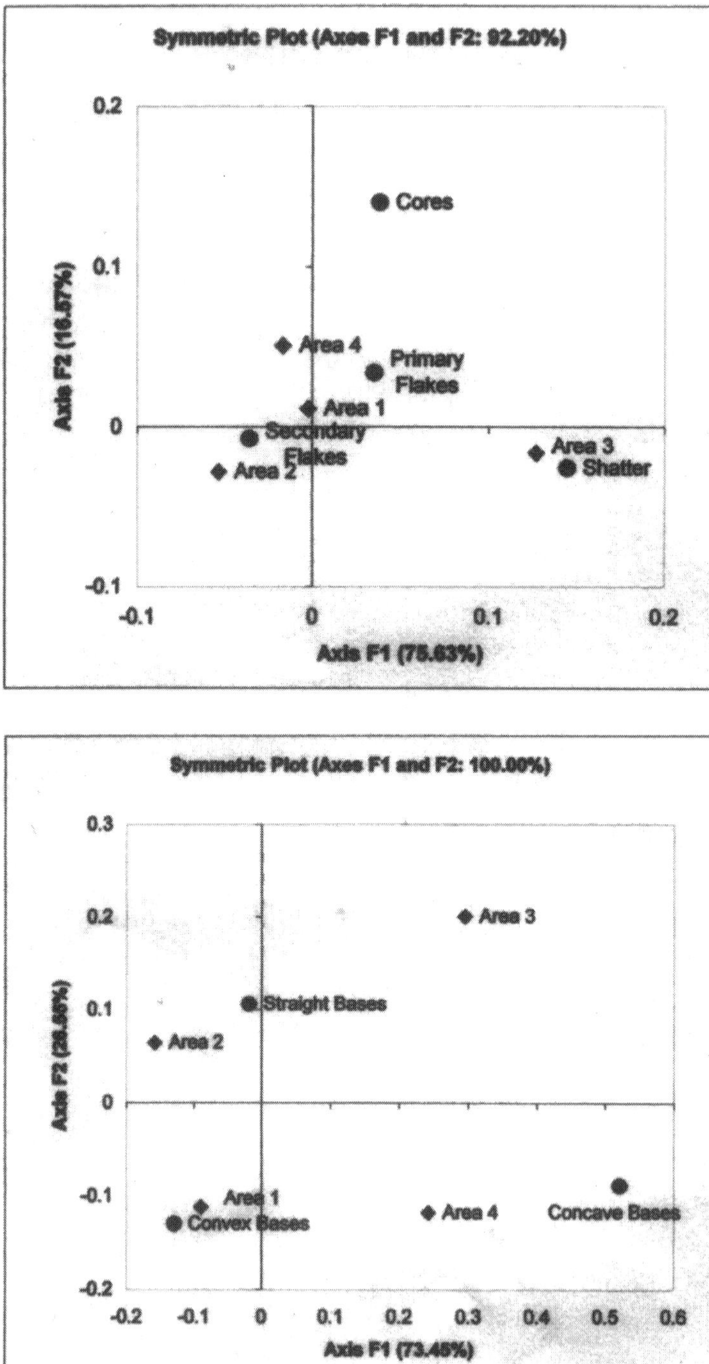

Figure 4.9. Correspondence analysis biplots comparing selected artifact attributes in pit features associated with four house clusters.

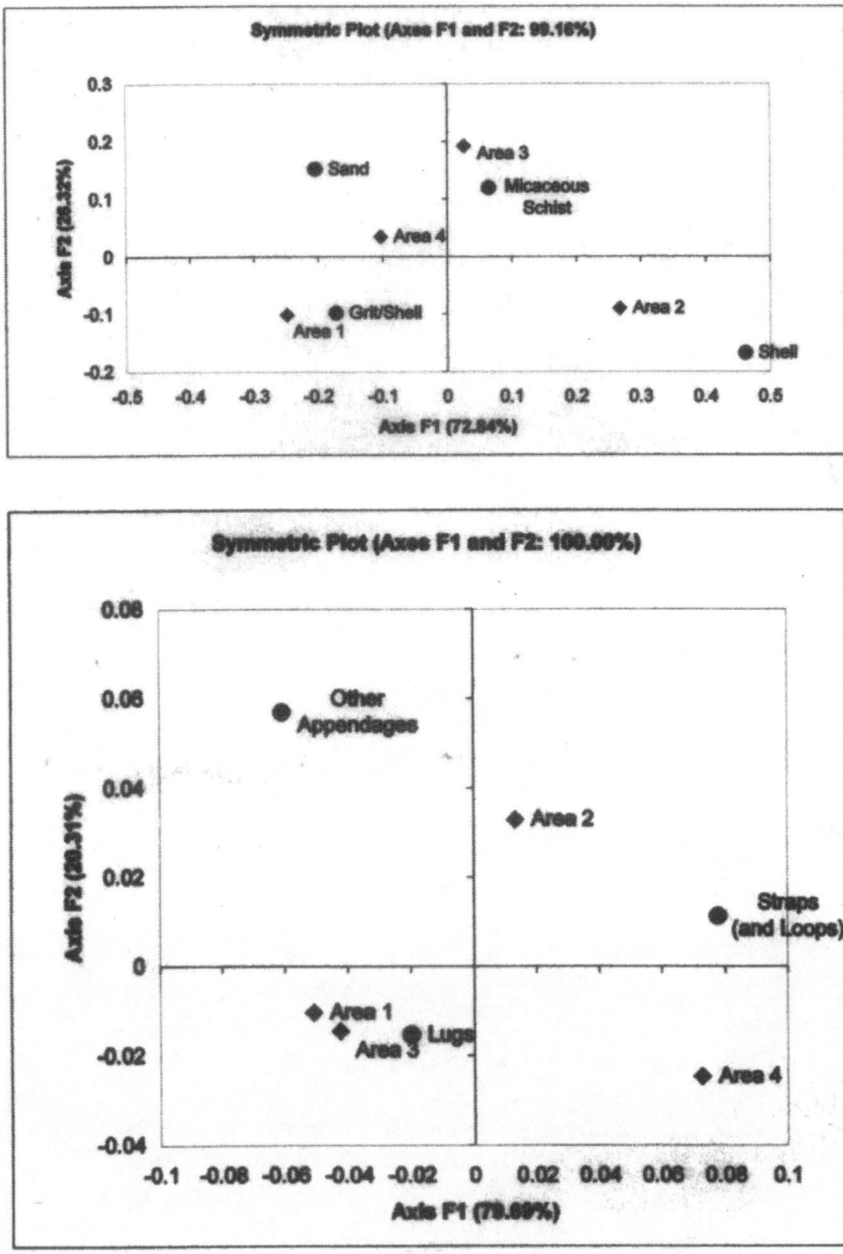

Figure 4.9. *Continued on the next page*

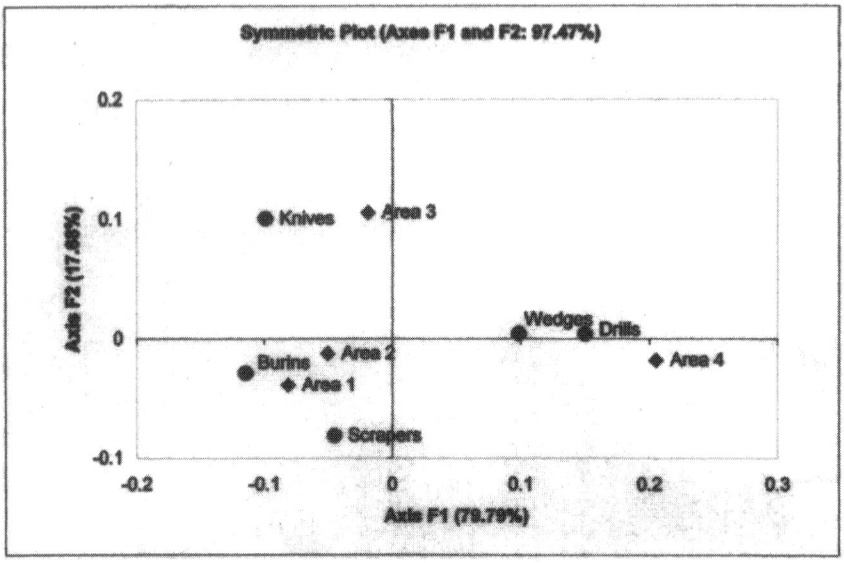

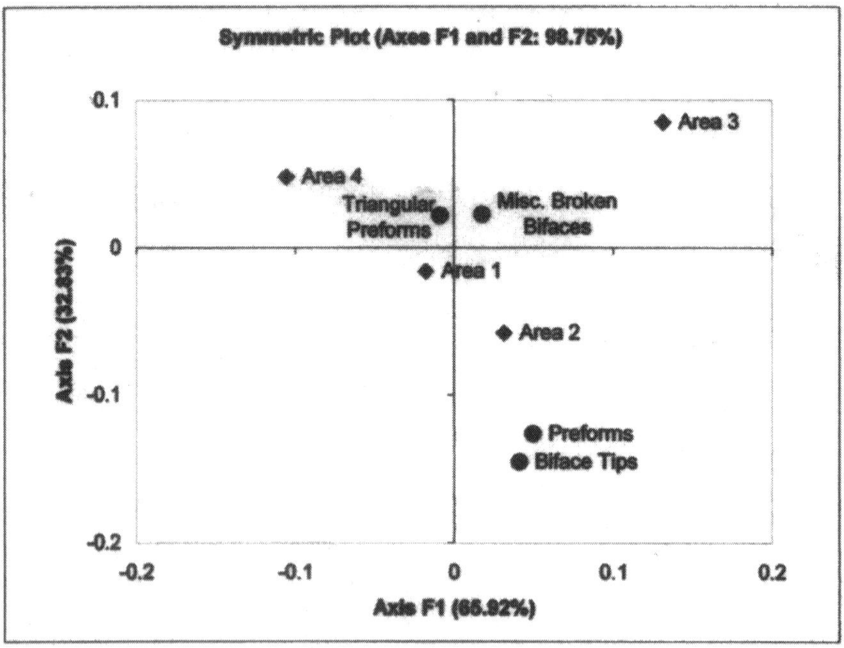

Figure 4.9. *Continued*

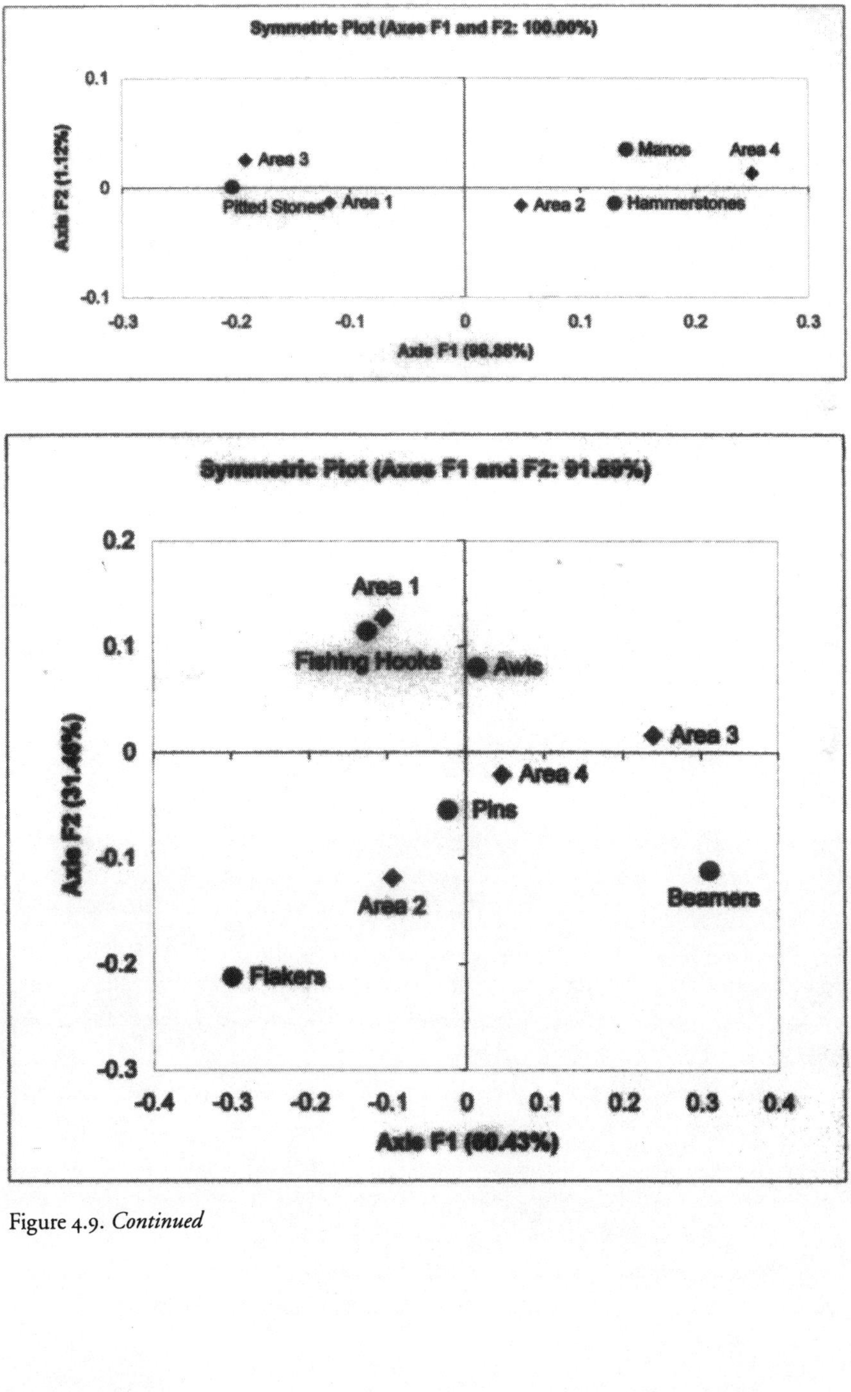

Figure 4.9. *Continued*

Areas 1 and 2
Correspondences include secondary flakes, scrapers, and burins. Associations include limestone discs, flakers, bear teeth and claws, shell disc and barrel beads, single slash, herringbone, and line-filled triangle (Type F) pottery designs.

Areas 2 and 4
Correspondences include hammerstones, manos, and pins. Associations include elk teeth, pottery bowls, negative-painted pottery designs, and curvilinear/rectilinear scroll pottery designs.

Areas 1 and 3
Correspondences include lug appendages and pitted stones.

Areas 3 and 4
Associations include abraders, antler point preforms, and curvilinear scroll pottery designs.

Areas 1 and 4
Associations include needles, shell spoons, and pinch pots.

Areas 2 and 3
The only association was with line-filled triangle (Type E) pottery designs.

Pit Feature Groups

Analytical pit feature groups were discerned through a consideration of visually distinguishable breaks, with the assistance of short-distance pottery refits (<25 feet), resulting in the demarcation of 26 analytical pit feature groups (Figure 4.10). (The avocational area was considered as one feature group due to data limitations [see Chapter 1]). In cases where a pottery refit connected clearly distinguishable groups, preference was given to the visually determined spatial boundary. This occurred in only two instances, in distinguishing Group 3.5 from 3.4, and Group 2.4 from 2.1, and is likely related to the close functional relationship between these areas (see Chapter 5).

Temporal and functional differentiation. Diagnostic artifact and feature attributes were studied in this spatial framework by examining natural breaks in their respective distributions (Figure 4.11). It is apparent from inspection of the maps that later attributes are generally more common in the north and west parts of the site, precisely those areas containing later radiocarbon dates and evidence for village expansion. These data are summarized in Table 4.2 in terms of the total number of associations per analytical pit feature group. For purposes

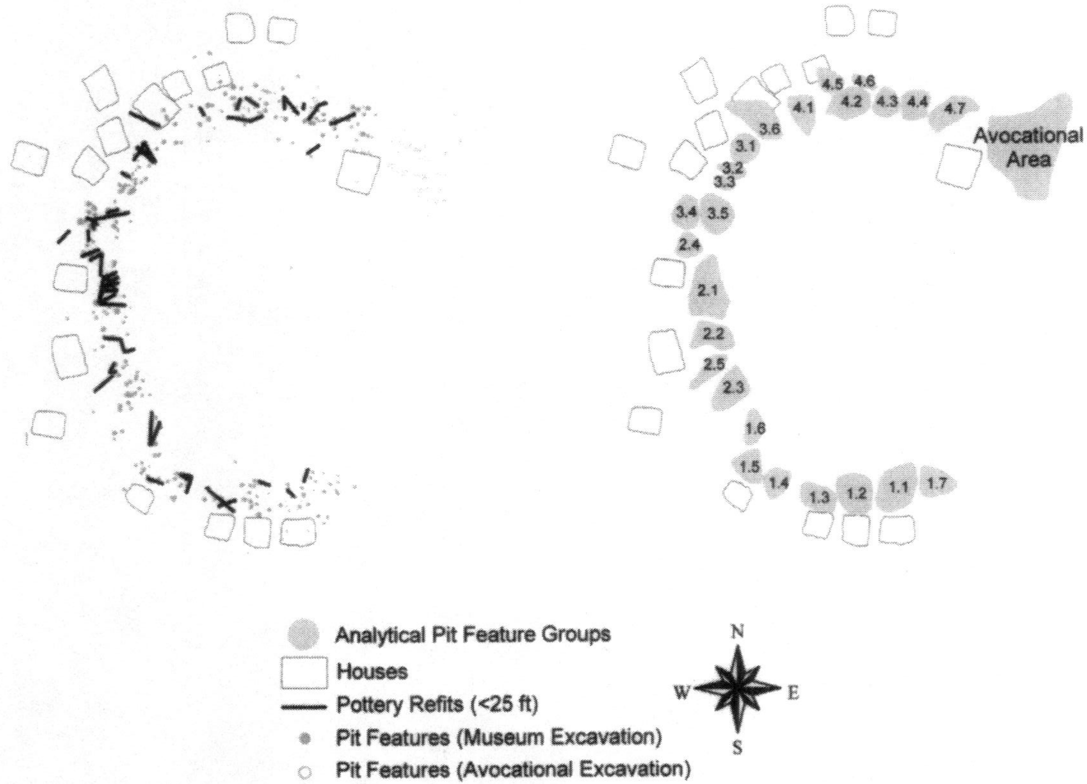

Figure 4.10. Map showing division of site into 26 analytical pit feature groups based on visually discernible breaks and short-distance (<25 feet) pottery refits. Due to lack of feature-specific data, the avocational area was not internally partitioned, despite recognition of two subareas.

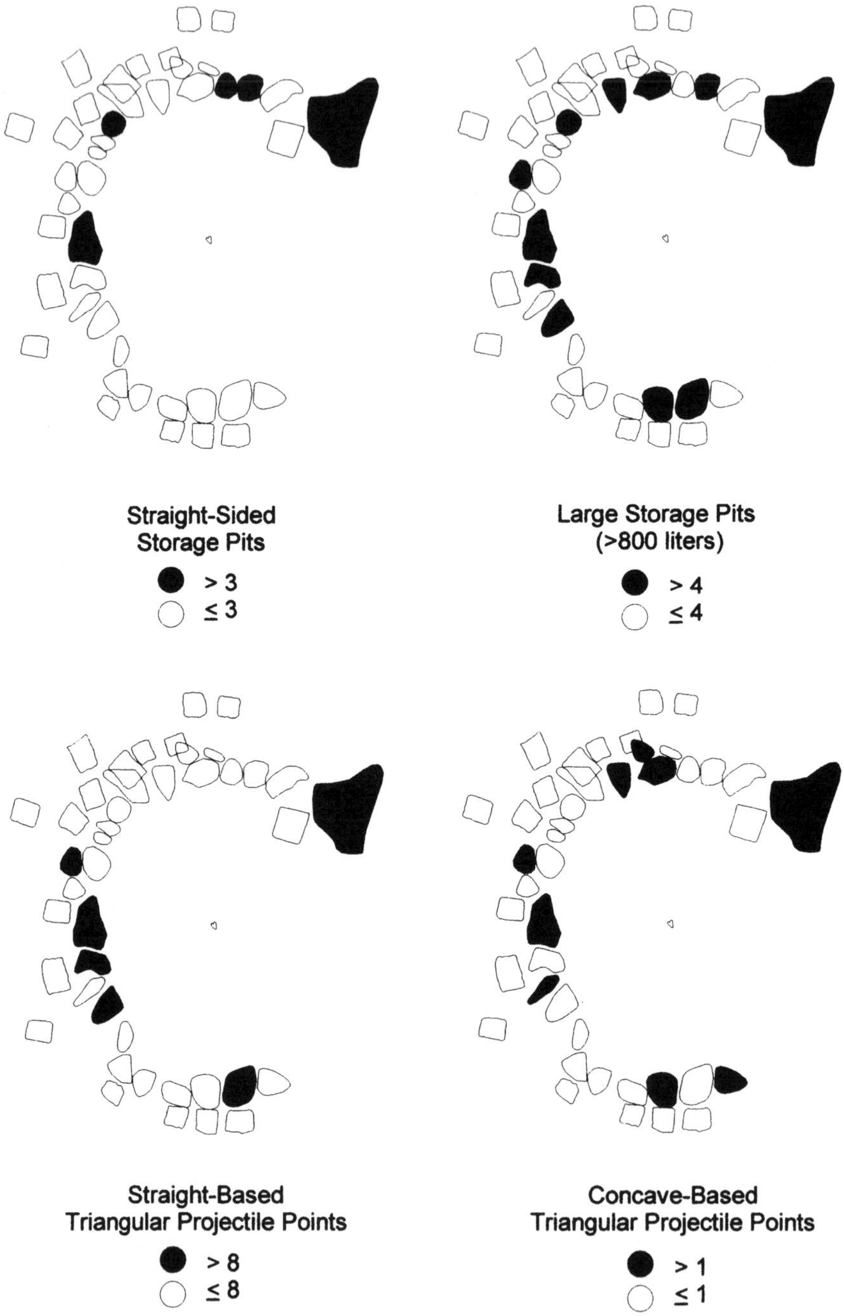

Figure 4.11. Maps showing distribution of diagnostic pit feature and artifact attributes in analytical pit feature groups. Frequency divisions were based on one natural break in each of the respective distributions.

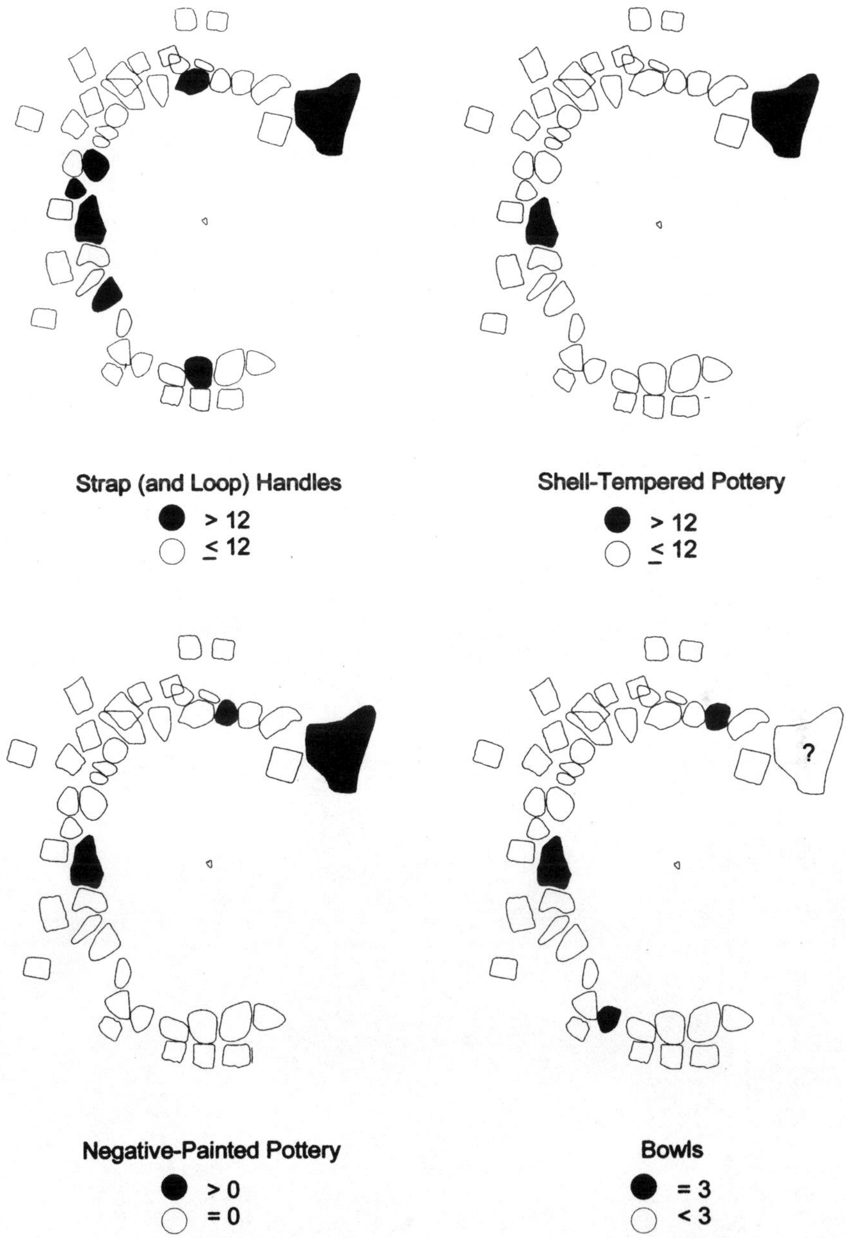

Figure 4.11. *Continued*

Table 4.2. Summary of the Occurrence of Later Attribute Diagnostics by Pit Feature Groups

Analytical Feature Group	Features		Projectile Points		Pottery				Total Number of Associations	Order of Occupation
	>800 liters	Straight storage	Straight base	Concave base	Shell temper	Negative paint	Bowl	Strap handle		
1.1			X						1	A
1.2	X	X		X				X	4	B
1.3									0	A
1.4							X		1	A
1.5					X				1	A
1.6									0	A
1.7				X					1	A
2.1	X	X	X	X	X	X	X	X	8	C
2.2			X					X	2	B
2.3	X		X		X			X	4	B
2.4					X			X	2	B
2.5				X					1	A
3.1	X	X			X				3	B
3.2		X							1	A
3.3									0	A
3.4	X		X	X	X				4	B
3.5					X			X	2	B

3.6									0	A
4.1		X	X	X					3	B
4.2	X			X				X	3	B
4.3		X				X			2	B
4.4	X	X					X		3	B
4.5				X					1	A
4.6			X						1	A
4.7								X	1	A
Avocational	X	X	X	X	X	X		X	7	C

Note: Order of occupation was based on the following: A (Initial) = 0–1 associations, B (First Addition) = 2–4 associations, C (Second Addition) = 7–8 associations.

of comparing the temporal relationship between houses and feature groups, areas were assigned to three different temporal points in the occupational sequence: A (13 pit feature groups) = 0–1 associations; B (11 pit feature groups) = 2–4 associations; and C (2 pit feature groups) = 7–8 associations. It is important to bear in mind that any attribute considered alone would be problematic due to the earlier occurrence of some of these criteria at Fort Ancient sites in southwest Ohio. However, the strength of this analysis is in the multiple lines of evidence used to determine temporality of pit feature groups and spatially comparing the results to the independently derived architectural data set.

Spatial comparison of the temporal sequences of house and feature groups along with medium-distance pottery refits (25–100 feet) revealed several relationships. In areas where the architectural sequence could be reliably discerned, more recently constructed pit feature groups and houses were located near one another (Figure 4.12). The south and west parts of the village were clearest in terms of their formation history. The northern part of the village contains many more houses and pit features, rendering the pattern more difficult to discern. Contemporaneity of all feature groups can be assumed on the basis of medium-distance pottery refits (25–100 feet) (see p. 51 and Figure 4.12). On this basis, we can assume that most houses in the village were in use at the end of the site occupation.

Correspondence analysis was used to compare the three stages of village occupation with the occurrence of artifacts not used for temporal affiliations (Figure 4.13). The following linkages were made between time periods and artifacts:

A	B	C
grit/shell temper	micaceous schist temper	quartzite temper
limestone/grit temper	fishing hooks	discoidals
pitted stones	beamers	shell disc beads
abraders	bone beads	shell discs
celts	drilled deer phalanges	single slash
bone needles	drills	scroll
shell pendants	bone pins	line-filled triangle (Types C, E, F)
line-filled triangle (Type A)	antler points	crosshatched
	awls	

A/B	B/C
scrapers	sand temper
manos	plain
hoes	bowls

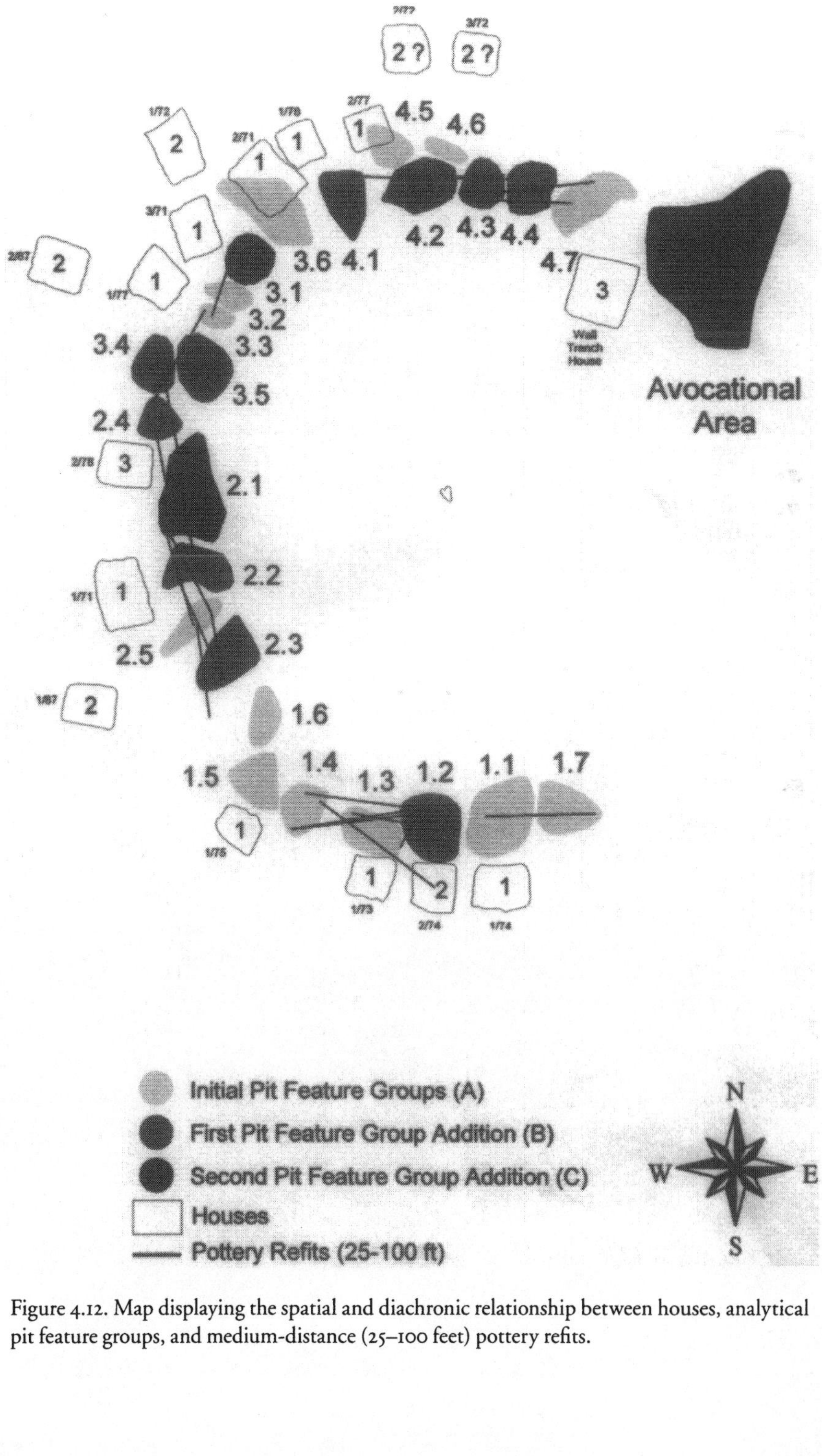

Figure 4.12. Map displaying the spatial and diachronic relationship between houses, analytical pit feature groups, and medium-distance (25–100 feet) pottery refits.

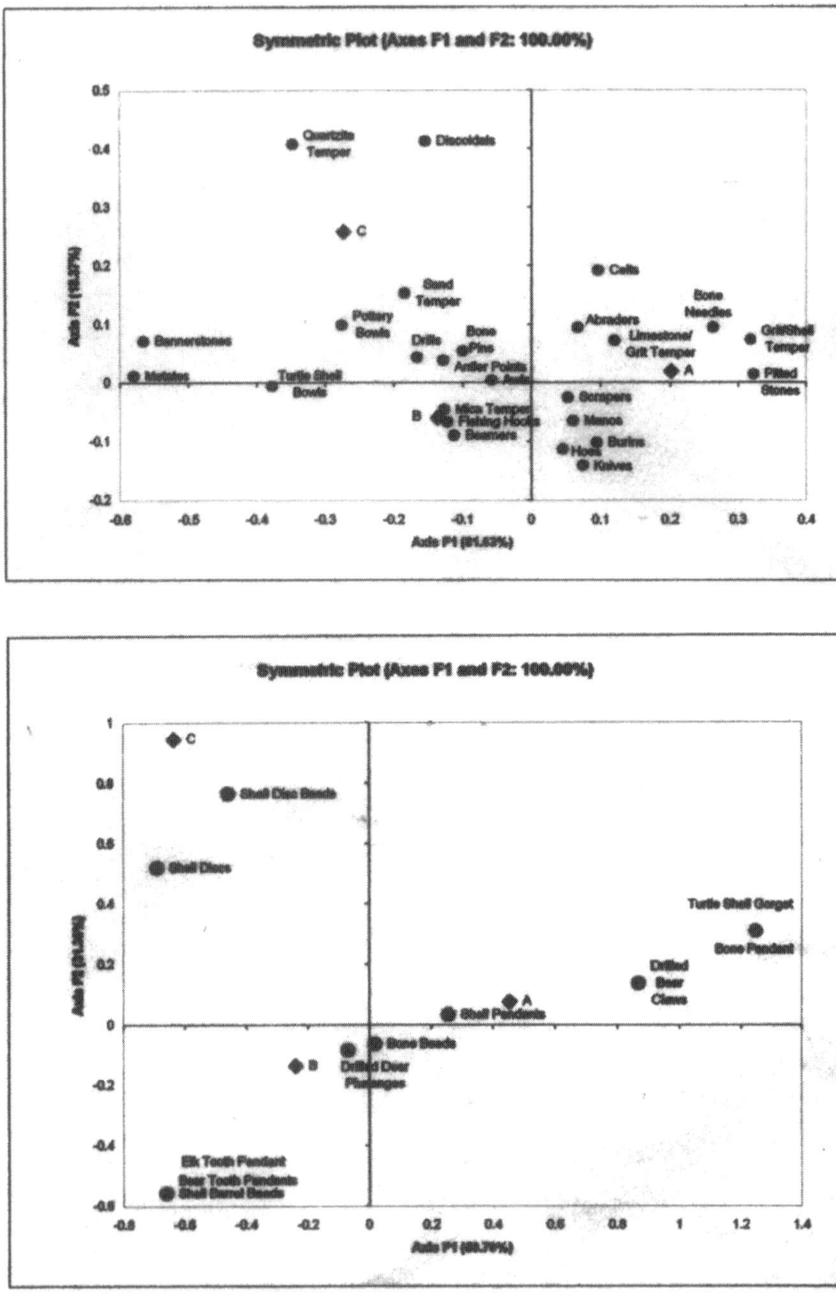

Figure 4.13. Correspondence analysis biplots comparing selected artifact attributes in pit features associated with the 26 analytical pit feature groups. (Mica refers to micaceous schist.)

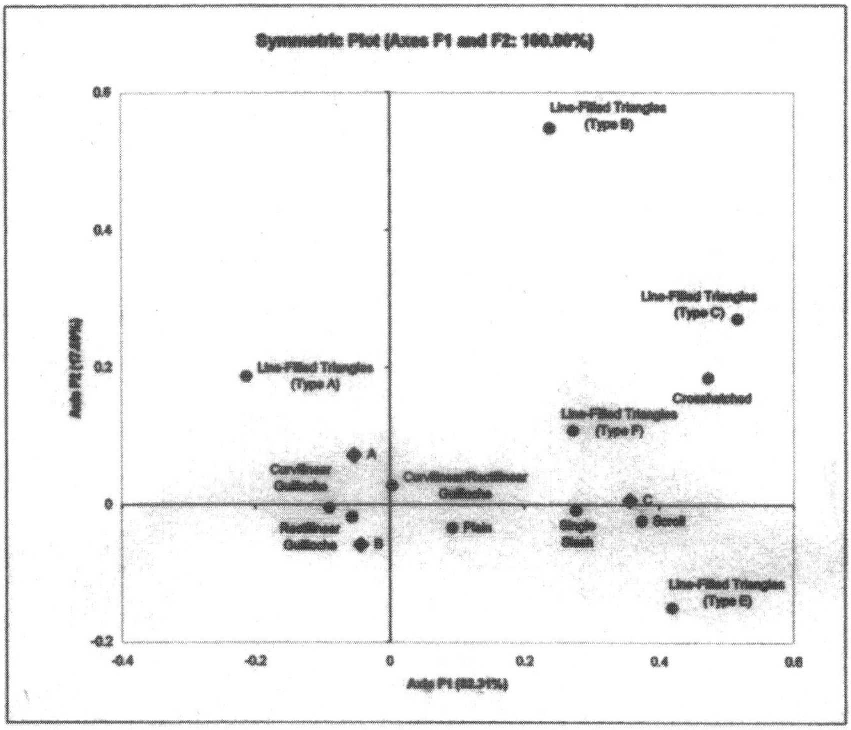

Figure 4.13. *Continued*

burins
knives
curvilinear guilloche
rectilinear guilloche
curvilinear/rectilinear guilloche
turtle shell bowls

These correspondence results were compared with the occurrence of artifact attributes in dated pit features (with the exception of Feature 2/05 [see above]). As stated at the beginning of this chapter, there are two distinct groups of radiocarbon dates and an outlier in the sixteenth century (see Figure 4.1). Median date ranges for the two main sets are as follows: Early (six pits) = A.D. 1112–1236; Middle (three pits) = A.D. 1332–1367; Late (one pit) = A.D. 1521. While the number of features varies, volume totals are comparable for the main two groups (Early = 4,738 liters; Middle = 4,222 liters; Late = 1,010 liters), allowing for general comparisons to be made (Table 4.3).

Table 4.3. Selection of Artifact Occurrences in Pit Features with Associated Radiocarbon Dates

	A.D. 1112–1236		A.D. 1332–1367		A.D. 1521	
Artifact	N	%	N	%	N	%
Groundstone						
Hammerstones	2	50	1	25	1	25
Pitted stones	5	71	2	29	0	0
Choppers	1	100	0	0	0	0
Celts	1	50	1	50	0	0
Bannerstones	0	0	1	100	0	0
Abraders	1	100	0	0	0	0
Lithic Reduction Debris						
Cores	14	34	24	39	3	27
Wedges	2	29	5	71	0	0
Shatter	65	36	109	60	8	4
Primary flakes	64	32	125	63	9	5
Secondary flakes	239	20	922	78	17	2
Triangle preforms	3	38	5	63	0	0
Other preforms	1	33	2	67	0	0
Chipped Stone Tools						
Triangular drills	2	50	2	50	0	0
Other drills	1	33	2	67	0	0
Scrapers	3	50	3	50	0	0
Knives	2	40	2	40	1	20
Burins	1	50	1	50	0	0
Bone and Shell Tools						
Awls	13	50	12	46	1	4
Flakers	2	67	1	33	0	0
Fishing hooks	5	71	2	29	0	0
Antler points	10	67	2	13	3	20
Pins	12	71	4	24	1	6
Needles	0	0	1	100	0	0
Beamers	4	50	4	50	0	0
Hoes	8	80	1	10	1	10
Bone and Shell Adornment						
Drilled bear claws	4	100	0	0	0	0
Shell pendants	2	100	0	0	0	0
Bone beads	1	100	0	0	0	0

Artifact	A.D. 1112–1236 N	A.D. 1112–1236 %	A.D. 1332–1367 N	A.D. 1332–1367 %	A.D. 1521 N	A.D. 1521 %
Drilled deer phalanges	0	0	1	100	0	0
Shell discs	0	0	1	100	0	0
Pottery						
Jars	324	45	367	51	33	4
Pinch pots	4	100	0	0	0	0
Bowls	0	0	4	100	0	0
Sand temper	4	100	0	0	0	0
Grit temper	291	44	344	52	31	4
Mica temper	7	44	8	50	1	6
Shell temper	2	12	15	88	0	0
Quartzite temper	4	80	0	0	1	20
Grit/Shell temper	20	83	4	17	0	0
Lugs	27	63	16	37	0	0
Straps (and loops)	5	28	12	67	1	5
Plain	25	24	74	72	4	4
Rectilinear scroll	0	0	2	100	0	0
Crosshatched	2	100	0	0	0	0
Herringbone	0	0	2	100	0	0
Single slash	5	56	4	44	0	0
Curvilinear guilloche	74	65	32	28	8	7
Rectilinear guilloche	44	51	34	40	8	9
Curv./Rect. guilloche	3	50	2	33	1	17
Line-filled tri. (Type A)	12	63	6	32	1	5
Line-filled tri. (Type B)	1	50	1	50	0	0
Line-filled tri. (Type C)	1	33	2	67	0	0
Line-filled tri. (Type D)	0	0	1	100	0	0
Line-filled tri. (Type E)	0	0	2	100	0	0
Line-filled tri. (Type F)	4	40	6	60	0	0

Note: Mica refers to micaceous schist.

Based on a consideration of both lines of evidence, the following artifacts are considered to be relatively early in the occupation of the site: pitted stones, abraders, shell pendants, grit/shell-tempered pottery, and line-filled triangle Type A pottery neck design. Relatively late occurrences at the site include shell discs, drilled deer phalanges, plain pottery necks, and three neck designs (scroll, line-filled triangles Types C and E).

Consideration of seasonality data within this chronological framework resulted in a significant finding. The majority of features associated with the first stage of village use is related to spring and summer (n = 11); only two winter pits were associated with this stage of occupation. However, the second (B) and third (C) uses of the site are collectively associated with even numbers of winter (n = 14) and spring/summer pits (n = 14). This is a statistically significant difference (x^2 [observed] = 4.5, x^2 [critical] = 3.8, DF = 1, p = 0.03). This finding supports one of the following two scenarios: (1) the occupation became more year round as it became larger; or (2) the village growth pattern represents a seasonal phenomenon in which aggregation occurred at this time of the year. The latter possibility would be the opposite expectation of a model proposing that SunWatch diminished in population during the winter months as many groups frequented hunting camps (Shane 1988; Shane and Wagner 1993; Wagner 1996). I favor the first scenario, and suggest that year-round sedentism developed over time as the village grew in size and complexity. The fact that straight-sided storage pits were shallower and smaller in volume than bell-shaped storage pits (see above) could be related to a winter association (i.e., it is more difficult to dig a deep pit in the colder months), but there was no clear linkage between feature form and seasonality (see above). There is also no apparent relationship between the placement of larger houses and winter pits, suggesting there is not a direct connection between these variables as has been proposed elsewhere (Carskadden 1992).

Burial Groups

Fifteen burial groups were identified (13 [6%] burials did not meet the criteria to be assigned to a burial group [see Chapter 3]) (Figure 4.14). The spatial restriction of burial groups was relatively clear, with the exception of Burial Groups 8, 9, and 10. While the distribution of burials is generally without a break in this part of the site, burials were segregated into these groups on the basis of the anomalous patterning associated with Burial Group 9, which is distinct from adjacent burial groups.

Based on the presence of various combinations of burial arcs and rows and one amorphous pattern I refer to here as a "cluster" (Burial Group 9), three

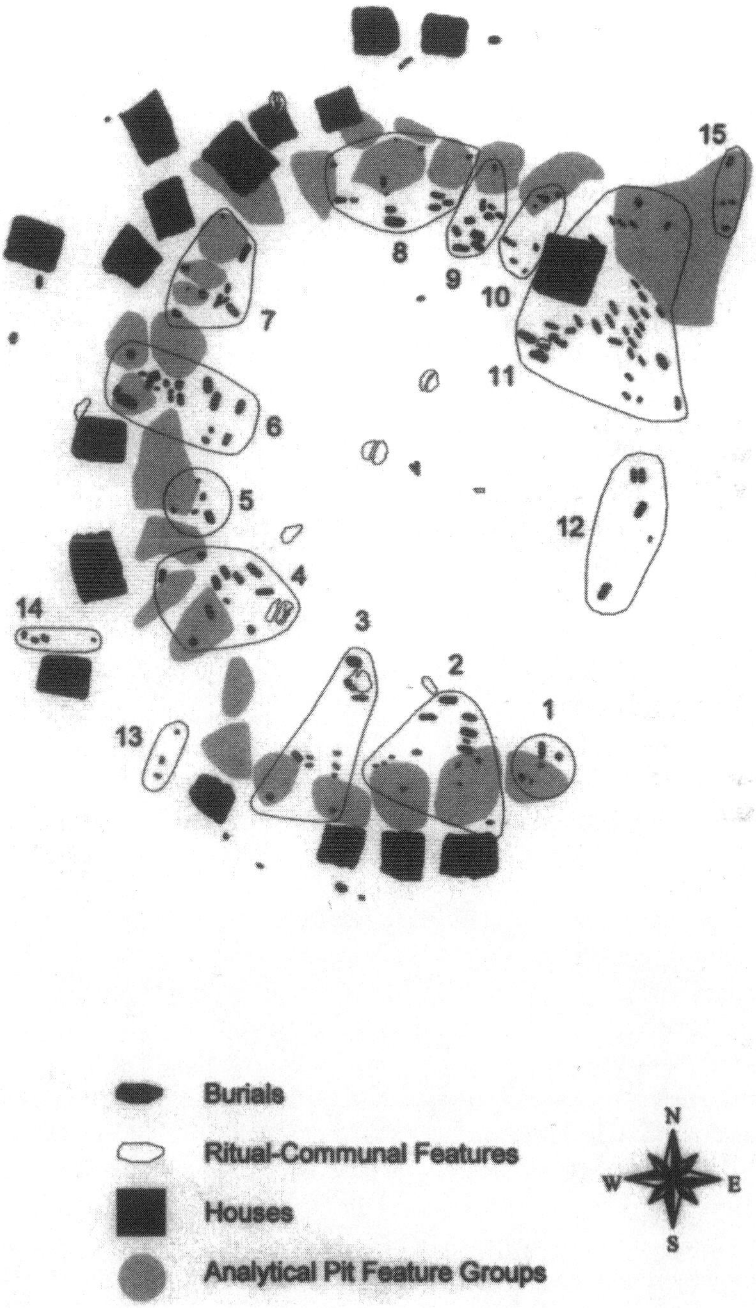

Figure 4.14. Map showing locations of burial groups in relation to houses and analytical pit feature groups.

Table 4.4. Burial Group Form and Interment Frequencies and Percentages

Burial Group	Type	N	%
1	indeterminate	6	3.3
2	arc-row	16	8.8
3	arc-row	15	8.3
4	arc-row	13	7.2
5	arc	5	2.8
6	arc-row	18	9.9
7	arc	14	7.7
8	arc-row	14	7.7
9	cluster	10	5.5
10	indeterminate	7	3.9
11	arc-row	34	18.8
12	indeterminate	5	2.8
13	indeterminate	3	1.7
14	indeterminate	4	2.2
15	indeterminate	4	2.2
other		13	7.2
Total		181	100.0

types of burial groups were defined (Table 4.4). The most common burial group type is the arc-row pattern. For comparative purposes, arc-row burial groups were oriented in the same direction with respect to the plaza (Figure 4.15). The superimposed arcs and lines (to indicate rows) reveal a pattern of conjoined arc-row segments focused on one or two burials located nearest the plaza. When there are two or more segments in a single burial group, they are usually associated with specific pit feature groups. Groups 2, 3, and 8 are notable in this respect (see Figure 4.14). Row patterns are clearest in Burial Groups 2, 4, 6, and 11. Ritual-communal structures are usually (83%) located in direct association or in close proximity to the arc-row burial groups. Recall that these are thermal features, which have often been described as "sweat lodges." The frequent connection with arc-row burial groups suggests that they were used as part of mortuary rituals.

Comparison of sex and age proportions reveals several distinctions between burial groups. Several groups are composed of males and children: Burial Group 6 (44% males, 56% children), Burial Group 1 (17% males, 83% children), Burial Group 15 (25% males, 75% children), Burial Group 12 (80% males, 20% children). Three groups are composed of children or indeterminate burials: Burial Group 5 is restricted to children, Burial Groups 13 and 14 consist of only chil-

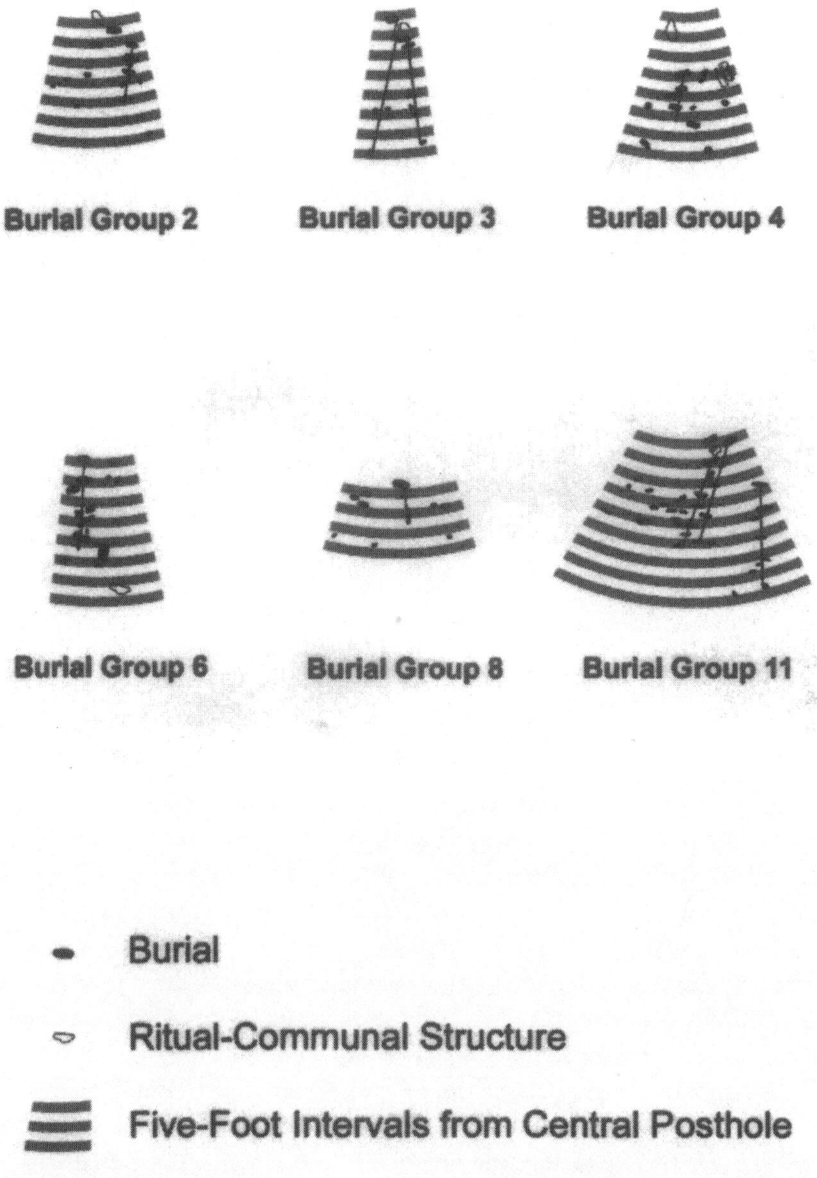

Figure 4.15. Internal spatial structures of the six arc-row burial groups. Note that burial groups are not shown in actual compass orientation; the curve of the arcs is related to the center pole.

dren and indeterminate cases (one in each group). Four burial groups are composed of relatively even proportions of males and females: Burial Group 2 (19% males, 19% females, 56% children, 6% indeterminate), Burial Group 4 (39% males, 31% females, 23% children, 7% indeterminate), Burial Group 11 (35% males, 35% females, 27% children, 3% indeterminate), Burial Group 7 (14% males, 14% females, 72% children). Remaining groups are composed of varying proportions of males, females, and children: Burial Group 3 (6% males, 27% females, 67% children), Burial Group 8 (14% males, 21% females, 65% children), Burial Group 9 (20% males, 10% females, 50% children, 20% indeterminate), Burial Group 10 (14% females, 72% children, 14% indeterminate).

Leg position varies considerably between burial groups. Six burial groups contain larger proportions of flexed burials: Burial Group 4 (69% flexed, 23% extended), Burial Group 6 (50% flexed, 44% extended), Burial Group 10 (57% flexed, 43% extended), Burial Group 12 (60% flexed, 40% extended), Burial Group 14 (75% flexed, none extended), and Burial Group 15 (75% flexed, 25% extended). Seven burial groups contain larger proportions of extended burials: Burial Group 7 (14% flexed, 57% extended), Burial Group 2 (25% flexed, 56% extended), Burial Group 3 (25% flexed, 38% extended), Burial Group 5 (40% flexed, 60% extended), Burial Group 9 (30% flexed, 60% extended), Burial Group 11 (37% flexed, 51% extended), and Burial Group 1 (50% flexed, 50% extended). Burial Group 8 (36% flexed, 36% extended) and Burial Group 13 (33% flexed, 33% extended) contain even proportions of flexed and extended burials. Secondary burials were present in Burial Group 2 (13%), Burial Group 4 (8%), Burial Group 7 (7%), and Burial Group 11 (6%). Remaining proportions of burial groups were indeterminate in terms of disposition of the legs.

All burials in Burial Groups 12 and 15 and large proportions of burials in Burial Groups 4 (69%), 6 (83%), 7 (64%), 10 (71%), and 11 (83%) contain limestone slab grave covers. Burials in other groups contained lower occurrences of limestone slabs: Burial Group 2 (50%), Burial Group 3 (25%), Burial Group 5 (40%), Burial Group 8 (43%), Burial Group 9 (60%), and Burial Group 13 (33%). No burials in Burial Group 14 contained limestone slabs. One grave in Burial Group 8 contained a cedar bark covering, which is the only occurrence of such a treatment for an individual in a burial group.

Correspondence analysis of burial groups of determinate form (Burial Groups 2, 3, 4, 5, 6, 7, 8, 9, 11) failed to produce many clear relationships between sex, body position, and grave covering (Figure 4.16). Burial Groups 6 and 11 are characterized as being more often flexed males with limestone slab grave covers. Burial Groups 7 and 9 are characterized as extended. Burial

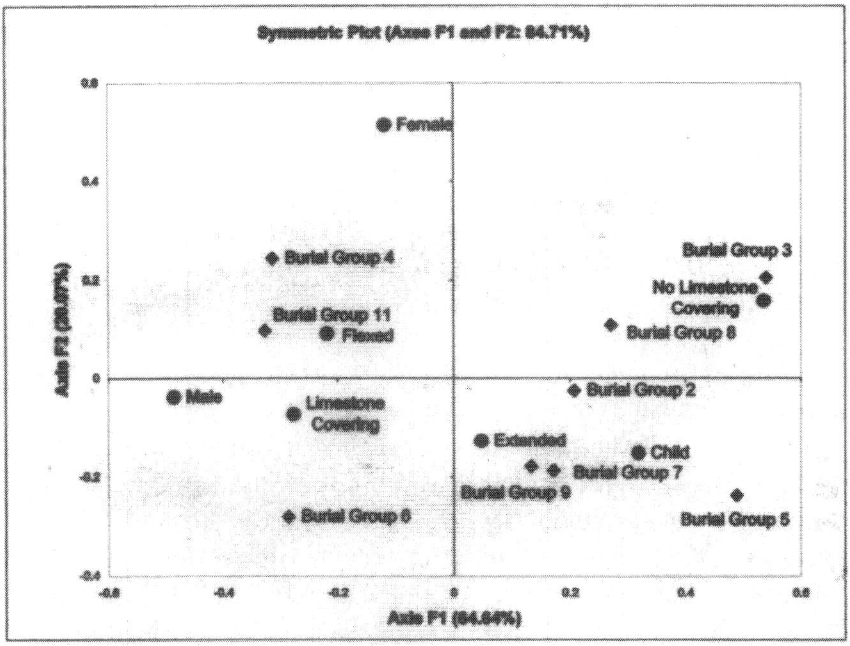

Figure 4.16. Correspondence analysis biplot comparing burial groups with body position, sex, and grave covering.

Group 3 is characterized as containing a low occurrence of limestone slab grave covers.

Artifacts are most common in Burial Groups 1 (50%), 2 (31%), 4 (39%), 6 (40%), 8 (43%), 9 (46%), 10 (43%), 12 (60%), 13 (33%), and 15 (50%). The occurrence of artifacts is less common in Burial Groups 3 (13%), 7 (14%), and 11 (3%); no artifacts are present in Burial Groups 5 and 14. Artifact diversity was considerably higher in Burial Groups 1 (n = 9), 6 (n = 14), 8 (n = 11), and 9 (n = 12). Burial Groups 2 (n = 5), 3 (n = 6), 4 (n = 5), 5 (n = 0), 7 (n = 2), 10 (n = 5), 11 (n = 6), 12 (n = 4), 13 (n = 1), 14 (n = 0), and 15 (n = 4) were much less diverse in terms of the number of artifact types present. These distinctions are not a simple function of greater burial frequency (see Table 4.4). If this were the case, Burial Group 11 should contain by far the most diverse artifact types. This group actually contains the lowest occurrence of artifacts.

The types of artifacts vary considerably between burial groups. The occurrence of certain artifacts was limited to particular groups or sets of neighboring groups. For discussion purposes, burial groups were segregated into the following partitions:

Partition	Burial Groups
north	7, 8, 9, 10, 11, 12, 15
west	4, 5, 6, 14
south	1, 2, 3, 13

Northern burial groups were the only ones to contain a slate pendant (Burial Group 10), a shell spoon (Burial Group 8), a burned stone (Burial Group 9), pottery vessels (Burial Groups 9 and 12), discoidals (Burial Group 9), turtle shell bowls (Burial Groups 8 and 9), wolf mandibles (Burial Groups 9, 11, and 15), unidentified animal teeth (Burial Groups 9 and 15), a drilled deer phalange (Burial Group 9), and a beamer/awl (Burial Group 10). Fish teeth were restricted to one burial in a western group (Burial Group 6). Deer sesamoids, antler flakers, and bobcat teeth were present only in a southern group (Burial Group 1). Artifact types restricted to the northeast and west groups include lithic projectile points (Burial Groups 4, 6, 8, 11, and 12), burned corn (Burial Groups 4, 6, 8, and 9), wolf and dog teeth (Burial Groups 6 and 9), shell pendants (Burial Groups 6 and 8), and antler projectile points (Burial Groups 4, 6, and 8). Artifacts occurring only in the south and west groups include bone awls (Burial Groups 1 and 6), hammerstones (Burial Groups 2 and 6), and whelk shells (Burial Groups 3 and 6). Items recovered only from north and south groups include shell barrel beads (Burial Groups 2, 3, 7, 10, and 11), shell tubular beads (Burial Groups 2 and 8), and smoking pipes (Burial Groups 1, 8, and 9). Marginella shells (Burial Groups 1, 2, 3, 4, 6, 7, 8, 9, 10, 11, 12, 15), shell disc beads (Burial Groups 1, 2, 3, 4, 6, 8, 10, and 11), perforated shell discs (Burial Groups 1, 3, 6, 8, 9, 12, and 13), bone pins (Burial Groups 1, 6, and 15), and ochre (Burial Groups 3, 6, and 11) were located in groups throughout the village.

Living with the Dead

This section describes the result of integrating the three data sets described thus far (chronological indicators, residential units, and burial groups) into one map from which to fully examine the utility of applying the localized corporate group model (Figure 4.17).

Burial Group 2 and Burial Group 3 are each linked to a series of analytical pit feature groups and house structures. (Burial Group 1 is too incomplete to fully assess its relationship with houses and pit feature groups, due to its proximity to the limits of excavation in the southeastern part of the village. However, it is associated with Pit Feature Group 1.7.)

Burial Group 2 is a corporate group composed of two distinct segments. The eastern segment is linked with Pit Feature Group 1.1 and House 1/74, and the

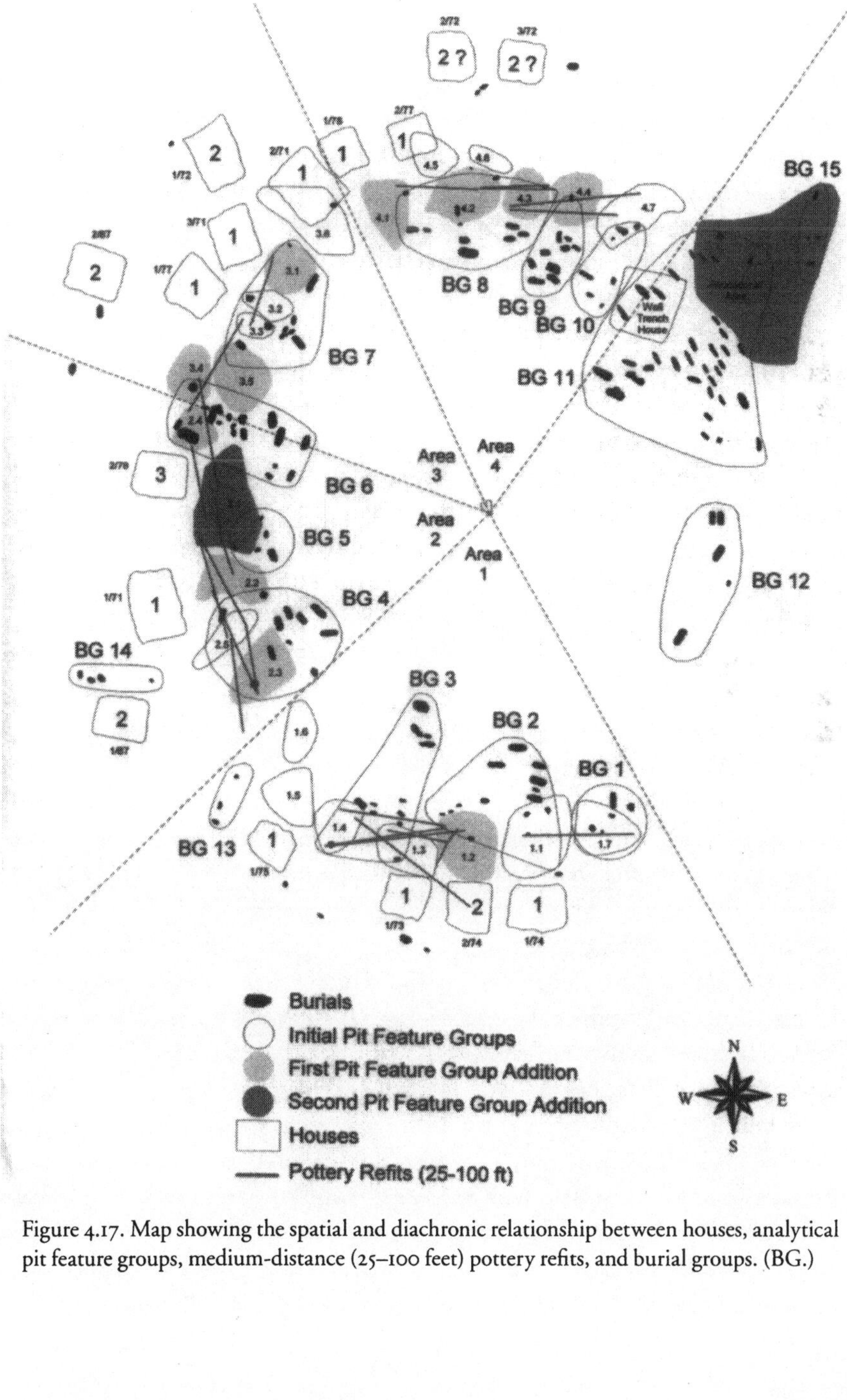

Figure 4.17. Map showing the spatial and diachronic relationship between houses, analytical pit feature groups, medium-distance (25–100 feet) pottery refits, and burial groups. (BG.)

western segment is connected with Pit Feature Group 1.2 and House 2/74. By all accounts the western segment is the newer of the two. This segment contains fewer burials, there is no indication of house rebuilding in the associated structure, and many diagnostic characteristics associated with the middle time period were located in the associated pit feature group. Burial Group 3 is a corporate group that is also composed of two segments. The eastern segment is linked with Pit Feature Group 1.3 and House 1/73, and the western segment is connected to Pit Feature Group 1.4 and House 1/75. However, there is no clear indication for one segment preceding the other as there are similar frequencies of adult burials and similar relative ages of both pit feature groups and houses.

Medium-distance pottery refits (25–100 feet) link pit feature groups associated with the two distinct burial groups (Burial Groups 2 and 3); in no case do they occur only within respective groupings. In particular, there appears to be a strong connection between House 2/74 and House 1/75 based on the high incidence of pottery refits between pit features associated with these two structures. This pattern could have arisen as a consequence of members of the newer House 2/74 being more closely linked with House 1/75 than was the case for House 1/73. Based on one refit, House 1/74 is linked with Pit Feature Group 1.7 and Burial Group 1.

House 1/75 and associated pit feature groups are set apart from others in Area 1, although this house is linked with House 1/73 via Burial Group 3. The uniqueness of the location of House 1/75 is partially related to time, as all temporal indicators suggest a very early appearance of this household. Furthermore, this house is the only one at the site to be positioned near the intersection of both stockades (see Figure 1.4), which appears to be one location for a village entrance. This house is also unique in terms of its relationship to the longest-distance pottery refits (>100 feet), which link it with the western part of the site (Figure 4.18). This could explain its senior position relative to the newest house in the area (House 2/74) as well as strong connections with the leadership precinct in the village (see Chapter 5). Long-distance pottery refits link most (71%) of the pit feature groups or associated houses in Area 1 with Area 2, leaving little doubt about the strength of this relationship. Moreover, these refits link areas associated with differing temporal affiliations.

Three burial groups (4, 5, 14) are clearly associated with Area 2, and I suggest that Burial Groups 6 and 13 are also most closely related to this area (see below). Burial Group 4 is associated with Houses 1/71 and 1/87 and Pit Feature Groups 2.2, 2.3, and 2.5. The spatial segmentation of this group is not clear. House 1/71 and Activity Area 2.5 were likely used throughout the village occupation, while House 1/87 and Pit Feature Groups 2.2 and 2.3 were later additions to the area.

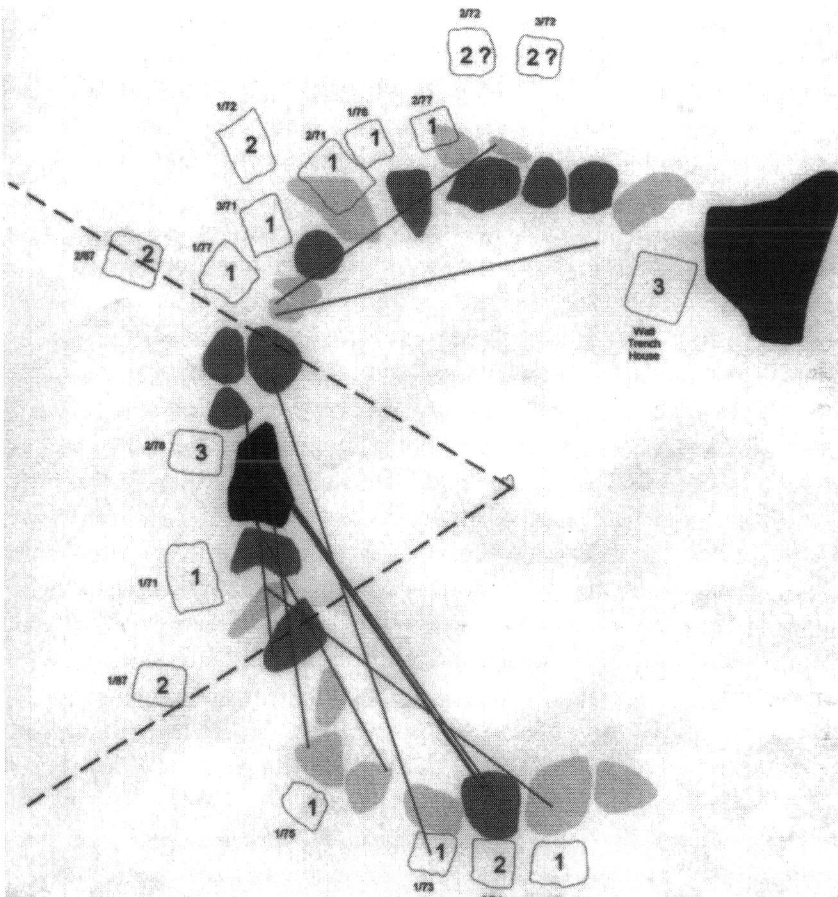

Figure 4.18. Map showing the spatial and diachronic relationship between houses, analytical pit feature groups, and long-distance (>100 feet) pottery refits.

Burial Groups 13 and 14, located on either side of House 1/87, are aligned with Pit Feature Group 2.3 and Burial Group 4 (albeit at some distance from it). The three tightly grouped burials in Burial Group 14 are located outside of the inner stockade, further affiliating these individuals with this house and the later stages of village use. Burial Group 4 appears to have had a long history at the site, as this group contained the highest percentage (69%) of flexed burials in the arc-row groups. Recall that this group is located very close to the hypothesized summer solstice alignment (see Figure 1.5).

Burial Group 5 is positioned between Pit Feature Groups 2.1 and 2.2. This small burial group (n = 5) consists exclusively of children and is positioned between the hypothesized equinox and planting/harvesting alignments (see Figure 1.5). Based on the later period of use associated with both pit feature groups, I suggest that this burial group developed later in the site occupation.

Burial Group 6 is associated with House 2/78 and Pit Feature Groups 2.1 and 2.4 (and possibly Pit Feature Groups 3.4 and 3.5). All indications suggest that Burial Group 6 developed late in the occupational sequence of the village, during a time of village expansion, the arrival of a small Middle Mississippian group, and the development of a ritual/leader area focused on House 2/78 (see below and Chapter 5). Burial Group 6 consists exclusively of males and children. This finding adheres well to the theoretical expectations of male ritualism and leadership forming along with village growth (Marcus and Flannery 1996:238–239; see also Chapter 5), expanding an earlier hypothesis regarding the development of a male-focused institution in the village (Robertson 1980:75–78) (see Chapter 1). Recall that this group is located near the hypothesized winter solstice alignment (see Figure 1.5).

Area 3 contains one burial group (Burial Group 7) with three segments associated with four houses and five pit feature groups (recall that House 2/71 could not be reliably associated with either Area 3 or 4). Based on nearest proximity between houses and pit feature groups, House 1/77 is associated with Pit Feature Group 3.3 and House 3/71 is associated with Pit Feature Group 3.2. I suggest that Burial Group 7 initially formed near these houses and expanded outward in both directions, which included the construction of Houses 2/87 and 1/72 and Pit Feature Groups 3.1, 3.4, and 3.5. This conclusion is based on the fact that there are more burials in the central portion, which is clearly associated with earlier pit feature groups and houses. Additionally, medium-distance pottery refits (25–100 feet) link older and newer pit feature groups in this part of the site.

Pit Feature Group 3.5 is least attributable directly to either of the houses in this area, most likely due to the unique nature of this pit feature group (see Chapter 5). House 2/71 and Pit Feature Group 3.6 are both associated with the earliest part of the site usage but are not directly relatable to a specific corporate group. This part of the site remains unclear. It appears to predate the remainder of the houses, pit feature groups, and burials in this part of the site, perhaps representing a development in the village before the more intensive village occupation(s).

Burial Group 8 consists of three distinct segments associated with three pit feature groups and four houses. The central burial segment overlaps with Pit Feature Group 4.2, the western burial segment overlaps with Pit Feature Group 4.1, and the eastern burial segment overlaps with Pit Feature Group 4.3. Houses 1/78, 2/77, 2/72, and 3/72 are associated with Area 4, but connections between individual burial segments and pit feature groups are unclear. There is also some discrepancy between the temporal indicators in this area, in contrast to other areas. Based on the mortuary pattern and pottery refits, it seems that the central segment of the burial group formed the nucleus to which adjacent portions were added, similar to Burial Group 7, although the temporal affiliation of associated pit feature groups could not be discerned. However, if only straight-sided storage pits are considered, which are consistently located in later areas of the site, the pattern is much clearer, as they are nearly absent from Pit Feature Group 4.2 and occur in abundance in neighboring groups (4.1, 4.3, 4.4, avocational area) (Figure 4.19).

Burial Group 11 contains two distinct segments, one of which is commingled with the wall trench house. This group cannot be subdivided into an earlier and later part; all indications are that it formed late in the site occupation. Burial rows are clearest in this area, which is not surprising given the fact that the Middle Mississippian association is strongest in this part of the site (i.e., there is a wall trench house). There is also a distinct concentration of burials around this house (see Chapter 5). The arrival of a small Middle Mississippian–style group is a plausible hypothesis, coinciding with the expansion of the corporate group initially represented by the central portion of Burial Group 8. Curiously, the most unusual burial group at the site (Burial Group 9)—located between Burial Group 8 and the wall trench house—is not a row pattern, and burials associated with it are the only ones at the site to contain discoidals and one of the two instances of a pottery vessel. The hypothesized mixture of social groups in this part of the site may explain why spatial and temporal associations between pit feature groups and houses are less clear than elsewhere in the village. Regarding potential solar phenomena, this group is concentrated with respect to the summer solstice alignment (see Figure 1.5 and Figure 5.1).

Area 4 is further distinguishable from the remainder of the site in terms of the distribution of wolf and dog remains. The five dog burials and all wolf and dog teeth and mandibles in human burials are concentrated in this part of the

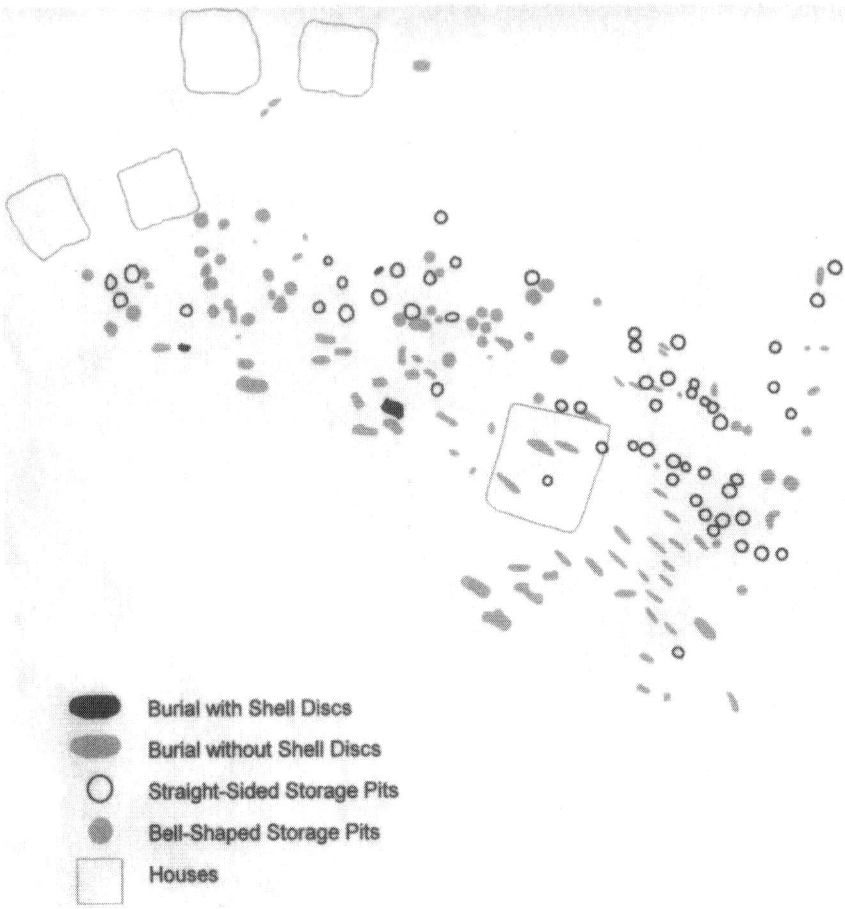

Figure 4.19. Spatial relationship between shell discs and straight-sided storage pits in the northern house cluster and avocational area.

village. There are only two exceptions, in Burial Group 6 (the only one of determinate form to contain only male and child burials) and in front of House 2/78, the red cedar house constructed late in the village occupation. Dog burials are most directly associated with Burial Groups 6, 9, and 11. The distribution of negative-painted pottery is consistent with this pattern, suggesting that there may be a relationship between these phenomena (Figure 4.20). Additionally, dog burials surround but are not inside the wall trench house (which is also the case for a set of human burials [see Chapter 5]). I suggest that a wolf clan–like group was located in this part of the site (see Evans-Eargle 1998; Heilman and Hoefer 1981; Lileas 1988b for earlier suggestions of a wolf clan). The strong

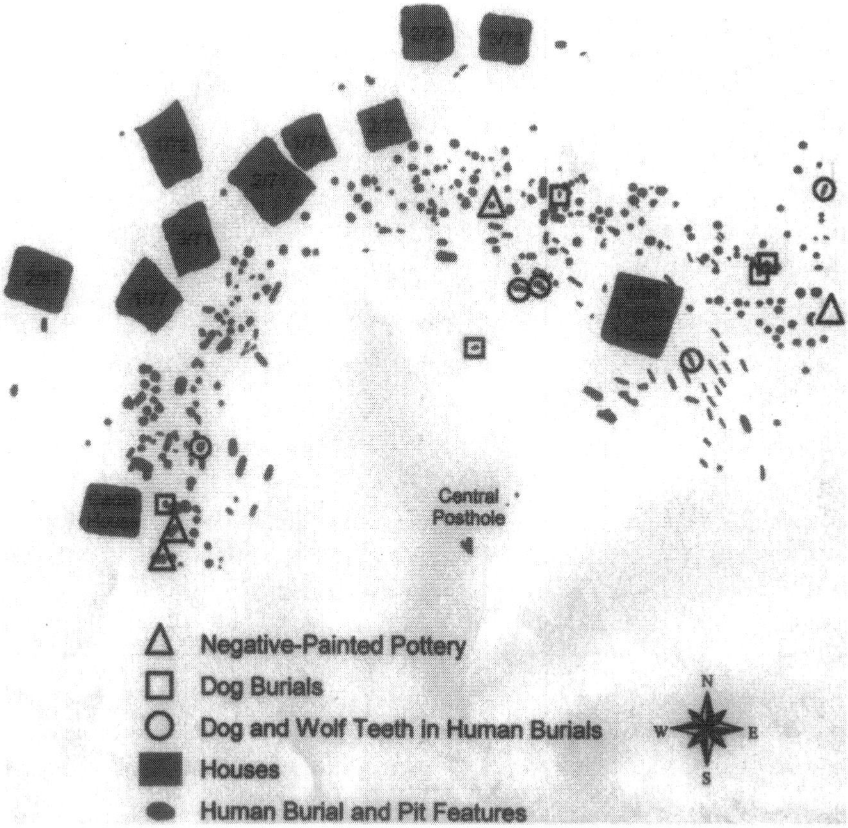

Figure 4.20. Spatial distribution of negative-painted pottery and wolf and dog remains in burials and pit features.

linkage of corporate behavior considerably strengthens this hypothesis. The location of a wolf clan in the northeastern portion of a village is consistent with the layout of Central Algonquian villages (Callendar 1978). Furthermore, this pattern is not an isolated one, as Essenpreis (1982:208, 285) has noted a burial containing multiple wolf jaws in the northern portion of the Anderson village site. While the conclusion is tentative, I suggest we can consider Fort Ancient villages to adhere to Keesing's Type IV village kinship model (see Chapter 1), as similar clans appear to be located in other Fort Ancient villages (Keesing 1975:42–43).

The Middle Mississippian–style wall trench house and spatially related artifacts in an area with several dog burials and wolf remains suggest that perhaps a small group moved into a wolf clan–like segment of the village. Alternatively, this pattern could have arisen in the context of short-term stays within these social groups: "If the traveler found members of his clan in the town, he spent the night in one of their households; if not, he spent the night in the town house" (Hudson 1976:314–315). Of course, the in-movement of individuals may have been more permanent (e.g., marriage alliances). The concentration of morphologically distinct shell-tempered pottery in these locales suggests that females may have moved into the village, perhaps as marriage partners (Cook and Sunderhaus 1999). A recent finding that shell-tempered pottery was produced some distance from the site lends additional support to this hypothesis (Cook and Fargher 2007).

Conclusion

Examination of multiple lines of evidence supports temporal distinctions observed in the radiocarbon sequence. The village was larger at the end of its use, temporally associated with a Middle Mississippian–style house and associated artifacts, and was used on a more year-round basis (the earliest occupation was most associated with spring and summer). Based on estimates for house use-life of 5 to 15 years (see Chapter 3), the site may represent a single occupation of between 10 and 30 years. Given the association of distinct architecture and artifacts, the later point in this occupation occurred at a time of considerable Middle Mississippian contact with Fort Ancient village. Based on radiocarbon dates, if there was a single occupation, it is most likely to have occurred between the late A.D. 1200s and early A.D. 1300s, approximately 100 years later than has been previously suggested, although of a similar overall duration. (It has long been suggested that the village was occupied in the latter part of the twelfth century for about 25 years [Essenpreis 1982:209; Heilman and Hoefer 1981].)

An equally plausible explanation is that there were two episodes of occupation. The initial occupation occurred in the late A.D. 1100s, consisted of about half the size of the final village population, occurred mostly during the spring and summer months, and lacked clear evidence for Middle Mississippian influence. The second occupation occurred in the late A.D. 1300s, consisted of a considerably larger population who utilized the site on a year-round basis, and possessed clear indicators of Middle Mississippian influence, including a wall trench house and negative-painted pottery. A series of Fort Ancient diagnostics (many but not all of which I suggest are also related to Middle Mississippian interactions) was also associated with this stage: shell-tempered pottery, strap and loop appendages, pottery bowls, a salt pan, and certain pottery designs (scroll, plain, a few line-filled triangle variants).

One of the difficulties of accepting a reoccupation that so carefully built on the earlier village is the suspicion that little would be visible after the intervening period of time. Reoccupation usually results in frequent feature overlap and staggered village plans. However, in this case the time involved may have been brief enough as to render much of the village visible. Depending on how much time is allotted, it is reasonable to conclude that the center pole, house basins, and possibly some pit features would have been visible. Site reuse is common in shifting agriculture systems because gardens are often reused after lying fallow for some time, as this is much easier than clearing virgin forest (Sahlins 1968:29–30). This has been suggested to be a general pattern that develops toward the beginning of the Middle Fort Ancient period (Henderson and Pollack 2001; Pollack and Henderson 2000). Regardless of whether site occupation was continuous or interrupted, the following sequence is postulated: (1) the village was established; (2) the village grew at a time when a small Middle Mississippian–style group arrived.

A close spatial relationship existed between the living and the dead in this Fort Ancient village. The center pole was a critical part of arranging cemeteries used by corporate groups. Corporate group behavior was most often expressed as arc-row groups containing two or three conjoined segments. These segments converged on one or two burials located closest to the central posthole. Each of these groups grew over the course of village occupation(s), based on the examination of site formation using a chronological framework derived through comparison of radiocarbon dates and temporally diagnostic artifact and feature attributes. The key question that remains is: How is the timing of the Middle Mississippian–style wall trench house related to leadership development in the village?

5
Development of Village Leadership

The examination of leadership at SunWatch focused on general characteristics of status in mortuary and architectural elements encoded in Middle Mississippian villages (see Chapter 2 and Chapter 3). Village layout is examined on the basis of spatial proximity of features to the central posthole, unique architecture, storage distinctions, and solar alignments. Findings are then compared to spatial dimensions associated with status differences in the mortuary realm.

Centering Power

Leaders often situate their houses in closer proximity to village centers and have more storage potential or differential access to storage. In some Middle Mississippian examples, positioning in relation to key solar alignments was also a factor in the location of leaders' houses. Leaders themselves are buried in these locales and are usually a definable group of higher-status male burials with supralocal status symbols. Obviously, the more of these criteria that are present, the stronger the case for the presence of leadership styles akin to Middle Mississippian analogues.

Proximity and Solar Alignments

To begin examining whether SunWatch contained any part of this "power package," circles were drawn on a map around the location of the central posthole in 5-foot increments enclosing the entire village area, using the ArcGIS buffer command. The resulting map was inspected to assess whether any houses or other features were positioned in closer proximity than the others to the central posthole. The 125-foot radius circle serves as a significant dividing line for pit features initially defined in Area 2 (Figure 5.1), as 95% of pit features in this area were within 125 feet of the central posthole, while only 5% of pits in the southern and northern portions of the site were within this boundary. Only one structure falls within the 125-foot radius: the wall trench house.

Solstice alignments were plotted to explore their relationship with features in closest proximity to the center pole (see Figure 5.1). The result is consistent

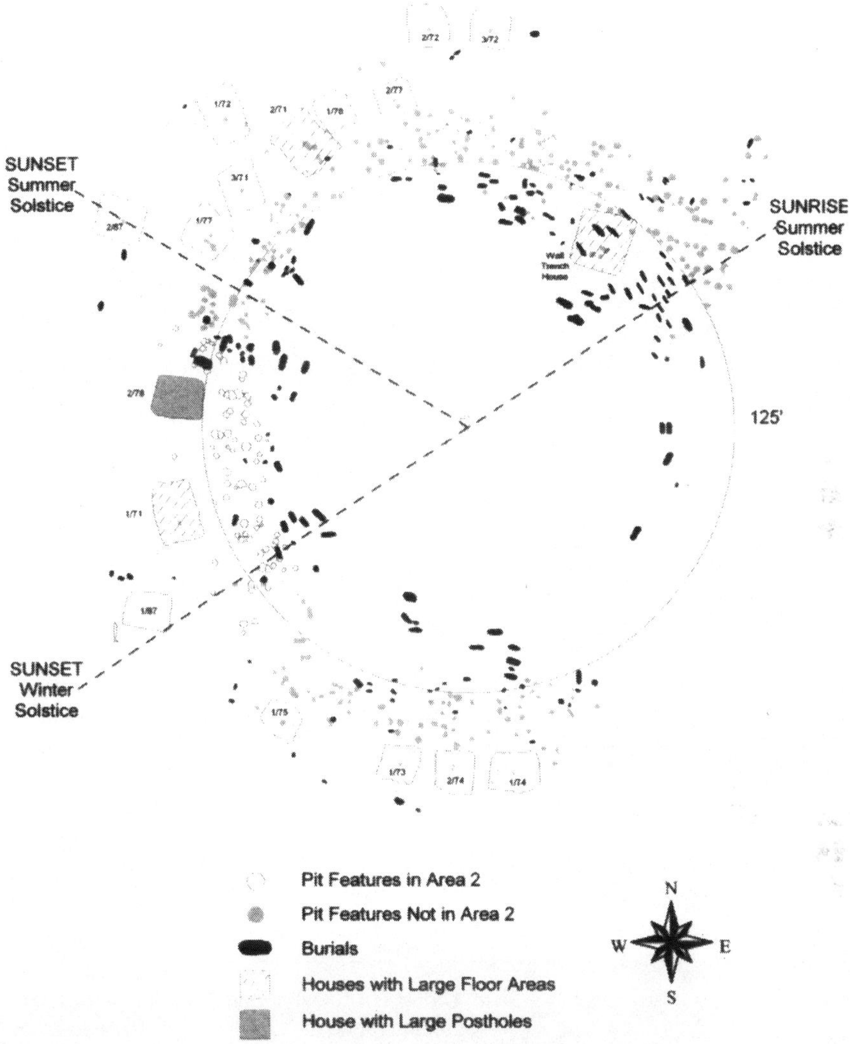

Figure 5.1. Map showing the 125-foot radius circle discovered through distance analysis (measured from the central posthole) and the location of large houses [see Figure 5.2 and Figure 5.3]).

with the 125-foot "proximity rule." The solstice alignments generally demarcate the set of pit features concentrated within the 125-foot radius circle (Area 2). A few burials in rows nearest these alignments and near the wall trench house are situated slightly closer to the center pole, although this distinction is not statistically significant. The wall trench house and associated burials are near the summer solstice sunrise alignment, but due to lack of extensive excavation in the eastern portion of the village this possibility cannot be further investigated.

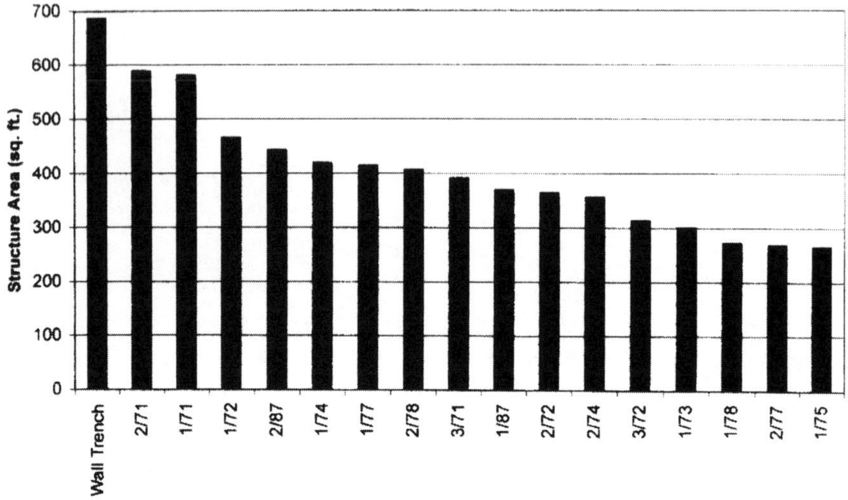

Figure 5.2. Bar graph showing range of house areas.

The combination of proximity and a close relationship with solstice alignments provides an effective means for segregating a leadership precinct; and the proximity rule (and possibly solar alignments) provides a direct connection between the western leader area and the wall trench house.

Unique Architecture

Distinctions in architectural construction were assessed in terms of house sizes and construction materials. One house was built from red cedar (House 2/78)—all other houses were built using primarily oak and hickory (Wagner 1979). Unfortunately, we do not know what type of wood was used in the construction of the wall trench house, but it was clearly constructed in a unique fashion as compared to other houses in the village.

House size was examined in terms of floor area and wall-post size (Cook 2005). House areas were distinctly larger for three structures (Wall Trench, 2/71, 1/71) (Figure 5.2). Posthole sizes were slightly larger for these same structures (the wall trench house was not included due to lack of data). However, the only significant difference in size for wall postholes was for the red cedar House 2/78, which contained much larger wall posts in terms of both depth and diameter measurements (Figure 5.3).

The wall trench house and House 2/78 are architecturally unique. The wall trench house is not only closer to the center pole but also larger and constructed in a different fashion than other houses in the village. The red cedar house is the second closest structure to the center pole, is made from a unique building material, and on the basis of posthole depth may have been considerably

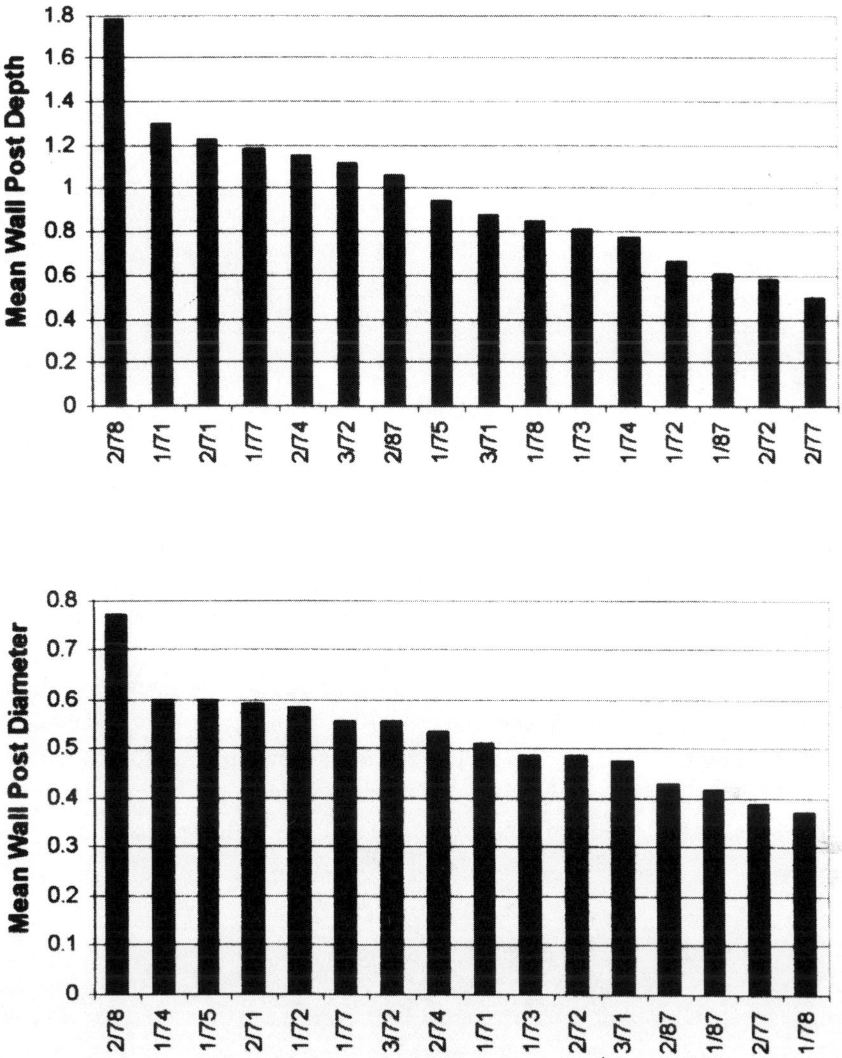

Figure 5.3. Bar graphs showing mean wall posthole depths and diameters for houses (measured in feet).

taller than other houses (although the depth and diameter of these posts could be a function of wood type). These two houses are also spatially associated with Middle Mississippian–style pottery (see Figure 4.11 and Figure 4.19), produced the latest radiocarbon dates for houses in the village (see Figure 4.1), and are associated with artifact (shell-tempered pottery) and mortuary distinctions (limestone slabs) that are specifically noted for some Middle Mississippian groups.

Storage

The volumes of all bell-shaped and straight-sided storage features with average depth >1.6 feet (see Chapter 4) were compared among the four site areas. The expectation was that in Area 2 the leadership precinct would contain more storage volume relative to house size, indicative of increased storage for a local leader (as noted by Nass and Yerkes 1995:77 on the basis of bell-shaped pits only). However, results considering both feature types do not support this distinction (Figure 5.4).

One potential storage distinction is associated with Area 3, near the border with Area 2. A series of postholes, which I interpret as a structure, encloses a group of pit features and is further defined on the basis of the pronounced row of burials in Burial Group 6. Moreover, this structure is intersected by the winter solstice sunrise alignment (Figure 5.5). Hence, the only potential storage distinction involves a previously unrecognized structure enclosing several storage pit features. Given its location in relation to the winter solstice alignment and adjacent red cedar house, a logical possibility is that this structure contained storage pits used during the winter months, perhaps under some control of a village leader. However, seasonal data from pit features located inside this structure support both a winter/summer (n = 1) and summer (n = 1) use, rendering such a conclusion unwarranted. One of these features contains several grit/grog-tempered pottery sherds, which, along with some of the negative-painted sherds, appear to be currently Middle Mississippian. The validity of this conjectural viewpoint is being tested in a petrographic analysis.

Burials

The mortuary program was investigated to assess the general parameters of the population and to determine if there was an identifiable segment that formed a "village leader" category and the extent to which this was similar to Middle Mississippian examples. Toward this end, a general comparison of mortuary treatment by sex and age is followed by a cluster analysis.

General Profile

The mortuary population consists of 181 individuals: 42 (23%) males, 34 (19%) females, 99 (55%) children, and 6 (3%) indeterminate. Ages range from fetal to 58 years. Half (50%) of the burial population died at 4 years of age or younger: fetal (6%), <1 (28%), 1–4 years (16%). Approximately one-third (32%) of the burial population is between 30 and 49 years of age: 30–34 years (10%), 35–39 years (12%), 40–44 years (7%), 45–49 years (3%). The remainder of the burial

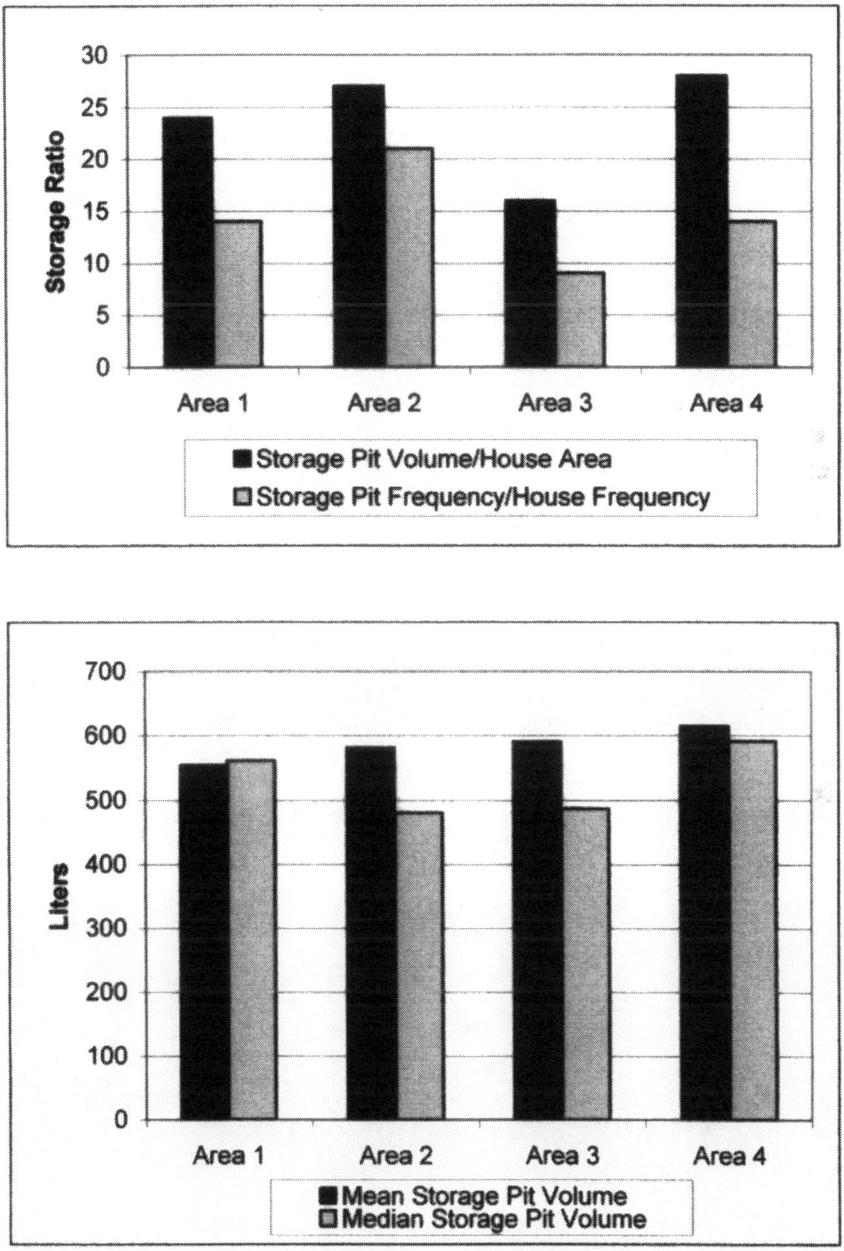

Figure 5.4. Bar graph comparing pit features and houses in terms of respective sizes and frequencies in four house clusters.

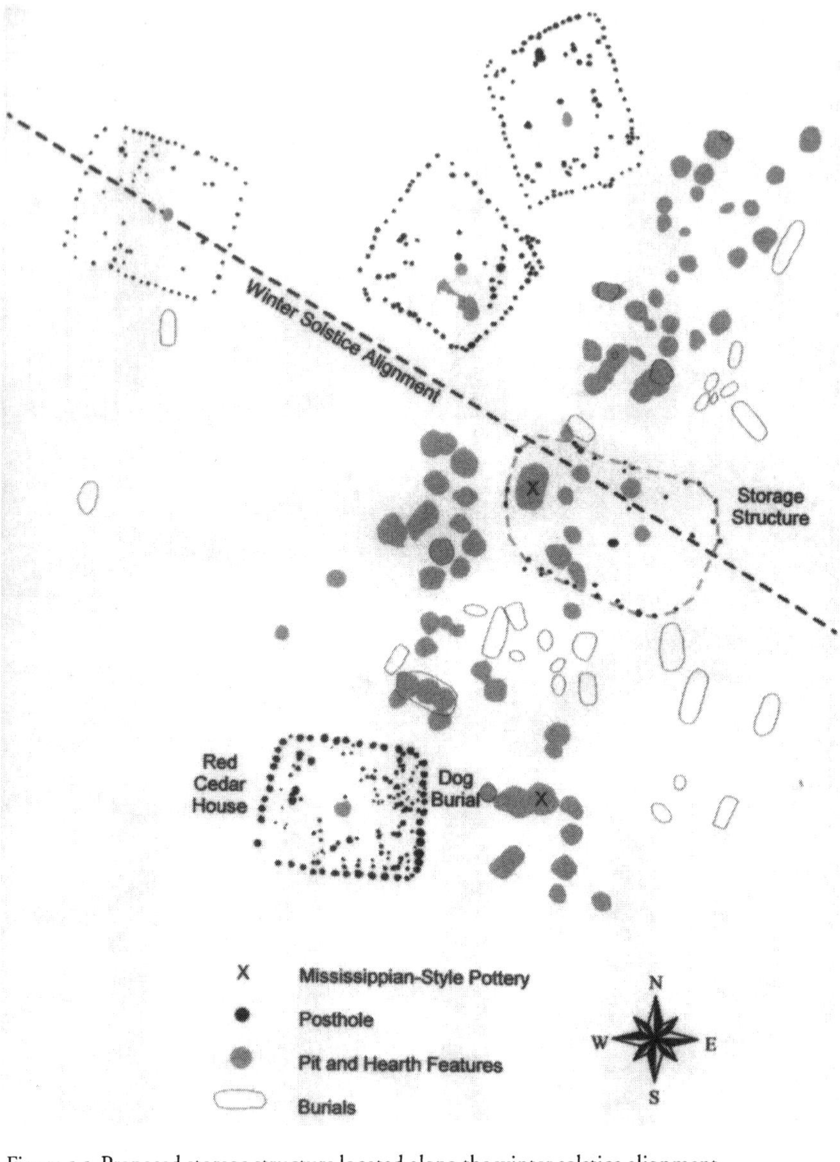

Figure 5.5. Proposed storage structure located along the winter solstice alignment.

population (18%) died at relatively even rates in other age intervals: 5–9 years (2%), 10–14 years (3%), 15–19 years (4%), 20–24 years (3%), 25–29 years (3%), 55–59 years (1%), indeterminate (2%). While there are a few more males in older age categories, there is no significant difference between the age of death for males and females.

Extended (45%) and flexed (41%) leg positions are nearly equally represented, and there is only a slight tendency for semiflexed (23%) over fully flexed (18%) variants. Disarticulated (5%) and secondary (3%) interments are uncommon, and only a small proportion of the burial population is indeterminate in terms of leg positioning (6%). Leg positions are similar for males (60% flexed, 31% extended) and females (53% flexed, 38% extended). Males (7%) and females (6%) are also equally represented as secondary burials. Children are more frequently extended (54%) than flexed (30%). Children are also disarticulated more often (8%) than females (3%) (no males are disarticulated), but rarely (1%) occurred as secondary burials. Leg position did not significantly vary by age, although there is a tendency for adults 40 years of age and older to be buried in flexed positions.

Grave coverings are associated with the majority of burials (64%). The most common occurrence is limestone slabs, which are present in 97% of the burials containing extant grave coverings. The remaining grave covers are log impressions (n = 2) and cedar bark (n = 1). There is a slight difference in the occurrence of limestone slabs between males (81%) and females (91%), but this is not statistically significant. However, there is a significant distinction between adults and children in this dimension of the mortuary program. Most adult graves were covered with limestone slabs (86%), whereas children were covered with limestone slabs about half as often (44%) (x^2 [observed = 32.1, critical = 3.8], DF = 1, $p<0.00001$). The occurrence of limestone slabs is also related to distance from the center pole. On average, burials covered with limestone slabs (116 feet) are closer than those lacking grave covers (130 feet), a difference that is significant according to a two-tailed t-test of means ($p = 0.001$).

Distances of male, female, and child burials from the center pole varied between 75 and 205 feet. On average, males were buried the closest (110 feet), followed closely by females (116 feet), with children being the most distant (129 feet). According to the results of a series of two-tailed t-tests, the difference in distance between males and children was significant ($p<0.0001$), as was the difference between females and children ($p = 0.02$); however, the difference between males and females was not significant ($p = 0.323$). Thus, the main distinction in terms of proximity of burial to the center pole is between adults and children.

Artifacts were present in one-fourth (26%) of the burials, and males were interred with artifacts more often than females or children (36% of the male burials contained artifacts, in comparison to 23% of the children and 21% of the females). The graves of children less than 4 years of age were most likely to contain artifacts, and both male and female burials were most likely to contain artifacts between the ages of 30 and 39.

There are differences in terms of the types of artifacts associated with different sexes and children. The following items were found only with adult male burials: fish teeth, wolf mandibles, deer sesamoids, deer phalange, antler flakers, bone awls, pipes, lithic projectile points, pottery vessels, a slate pendant, and a beamer. Several items were found only with child burials: a shell pendant, a bobcat tooth necklace, wolf teeth, a dog tooth, and discoidals. The only artifact type restricted to a female was a shell spoon. A series of artifacts was associated with male burials and child burials (but not female burials), including: whelk shells, shell discs, bone pins, antler projectile points, and ochre. Turtle shell bowls were interred only with a female and a child. Burned corn was present only with males and females. The remainder of the artifact types (marginella shells, tubular shell beads, disc shell beads, barrel shell beads, and hammerstones) occurred in varying proportions with males, females, and children.

Specific adult ages are associated with specific types of artifacts. Males 30 years of age or older were the only ones to be interred with pipes (consistent with data from Madisonville [Drooker 1997:242–243, 246–247]), lithic projectile points, pottery vessels, and bone awls (a deer phalange, deer sesamoids, fish teeth, a slate pendant, an antler flaker, and a beamer/awl are also restricted to males in this age range but are each represented in only one burial). The female with the shell spoon was also in an older age category (45–49 years).

Cluster Analysis

Twenty-one artifact types are present in two or more burials, meeting the criteria developed for inclusion in the cluster analysis (see Chapter 3), including: antler projectile points, shell barrel beads, bone awls, bone pins, burned corn, shell disc beads, discoidals, hammerstones, lithic projectile points, marginella shells, ochre, pipes, pottery vessels, shell discs, triangular shell pendants, tubular shell beads, turtle shell bowls, unidentified animal teeth, whelk shells, wolf mandibles, and wolf teeth. Several cluster solutions were explored, but the five-cluster solution produced the clearest distinctions.

Artifact associations are marked for several clusters (Table 5.1). Cluster 1 has all occurrences of discoidals and unidentified animal teeth and the majority of lithic and antler projectile points. Cluster 2 has all occurrences of shell barrel beads and a relatively large proportion of shell disc beads. Cluster 3 has all occurrences of burned corn and relatively large proportions of marginella shells and hammerstones. Cluster 4 has all occurrences of triangular shell pendants, all but one occurrence of bone awls, shell discs, and whelk shells (the whelk shell is with a child less than one year in age), and a relatively large proportion of marginella shells. The individual that constitutes Cluster 5 has the remaining bone awl, shell disc, and whelk shell (the only one that is complete [see Figure 3.5]).

Clusters 1, 2, and 3 are made up of representative proportions of children, females, and males. However, ages vary between them (Table 5.2). Cluster 1 con-

Table 5.1. Occurrence of Artifact Types Used in the Five-Cluster Solution for Burials

	Burial Cluster											
	1		2		3		4		5		Total	
Artifact	N	%	N	%	N	%	N	%	N	%	N	%
Marginella	0	0.0	1	3.7	19	70.4	7	25.9	0	0.0	27	100.0
Shell disc bead	2	16.7	5	41.7	2	16.7	3	25.0	0	0.0	12	100.1
Shell disc	0	0.0	0	0.0	0	0.0	10	90.9	1	9.1	11	100.0
Shell barrel bead	0	0.0	10	100.0	0	0.0	0	0.0	0	0.0	10	100.0
Lithic projectile point	4	66.7	0	0.0	0	0.0	1	16.7	1	16.7	6	100.1
Bone pin	1	20.0	0	0.0	1	20.0	2	40.0	1	20.0	5	100.0
Antler projectile point	4	80.0	0	0.0	0	0.0	0	0.0	1	20.0	5	100.0
Hammerstone	0	0.0	0	0.0	4	80.0	0	0.0	1	20.0	5	100.0
Burned corn	0	0.0	0	0.0	4	100.0	0	0.0	0	0.0	4	100.0
Tubular shell bead	0	0.0	1	33.3	2	66.7	0	0.0	0	0.0	3	100.0
Unid. animal teeth	3	100.0	0	0.0	0	0.0	0	0.0	0	0.0	3	100.0
Wolf mandible	2	66.7	0	0.0	1	33.3	0	0.0	0	0.0	3	100.0
Pipe	1	33.3	0	0.0	1	33.3	1	33.3	0	0.0	3	99.9
Ochre	1	33.3	1	33.3	0	0.0	1	33.3	0	0.0	3	99.9
Whelk	0	0.0	0	0.0	0	0.0	1	50.0	1	50.0	2	100.0
Tri. shell pendant	0	0.0	0	0.0	0	0.0	2	100.0	0	0.0	2	100.0
Turtle shell bowl	1	50.0	0	0.0	1	50.0	0	0.0	0	0.0	2	100.0
Wolf tooth	1	50.0	0	0.0	0	0.0	1	50.0	0	0.0	2	100.0
Bone awl	0	0.0	0	0.0	0	0.0	1	50.0	1	50.0	2	100.0
Discoidal	2	100.0	0	0.0	0	0.0	0	0.0	0	0.0	2	100.0
Pottery vessel	1	50.0	0	0.0	1	50.0	0	0.0	0	0.0	2	100.0

Table 5.2. Sex, Age, Leg Position, and Grave Cover Comparisons by Burial Cluster

Characteristic	Burial Cluster									
	1		2		3		4		5	
Sex	N	%	N	%	N	%	N	%	N	%
Child	76	55.9	4	40.0	13	56.5	6	54.5	0	0.0
Female	25	18.4	3	30.0	6	26.1	0	0.0	0	0.0
Male	31	22.8	1	10.0	4	17.4	5	45.5	1	100.0
Indeterminate	4	2.9	2	20.0	0	0.0	0	0.0	0	0.0
Total	136	100.0	10	100.0	23	100.0	11	100.0	1	100.0
Age										
Fetal	11	8.1	0	0.0	0	0.0	0	0.0	0	0.0
<1	38	27.9	3	30.0	5	21.7	5	45.5	0	0.0
1–4	19	14.0	1	10.0	7	30.4	1	9.1	0	0.0
5–9	5	3.7	0	0.0	0	0.0	0	0.0	0	0.0
10–14	4	2.9	0	0.0	1	4.3	0	0.0	0	0.0
15–19	5	3.7	3	30.0	0	0.0	0	0.0	0	0.0
20–24	5	3.7	0	0.0	0	0.0	0	0.0	0	0.0
25–29	3	2.2	1	10.0	0	0.0	1	9.1	0	0.0
30–34	11	8.1	0	0.0	6	26.1	1	9.1	0	0.0
35–39	17	12.5	1	10.0	2	8.7	1	9.1	1	100.0
40–44	11	8.1	0	0.0	0	0.0	2	18.2	0	0.0
45–49	4	2.9	1	10.0	1	4.3	0	0.0	0	0.0

50–54	0	0.0	0	0.0	0	0.0	0	0.0	0	0.0
55–59	1	0.7	0	0.0	0	0	0	0	0	0
Indeterminate	2	1.5	0	0.0	1	4.4	0	0	0	0
Total	136	100.0	10	100.0	23	99.9	11	100.1	1	100.0
Leg Position										
Fully flexed	26	19.1	0	0.0	4	17.4	3	27.3	0	0.0
Semiflexed	33	24.3	2	20.0	5	21.7	2	18.2	0	0.0
Disarticulated	9	6.6	0	0.0	0	0.0	0	0.0	0	0.0
Extended	53	39.0	8	80.0	14	60.9	6	54.5	1	100.0
Secondary	6	4.4	0	0.0	0	0.0	0	0.0	0	0.0
Indeterminate	9	6.6	0	0.0	0	0.0	0	0.0	0	0.0
Total	136	100.0	10	100.0	23	100.0	11	100.0	1	100.0
Grave Cover										
Limestone slabs	80	58.8	8	80.0	17	73.9	7	63.6	1	100.0
Log impressions	1	0.7	0	0.0	1	4.3	0	0.0	0	0.0
Cedar bark	1	0.7	0	0.0	0	0.0	0	0.0	0	0.0
Absent	54	39.7	2	20.0	5	21.7	4	36.4	0	0.0
Total	136	100.0	10	100.0	23	100.0	11	100.0	1	100.0

tains all of the fetuses, most children are between 0 and 4 years in age, and most adults are between 30 and 44 years. Cluster 2 is made up of a high proportion of individuals 0 to 1 and 15 to 19 years. Cluster 3 contains a high proportion of individuals 0 to 4 and 30 to 34 years. Cluster 4 contains only males and children; males were between the ages of 25 and 44, and children were most often less than one year. Cluster 5 is composed of a 35-year-old male.

The spatial distribution of burial clusters varies (Figure 5.6). Cluster 1 burials are located throughout the site. Cluster 2 burials are concentrated around the wall trench house (60%); no burials are within it, suggesting it was being used at the time of these interments. Other Cluster 2 burials are generally located in prominent positions in the southern part of the site (i.e., closest to the central posthole). Interestingly, all Cluster 2 burials in the southern part of the site are adults, and those individuals located near the wall trench are mostly children 15 years old or younger (there is only one exception, a 38-year-old female in an extended position with no grave covering). The southern group of Cluster 2 burials includes two females (19 and 26 years of age); both burials are extended and covered with limestone slabs (in Burial Group 2). The only other Cluster 2 burial located in this part of the site is a 47-year-old male in a semiflexed position who is also covered with limestone slabs (in Burial Group 3). Cluster 3 burials are concentrated in four locales that are roughly evenly spaced throughout the village. Cluster 4 burials also appear to exhibit this type of distribution, but less clearly. There are two closely spaced burials in the east and west, with the remainder scattered throughout the northern and southern parts of the village. The burial in Cluster 5 is located in the western part of the village and is the nearest burial in proximity to the red cedar house, near the "restricted storage" structure.

I interpret Clusters 4 and 5 as being higher in authority than the other clusters, based on the fact that they contain only males and children and the only occurrences of a supralocal artifact type (whelk shells). The individual in Cluster 5 appears to be the village leader (see also below), who was associated directly with Cluster 4, a group of males and children marked with a single artifact type (shell discs). This group is more often flexed, perhaps indicative of a more local or earlier affiliation. In the absence of supralocal symbols, I consider Clusters 1, 2, and 3 to be of lower rank than Clusters 4 and 5. Some level of ascriptive status is implicated in the association of certain shell artifacts with children, a finding that has also been noted in a rural Middle Mississippian cemetery (Goldstein 1980:135).

Cluster 2 is most interesting for the information it reveals in connection to the wall trench house, with which it is clearly associated. This spatial finding is considerably strengthened by the fact that this cluster contains a high propor-

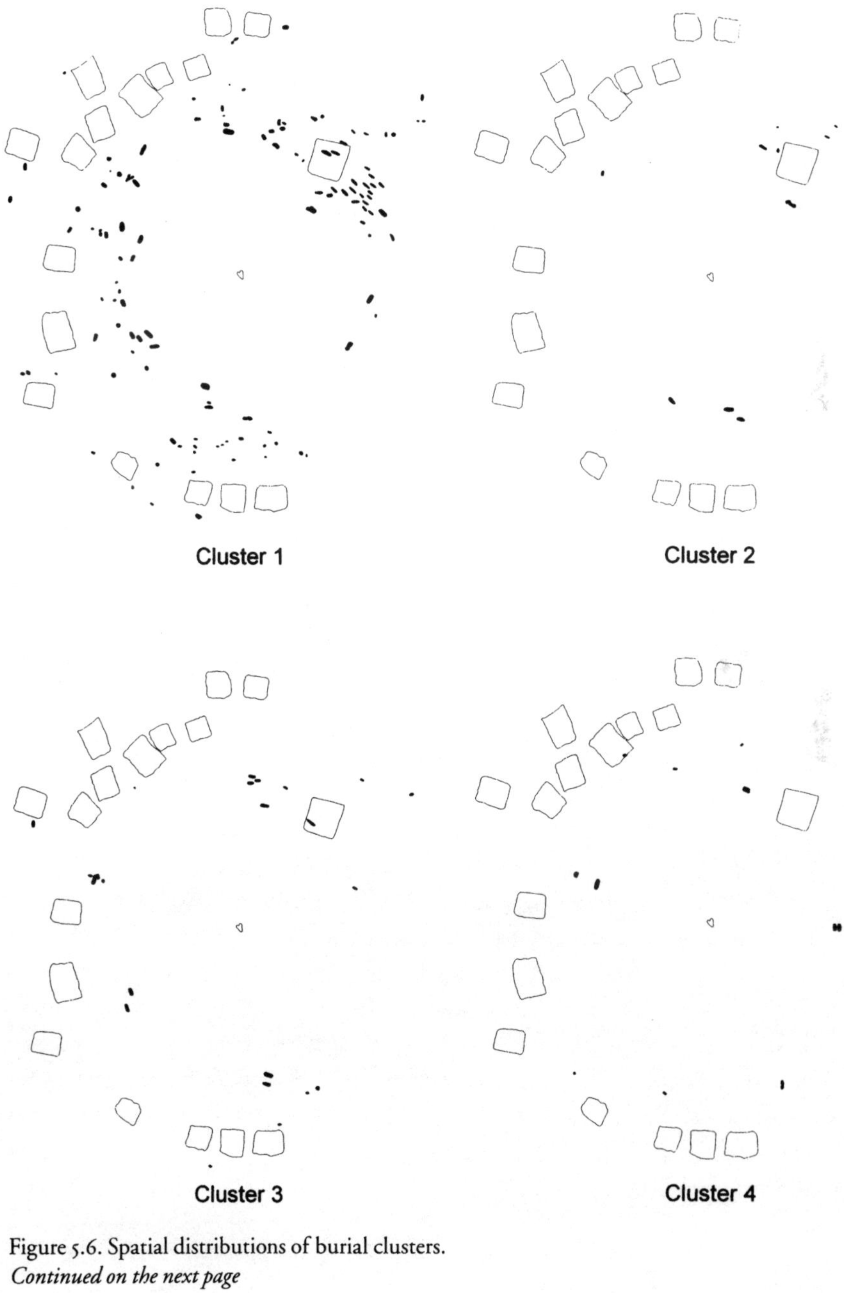

Figure 5.6. Spatial distributions of burial clusters.
Continued on the next page

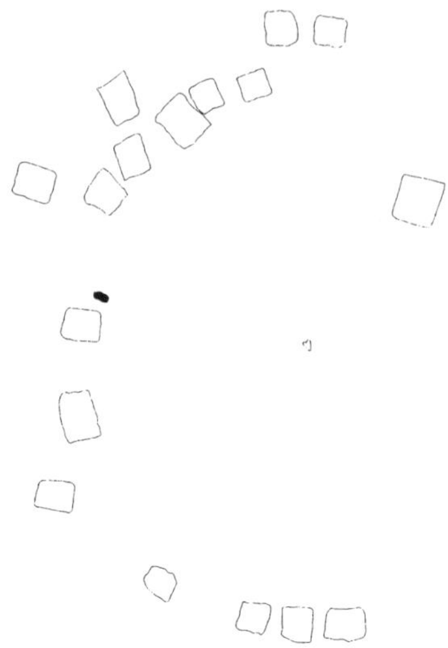

Figure 5.6. *Continued*

tion of shell disc beads, a common type of Middle Mississippian adornment. The predominance of limestone slab grave covers and extended leg positions in this cluster is also consistent with a later association for Cluster 2 (slabs are a strong Middle Mississippian marker, particularly with respect to Middle Cumberland sites [I. Brown 1981]). The presence of two relatively young females in the southern part of the site but associated with this cluster is intriguing, perhaps revealing marriage alliances between the "newcomers" and the "locals." This is conjectural but could be examined perhaps through DNA analysis.

Individuals associated with Clusters 1 and 3 are undoubtedly marked by a series of achieved status distinctions. Cluster 3 is more exclusive and is marked by some interesting characteristics, not the least of which is the concentration of individuals in particular areas within each segment of the village. Moreover, the association of burned corn with several of these individuals and a high proportion of marginella shells set this group apart. A large proportion of these individuals are also buried near the wall trench house (39%). However, in contrast to Cluster 2, this group clearly forms an integral part of the entire mortuary pattern in the village.

Craft Production and the Emergence of Power

The two burials with the most diverse sets of artifacts (indicative of more statuses [see Chapter 2]) were positioned in the western and southern parts of the village (Figure 5.7), in two of the burial groups restricted to adult males and children (Burial Groups 1 and 6). These two individuals were both extended adult males with limestone slab covers. The individual in Burial Group 6 and Cluster 5 (Burial 5/78) was 35 years old; his grave contained a drilled whelk shell positioned near the top of the head (with a bone pin used to attach it, presumably to the hair), shell discs placed at both ears (ear adornment), and a fish teeth "mosaic" near the top of the head (part of a headdress?). A hammerstone was also placed near the head. A bone awl, an antler tip projectile point, a triangular projectile point, a lithic preform, and a hammerstone were placed at the foot of the grave, and two bone pins were located near the grave edges. The individual in Burial Group 1 and Cluster 4 (Burial 8/74) was 41 years old; his grave also contained shell discs at each ear, and 24 shell disc beads (12 at each wrist), an antler flaker, two bone pins, two bone awls, red ochre, deer sesamoids, and a platform pipe were all placed near the top of his head (the platform pipe is somewhat similar in form to one referred to as a "Middle Mississippian type" at the Turpin site [Oehler 1973:Photo 10]).

Based on the location of the two individuals with the most diverse artifact sets, one could conclude a relationship between the southern and western parts of the site with respect to village leadership (perhaps the leader was from a southern kin group). However, other dimensions further support such a connection. I began by plotting the distribution of the two whelk shells, the major supralocal symbols present at the site. This type of shell was present only in burials located in the western and southern parts of the village. Knick's (1977) investigation of paleopathology in SunWatch individuals concluded a close genetic relationship between the south and west parts of the village, providing additional support for this argument. (Also, recall the strong pottery refit pattern between these parts of the site [see Figure 4.18].)

One of the "technomic" artifact types associated with the highest-status individual was a hammerstone. In examining the distribution of this artifact type (which was present in mostly male burials but also occurred with a female and a child) along with antler flaking tools and debitage concentrations, a connection became apparent (see Figure 5.7). Cumulatively, these data support a close connection between the southern and western parts of the village in terms of leadership and tool making. Based on this evidence, I suggest that village-level leadership developed in tandem with long-distance exchange and craft production.

The final part of the analysis involved assessing whether leadership emerged toward the end of the village occupation, in tandem with the appearance of the suite of Middle Mississippian–style features, artifacts, and ideas presented thus far in the study. General theoretical expectations hold that the emergence of leaders should occur over time, particularly with respect to administering a

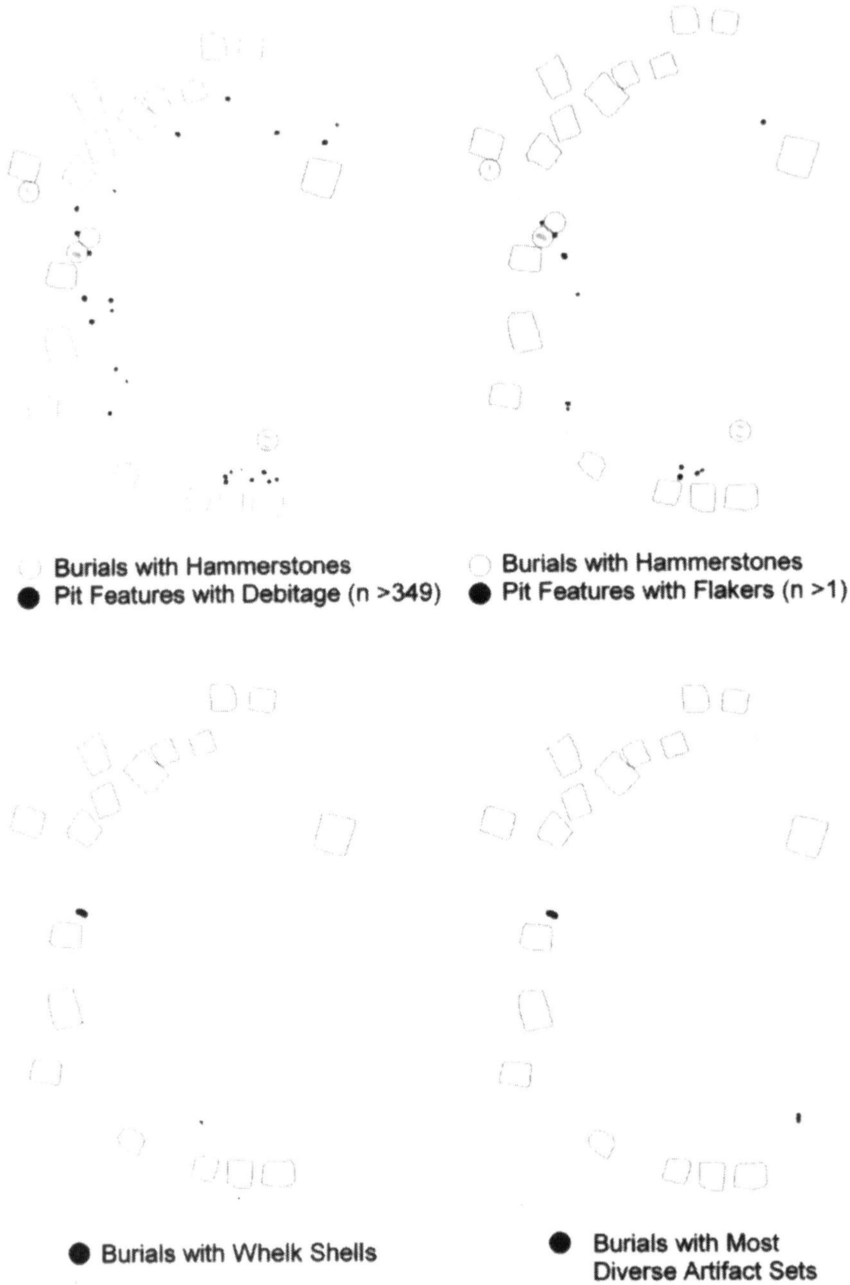

Figure 5.7. Selected mortuary relationships between the southern and western portions of the village.

growing local population (see Chapter 1). It was reasoned that the best method for assessing this was to directly date individual burials. To test this hypothesis, collagen samples from rib fragments of two individuals were submitted for AMS dating. I chose the two individuals that I felt were of the highest status as indicated by the most diverse artifact sets (Burial 8/74 [41 years old] and Burial 5/78 [35 years old]); the latter one also contained a supralocal Mississippian-style symbol (whelk shell). Burial 8/74 produced a calibrated two-sigma range of A.D. 1407–1513. Burial 5/78 produced a calibrated two-sigma range of A.D. 1394–1475. This finding is consistent with theoretical expectations and fits well with the last uses of the site, including the appearance of the Middle Mississippian–style house and artifacts.

Conclusion

The SunWatch site presents several similarities to and a few distinctions from the general pattern represented by Middle Mississippian villages. The mortuary pattern appears to be similar to that noted in the Middle Cumberland and eastern Tennessee areas than in Middle Mississippian communities to the west. The clearest line of support for this hypothesis is that the Middle Cumberland region is also known for its use of stone slabs as grave covers. At SunWatch there is a higher occurrence of limestone slabs in Burial Groups 6 and 11 and specifically in Burial Cluster 2, which includes several individuals around the perimeter of the wall trench house. These spaces are all associated with the later occupation of the site.

Most children with grave goods are less than 4 years old, which may have marked an important transition into beginning to learn adult behaviors, with a second transition occurring in early adulthood, marked by projectile points, pipes, and tool-making kits. SunWatch males had a much higher incidence of artifacts than did females, which is very consistent with findings at the Ledford Island and King sites (Hally 2004 and Sullivan 1995, respectively). Adult males and children were the only ones to be buried by a communal/leader house at the King site (Hally 2004:170), which is also the case at SunWatch, although not as marked (i.e., the house is not as large or as centrally located). SunWatch "leaders" are found in several locations within the village, which is also the case at the King site (e.g., 169, 175). Higher-status Middle Mississippian males are often accompanied by exotic marine shells (see Chapter 2), which is also the case at SunWatch. There is a distinct connection between adult male status and tool-making implements at SunWatch, which is common in lower-order Middle Mississippian cemeteries and villages (Goldstein 1980:135; Hally 2004:172; Milner 1984:477). Intensified craft production is often stimulated by leaders who use the products for intersocietal exchange (Schortman and Urban 1998:112). While a case can be made for a relationship between craft production and leadership at SunWatch, there is no clear evidence for craft specialization (Nass and Yerkes 1995).

There are two notable differences between Middle Mississippian and SunWatch mortuary practices. First, pottery is present with only two burials at SunWatch, while this artifact type is common in Middle Mississippian burials (although it does become much more common in Late Fort Ancient burials [see Chapter 2]). Second, those of children were the only burials with discoidals, which does not fit with a Middle Mississippian example, in which this item is associated with adult males who may have gained status through excelling in the game of chunky (Hally 2004:172–174).

The presence of male village leaders emerging later in the site's occupation meets general expectations about social evolution (Marcus and Flannery 1996:239) and provides additional support for a previous analysis at the site (Robertson 1980:71–72). The increase in village population occurred in tandem with the construction of the wall trench and red cedar houses, which could have served as the residence of a villagewide leader and/or men's council house. Such institutional transformations are precisely the expectation as a growing population exceeds the scalar threshold of household-level organization (Johnson 1982). A specific Middle Mississippian connection with this process is warranted based on the SunWatch case.

Additionally, a case has been made for a village leader emerging from a corporate group located in the southern portion of the site. Differential ranking among kin groups, with one becoming dominant, was discussed earlier as a general pattern (see Chapter 1). A specific connection between leaders and kin groups in southern parts of Algonquian villages has long been recognized (Callendar 1978).

6
Periphery Peers

This chapter examines the extent to which other Fort Ancient sites in the Miami Valleys exhibit characteristics documented at SunWatch. This examination is limited in two major ways. First, there have been no systematic surveys in the region; surveys that have been completed are in central Kentucky (Henderson 1998) and southeastern Ohio (Graybill 1981). Second, broad-scale excavations are limited to a few sites, and these are often poorly documented. Most sites in the sample were investigated in the late nineteenth and early twentieth centuries, using methodologies focused on artifact and burial recovery, greatly limiting the range of information of use in comparing with SunWatch. After brief descriptions of the site, chronological aspects are examined, followed by comparisons of a series of architectural characteristics and Middle Mississippian–style artifacts. The chapter concludes with an examination of these data against the periphery peer model.

Site Descriptions

The regional Fort Ancient sample was limited to sites concentrated along the Great Miami and Little Miami rivers and tributaries (n = 34 sites [including SunWatch]). Site density is highest in the lower, central, and upper portions of the two river systems (Figure 6.1). Due to the limited excavations at the majority of sites, functional differences between sites are difficult to fully assess, although it is clear that both villages (n = 26 [76%]) and smaller, nonvillage sites (n = 8 [24%]) exist in the region. Smaller sites likely fulfilled a variety of functions, including seasonal uses for summer farming, fall/winter hunting and gathering, and ritual activity (see below). Nonvillage sites are most common in the upper portion of the Little Miami drainage (n = 5), although they occur in lower reaches of these systems as well (n = 3).

Three sites are located in the lower portion of the Great Miami River: Guard, Haag, and State Line. The Guard site is a small residential site consisting of two houses, several burials, and several pit features (Robert Genheimer, personal communication 2006). The Haag site consists of a large Fort Ancient village

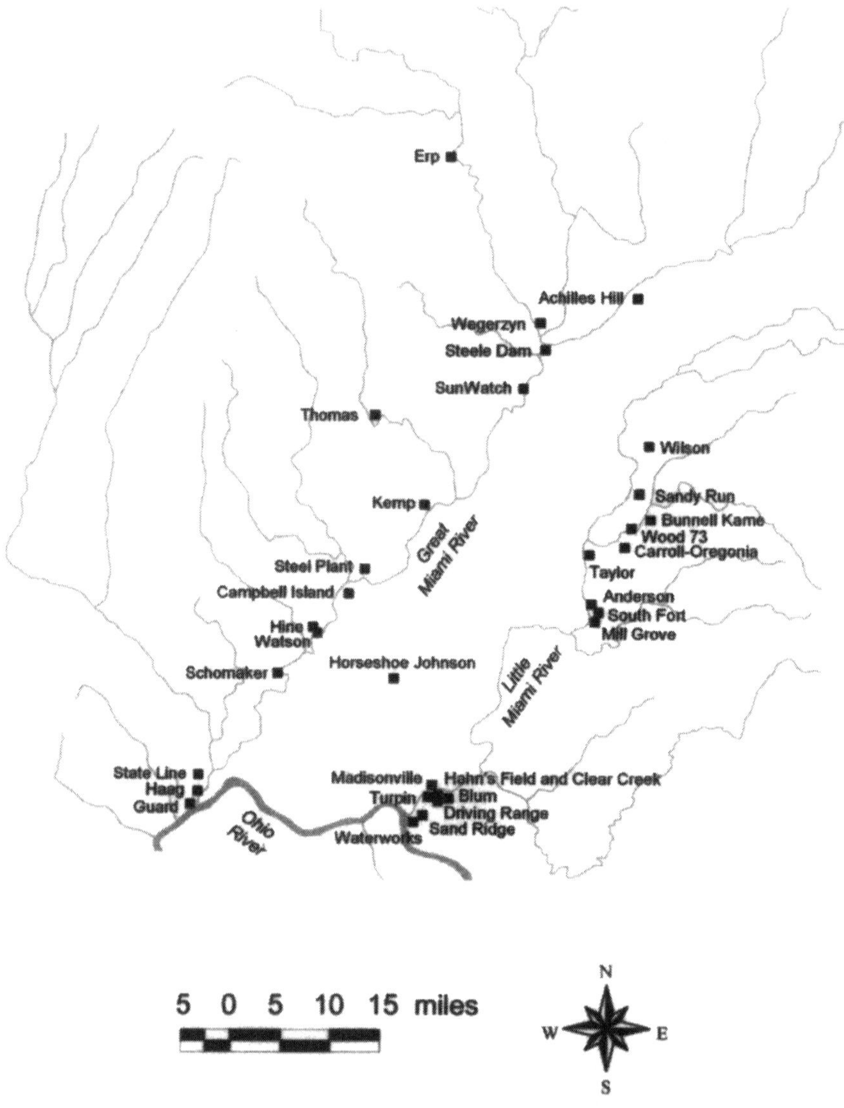

Figure 6.1. Fort Ancient site locations used in the regional comparison. (Map produced with assistance from William Kennedy.)

overtop a substantial Late Woodland occupation. Excavations were conducted by Indiana University (1972, 1973) and the University of Notre Dame (1972). Excavations were focused on midden deposits, including the excavation of numerous pits, burials, and postholes (Reidhead and Limp 1974). The State Line site is a large village that was briefly investigated by Black (1934) and subjected to two salvage excavations. The first of these efforts was led by the Cincinnati Museum of Natural History (now Cincinnati Museum Center) between 1974 and 1975, when a portion of the site was being removed for highway construction fill; the second effort was led in advance of the construction of a warehouse in 1979 by key personnel of the Miami Purchase Association (now Cincinnati Preservation Association) and the Department of Anthropology at the University of Cincinnati. The site includes several mounds and wall trench houses, most pottery is shell tempered (86%), and there is a wide variety of Middle Mississippian–style artifacts (Vickery et al. 2000:274; see below).

Five villages are located in the central portion of the Great Miami River: Campbell Island, Hine, Schomaker, Steel Plant, and Watson. Excavations at the Schomaker village site were limited to a small portion of the southwestern quadrant, although many additional features were identified and excavated by avocational archaeologists (Cowan et al. 1990:Figure 1). Campbell Island and Hine were both excavated by H. C. Shetrone during one field season (Shetrone 1926). Campbell Island appears to be a fairly typical village, as suggested by the locations of 31 pit features and 21 burials in a circular pattern; no mound was present (Cowan 1986; Shetrone 1926; see Figure 6.5 below). Hine village contained a burial mound (diameter = 60 feet, height = 7 feet), but the site was not as extensively excavated as Campbell Island. Steel Plant is known only on the basis of three small pottery vessels, which were most likely placed with burials (Griffin 1943:160).

Four villages are located in the upper portion of the Great Miami River: Erp, Steele Dam, SunWatch, and Wegerzyn. John Allman excavated the Erp village; no structures were located but several features and a dense midden were identified within a ditch enclosure (Allman 1959, 1960). August Foerste conducted limited excavations at the Steele Dam site, most likely a large village, recovering materials from several trash pits and burials (Foerste 1885:838–844). Wegerzyn has been excavated by various members of the Dayton Society of Natural History (1976, 1993–present). The site appears to be a small village, based on features located in excavations in the northern portion of the site and identification of a series of anomalies likely to be pit features in the southeastern part of the site through magnetic resistance survey (William Kennedy, Lynn Simonelli, and Jarrod Burks, personal communication 2006 [see Figure 6.5]).

The Kemp and Thomas sites are villages positioned between the central and upper concentrations of Fort Ancient sites located along the Great Miami River. The Kemp site was partially excavated by Emerson Greenman, focusing on pit and burial features (Shetrone 1930:367). The Thomas site was excavated in the mid-1980s by J. Heilman and the Dayton Society of Natural History as a salvage project in advance of gravel quarrying activities. Fourteen pit features and a burial containing several pottery vessels were located in what appears to be a circular village. A recently submitted carbon sample from a pit feature produced a calibrated two-sigma range of A.D. 1251–1391.

Ten sites are located in the lower portion of the Little Miami River: Blum, Clear Creek, Driving Range, Hahn's Field, Madisonville, Sand Ridge, Turpin 1, Turpin 2, Turpin 3, and Waterworks. Madisonville is composed of a series of villages that were initially excavated by Charles Metz between 1879 and 1881, under the auspices of the Literary and Scientific Society of Madisonville, Ohio. At this point, Metz was hired by F. W. Putnam to continue the excavation for Harvard's Peabody Museum, work that was conducted intermittently until 1911 (Griffin 1943:119). Wes Cowan conducted limited excavations at the site for the Cincinnati Museum Center. In the past few years, small-scale excavations have been conducted at Madisonville in advance of various construction projects, although most of these were in previously excavated portions of the site (Matthew Purtill, personal communication 2005).

The Turpin site actually consists of at least three different villages (Drooker 1997:Table 4.4; see also Miller 1997). The best known of the three villages is Turpin 1, which was partially excavated by the Cincinnati Museum of Natural History during the 1940s and 1960s (Oehler 1973); more recently a small-scale stratigraphic excavation was conducted there (Riggs 1986, 1998). The village consists of a burial mound in the center of a plaza, which is surrounded by burials oriented perpendicular to the plaza (Oehler 1973:Photo 54; Riggs 1977). This Fort Ancient village lies over a Late Woodland village (Oehler 1973:51). Turpin 2 is a village situated to the east of Turpin 1, although we know little about it except that it contains Madisonville and Anderson shell-tempered ceramics and at least one disk pipe (Drooker 1997:92; Nickerson 1885). Turpin 3 is also a poorly known village site, possibly located on a nearby ridgetop (Griffin 1943; Metz 1881, 1885; Starr 1960).

Driving Range and Clear Creek are both nonvillage sites. The Driving Range site is situated on a low terrace above the Little Miami River floodplain near Newtown, Ohio. The site was excavated as part of a sewer line mitigation project and is composed of a several pit features, a possible house, and a mortuary zone containing three burials; it appears to represent a fall/winter use (Kreinbrink et al. 1993; Purtill 1999). Clear Creek is located a few hundred meters southeast of Hahn's Field, across a slight depression. A portion of the site was excavated by the Cincinnati Museum Center prior to grading for a soccer field complex. The site may also have been used seasonally. One burial and numerous pit features were located, although no houses were present (Robert Genheimer, personal communication 2006).

Blum, Hahn's Field, Sand Ridge, and Waterworks are poorly known but appear to be large villages. Blum is the poorest known of this set (Metz 1878, 1881; Starr 1960). Hahn's Field contains many pit features and at least 31 burials (Metz 1881:299–300, 1885). Sand Ridge contains at least 23 burials (Metz 1881:302); Rodney Riggs also conducted limited excavations at this site, largely focusing on stratigraphic relationships (Riggs 1986, 1998). The Waterworks site is known only from brief accounts (Metz 1878, 1881; Starr 1960:70–71).

Nine sites are also located in the upper portion of the Little Miami River, including four villages (Anderson, Mill Grove, South Fort, Taylor) and five nonvillage sites (Bunnell Kame, Carroll-Oregonia, Sandy Run, Wilson, and Wood 73). Anderson village was initially excavated by C. C. Anderson, a former landowner. Professional work began with W. K. Moorehead, who excavated a large portion of the site between 1887 and 1889, mainly to procure items for the World's Columbian Exposition (Griffin 1943:92; Moorehead 1887, 1890, 1892, 1902, 1908). In addition to excavating an oval pattern of pit and burial features, Moorehead noted the existence of three villages separated by sterile soils (Moorehead 1892:84–87), although subsequent researchers have failed to identify these strata using more current excavation techniques (Essenpreis 1982:60–62), and there have been no clear differences in artifact types between the alleged strata (Griffin 1943:93). However, Essenpreis (1982:71) suggested that there was a slight horizontal distinction in artifact attributes between the southern and western parts of the site, concluding that village location may have shifted slightly over time (see below). Limited excavations have been completed at Mill Grove and Taylor, both of which are large villages. Mill Grove was initially reported by Moorehead (1892), which was later confirmed during a brief surface collection made by Griffin in 1938 (Griffin 1943:113). Taylor was subjected to intensive investigation, including a trench excavated through a sizeable central burial mound (70 x 35 x 7 feet high), and numerous pit and burial features were located in a circular village surrounding this feature, covering a total area estimated to be about 600 feet in diameter: "more specimens can be picked up on the surface than at any other spot with which I am familiar" (Moorehead's field notes, as reported by Griffin 1943:102).

Nonvillage sites have been explored most intensively in this region. Carroll-Oregonia, Sandy Run, Wilson, and Wood 73 appear to be small, seasonally used resource-procurement sites. Carroll-Oregonia was excavated in 1977 by the Cleveland Museum of Natural History. The site is located along a slight knoll east of Caesar Creek. No houses were located, but based on artifact and faunal/floral assemblages, it has been interpreted as a fall/spring hunting camp, most likely occupied by people from Taylor village (Brose and White 1983:22). Wood 73 represents a spring/summer gathering locale and also includes one burial (Brose and White 1983). Sandy Run and Wilson are located along the Little Miami River north of Taylor village. Wright State University field school students excavated these two sites between 1977 and 1979. According to Riordan (2000:420), both sites represent the remains of either resource-procurement camps (possibly seasonal) by members of nearby villages, or scattered homesteads whose occupants had social, economic, and/or seasonal relationships with other sites. Sandy Run contains two circular houses near a large pit feature; a summer use is inferred on the basis of a lack of hearths inside the houses (Riordan 2000). Few faunal remains and no cultigens were present. Wilson consists of a hearth and a windbreak rebuilt several times, suggestive of a transitory camp used on several occasions (Riordan 2000). The Bunnel Kame site is an unusual nonvillage site in that it is a glacial kame (62.5 x 7.8 meters) repeatedly used by Fort Ancient peoples for burial purposes (n = 9 burials), in contrast to all other nonvillage sites, which were used by smaller groups for residential or food-procurement purposes. However, this finding is similar to the use of gravel knolls at Taylor for burials (Brose and White 1983:11).

The only site in the sample not located along either of the Miami River systems is the Horseshoe Johnson site, documented during salvage excavations in advance of the construction of an industrial park in 1990 (Hawkins 1998) (see Figure 6.5). This small village is located on an alluvial terrace on the East Fork of the Mill Creek, a small stream that drains directly into the Ohio River on the western side of Cincinnati. This site consists of several houses and pit features, one of which is a large structure located in the western portion of the site.

Chronology

Assessing the chronology of southwest Ohio Fort Ancient sites is problematic due to limited excavations and the generally poor provenience of extant data. Additionally, given what has been learned about SunWatch in the present investigation, I prefer not to place entire sites into discrete temporal categories, as site reuse is a regular part of the Fort Ancient pattern. Penelope Drooker (1997:76–95, 2000) has recently accomplished much of what can be done with the meager data, carefully seriating many of these sites based on associations between radiocarbon dates and diagnostic artifacts. This effort resulted in temporal associations of sites into the following six overlapping time periods: A.D. 1000–1200, A.D. 1100–1300, A.D. 1200–1400, A.D. 1300–1500, A.D. 1400–1550, and A.D. 1500–1650. I utilized this chronological sequence, with the addition of seven sites based on similar criteria (Blum, Clear Creek, Driving Range, Sandy Run, Thomas, Wegerzyn, Wilson). Results indicate that the majority of sites can be associated with multiple time periods. A total of 96 temporal periods are represented at the 34 sites: 4 sites (12%) are associated with one time period, 8 sites (24%) are associated with two time periods, 13 sites (38%) are associated with three time periods, 5 sites (15%) are associated with four time periods, 1 site (3%) is associated with five time periods, and 2 sites (6%) are associated with all six time periods (Table 6.1). One site (3%) was indeterminate in terms of temporal affiliation.

A comparison of site component frequencies by time period clearly indicates that the majority of occupations occurred between A.D. 1200 and 1500 (see Table 6.1), which corresponds with the "crest" of Middle Mississippian developments (Griffin 1985:63). Most of the sites are represented by two or more time periods (85%). A consideration of the spatial distribution of temporal components reveals that the earliest site uses occurred throughout both river systems, with the region filling in between A.D. 1200 and 1400 (Figure 6.2). The earliest sites in the region included both villages (Haag, Madisonville, South Fort, SunWatch, Wegerzyn) and a nonvillage site (Wood 73). The second stage included the addition of 7 villages (Anderson, Hine, Horseshoe Johnson, Schomaker, State Line, Taylor, Turpin 1) and a nonvillage site (Guard). The next stage included the addition of 10 villages (Erp, Kemp, Mill Grove, Sand Ridge, Steele Dam, Thomas, Turpin 2, Waterworks, Watson) and 4 nonvillage sites (Bunnell Kame, Carroll-Oregonia, Sandy Run, Wilson). The next stage included the addition of a village (Blum) and a nonvillage site (Driving Range). The next stage included the addition of 1 nonvillage site (Clear Creek). After this point, no additional sites were occupied, and after A.D. 1400 the trend is for fewer sites to be used. After A.D. 1500, site distribution is reduced to three locales (see Figure 6.2). Interestingly, no new sites appear to have been established after the Middle Fort Ancient period.

Architecture and Village Layout

Architecture and site layout were compared, including the presence/absence of the following characteristics: circular village plan, central postholes, mounds, "big houses," wall trench houses, and burial rows (Table 6.2). SunWatch and Madisonville were the only sites in the sample to contain central postholes (the

Table 6.1. Temporal Affiliations of Sample of Fort Ancient Sites

Site Name	A.D. 1000–1200	A.D. 1100–1300	A.D. 1200–1400	A.D. 1300–1500	A.D. 1400–1550	A.D. 1500–1650
Anderson		X	X	X		
Blum				X		
Bunnell Kame			X	X		
Campbell Island			X	X	X	X
Carroll-Oregonia			X	X	X	
Clear Creek					X	X
Driving Range				X	X	
Erp			X	X	X	
Guard		X	X			
Haag	X	X	X			
Hahn's Field				X	X	X
Hine		X	X	X	X	
Horseshoe Johnson		X	X	X		
Kemp			X	X		
Madisonville	X	X	X	X	X	X
Mill Grove			X	X		
Sand Ridge			X	X	X	
Sandy Run			X	X	X	
Schomaker		X	X	X	X	
South Fort	X	X	X	X	X	X
State Line		X	X	X		
Steel Plant					X	X
Steele Dam			X			
SunWatch	X	X	X	X	X	
Taylor		X	X	X	X	
Thomas			X			
Turpin 1		X	X	X		
Turpin 2			X	X	X	X
Turpin 3						
Waterworks			X	X	X	
Watson			X	X		
Wegerzyn	X	X	X			
Wilson			X	X	X	
Wood 73	X					

Note: Temporal affiliations are based on radiocarbon dates and burial mounds (A.D. 1100–1300), Anderson-like pottery (A.D. 1200–1400), Anderson shell-tempered pottery (A.D. 1300–1500), Madisonville-type pottery (A.D. 1400–1550), and "classic" Madisonville pottery (A.D. 1500–1650). (After Drooker 1997:Table 4.2.)

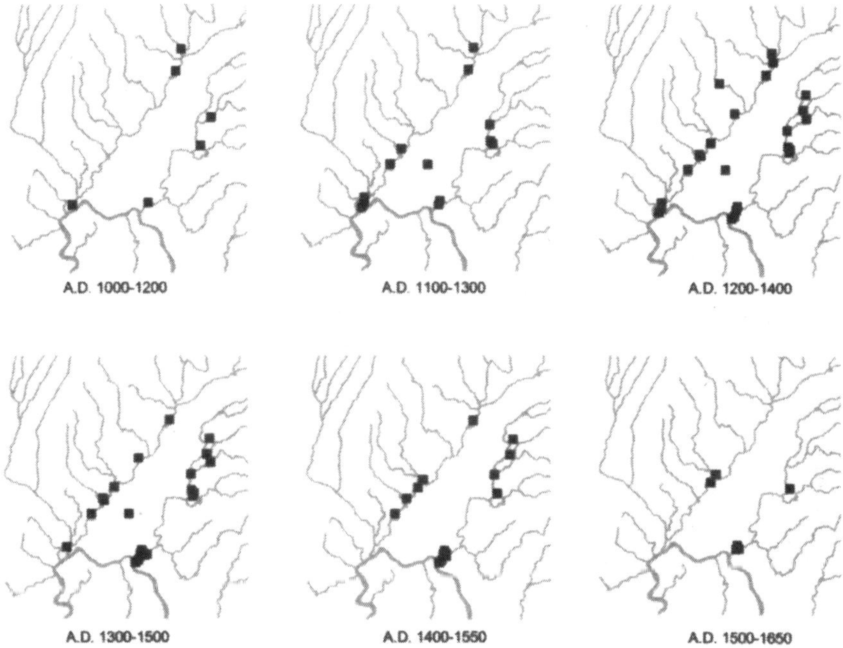

Figure 6.2. Maps showing the distribution of Fort Ancient sites sample by time period.

small feature located in the plaza at Horseshoe Johnson [see Figure 6.5] is not a central posthole [Rebecca Hawkins, personal communication 2006]). Circular plazas were present at Anderson, Campbell Island, Haag, Hine, Horseshoe Johnson, Madisonville, Schomaker, SunWatch, and Turpin 1. Plaza diameters have been estimated between 20 and 70 meters (see Drooker 2000:Table 7.3), although these numbers are misleading given the multiple occupations of known villages (examined further below). "Big houses" are present at SunWatch and Horseshoe Johnson (Hawkins 1998). Wall trench houses were present at Madisonville, Schomaker, State Line, SunWatch, and Turpin 3. Each of these sites contains one wall trench house, with the exception of State Line (n = 4). Mounds were present at a minimum of five sites (Guard, Hahn's Field, State Line, Taylor, Turpin 1), and glacial kames used for burial interment were present at three sites (Bunnell Kame, Hine, Taylor). Mounds are more common in the southern and western portion of the region (Drooker 2000:246).

The identification of the spatial structure of SunWatch provides a specific model with which to examine other Fort Ancient village plans. The SunWatch pattern was initially compared with site plans for Anderson and Madisonville,

Table 6.2. Architectural Characteristics of Sample of Fort Ancient Sites

Site Name	Circular Plan	Central Posthole	Mounds	Wall Trench Houses	Burial Rows	"Big Houses"
Anderson	X				X	
Blum						
Bunnell Kame			knoll			
Campbell Island	X					
Carroll-Oregonia						
Clear Creek						
Driving Range						
Erp						
Guard			1			
Haag	X					
Hahn's Field			1			
Hine	X		knoll			
Horseshoe Johnson	X					
Kemp						X
Madisonville	X	X		1 (NE area)	X	
Mill Grove						
Sand Ridge						
Sandy Run						
Schomaker	X			1 (SW area)		
South Fort						
State Line			5–6	4		
Steel Plant						
Steele Dam						
SunWatch	X	X		1 (NE area)	X	X
Taylor			2 (1 knoll)			
Thomas						
Turpin 1	X		1			
Turpin 2			1?			
Turpin 3			1?	1		
Waterworks						
Watson						
Wegerzyn						
Wilson						
Wood 73						

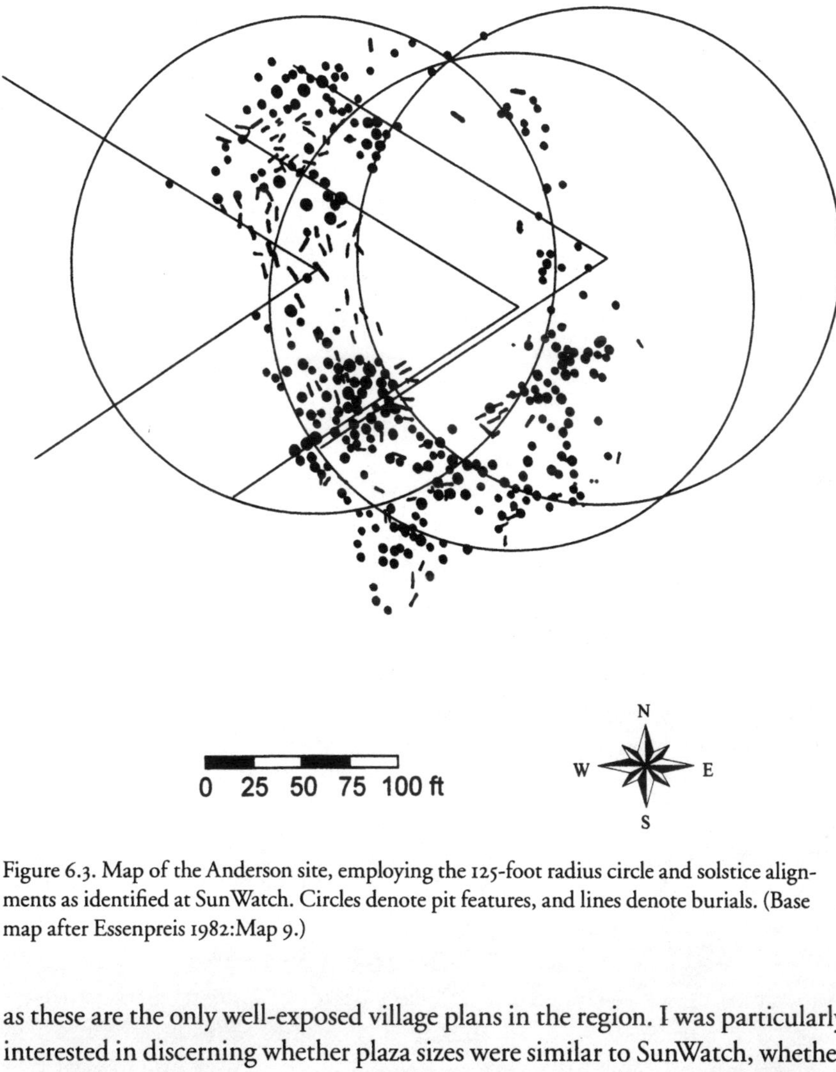

Figure 6.3. Map of the Anderson site, employing the 125-foot radius circle and solstice alignments as identified at SunWatch. Circles denote pit features, and lines denote burials. (Base map after Essenpreis 1982:Map 9.)

as these are the only well-exposed village plans in the region. I was particularly interested in discerning whether plaza sizes were similar to SunWatch, whether row patterning was present in burials, and whether some houses, pits, and burials were closer to the site center (and a central posthole when present), particularly in western portion of villages.

Exploring the circular layout of Anderson village was difficult due to the lack of a central posthole. I began the examination with the 125-foot radius circle, which defined two strong arcs of pit features (Figure 6.3). This pattern is strengthened considerably after considering the positioning of solar alignments: the winter solstice alignment demarcates another concentration of pit features for both cases. Moreover, the gap between the two main concentrations of burials and pit features is generally bordered by the solar alignments. There is a low occurrence of features in the area between the solar alignments, which could be due to a shorter length of occupation than SunWatch (i.e., that the leadership precinct was less developed), or the fact that this area contained more "disturbed" burials than other portions of the village (Essenpreis 1982: Map 9).

Despite the clarity of this finding, a serious question remains. If the village fits the SunWatch pattern, why are there numerous pit features on the eastern sides of the two village patterns in the middle of the plazas? I continued to use the 125-foot circle and discovered that if the circle was shifted to the west, it also defined the eastern boundary of the site (Essenpreis [1982:71] notes that the village may have shifted slightly in location over time, although always regarded the plaza as being oval). Applying spatial rules derived from SunWatch resulted in the identification of three incomplete village plans, exactly the number that was previously noted but not discernible stratigraphically. It is not just that houses are missing, but large sections of the eastern portions of two of the village plans and the entire western portion of the third village plan are also absent. The finding of a similar-sized village plan further supports a series of strong similarities noted between SunWatch and Anderson in terms of pottery styles and mortuary patterns (206–219).

Madisonville started out as a more straightforward case, in that it contains a central posthole from which to orient the SunWatch-sized plaza circle. Upon initial inspection, the 125-foot radius circle seemed too large to explain the division between pit feature and burial placements (Figure 6.4). Indeed, this is true for the site as a whole; however, it clearly separates a large group of pit features and burials in the westernmost portion of the village. A much smaller circle with a 62.5-foot radius (half of the 125-foot circle) serves to divide burials from pit features in the innermost circular pattern. Unfortunately, due to overlap of earlier and later burials at the site, it is not possible to determine which of these patterns came first (Drooker 1997:196). There were other plazas that did not contain central postholes, and the occupational history is complex (for a summary of the growth of Madisonville over time see Drooker 1997:200–202). Interestingly, the only other site to contain a central posthole also has pronounced burial rows, many of which are closer to the central posthole, and a single wall trench house located in the northeastern part of the village plan, albeit at Madisonville this structure is further away from the plaza (unless it was in a different village plan [see Figure 6.4]).

For the Madisonville village plan with a smaller plaza, it is particularly clear that there are two main groups of burials in closer proximity to the central post-

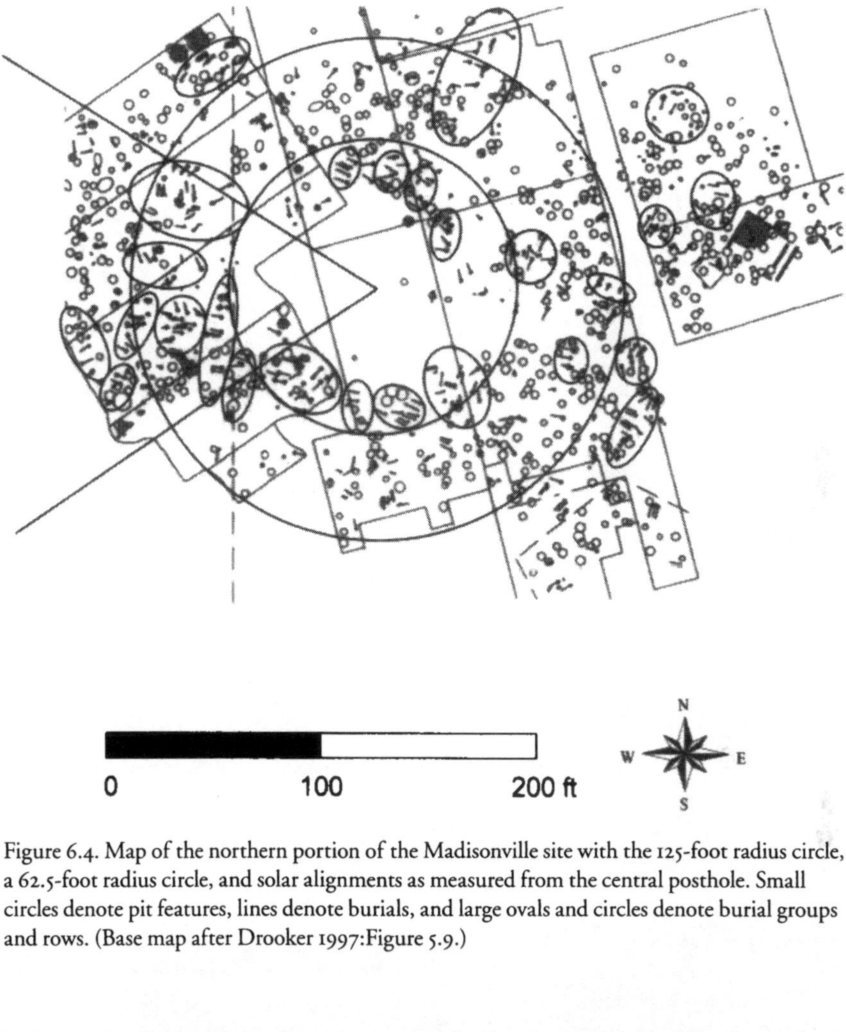

Figure 6.4. Map of the northern portion of the Madisonville site with the 125-foot radius circle, a 62.5-foot radius circle, and solar alignments as measured from the central posthole. Small circles denote pit features, lines denote burials, and large ovals and circles denote burial groups and rows. (Base map after Drooker 1997:Figure 5.9.)

hole, one in the north and one in the south. For the larger SunWatch-sized village, it is clear that burials in the western part of the village are closer to the site center, while the locations of other burial groups are outside this zone, with the exception of a group in the northeastern and southeastern part of the site. This is very consistent with the SunWatch pattern.

Armed with the knowledge that Fort Ancient villages come in at least two sizes, I turned my attention to three sites that were less amenable to detailed examination—Campbell Island, Horseshoe Johnson, and Wegerzyn (Figure 6.5). When the two plaza sizes were examined, it was clear that the smaller of the two best accounted for the distribution of features within each village.

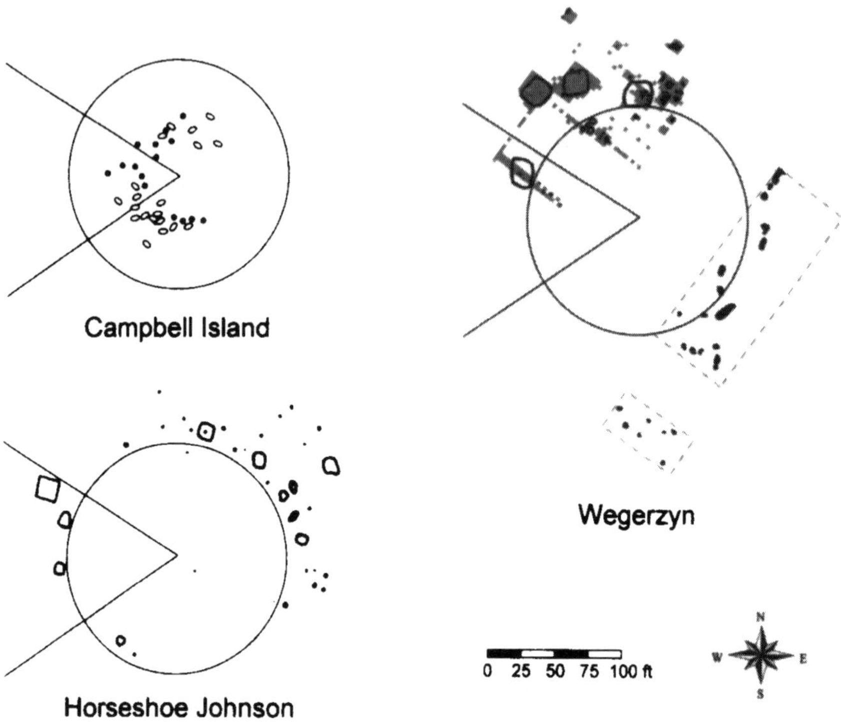

Figure 6.5. Maps comparing Campbell Island, Horseshoe Johnson, and Wegerzyn with the 62.5-foot radius circle. For Campbell Island, black circles denote pit features, and open ovals denote burials. For Horseshoe Johnson, houses and pits with black circles and ovals are denoted with open circles and squares; no burials were present. For Wegerzyn, black circles and ovals denote confirmed and suspected pit features, open circles denote burials, and open squares denote houses; excavation limits are shaded in the northwestern area and magnetometry limits are defined by dashed lines in the southeastern area. (Campbell Island base map after Shetrone 1926:3; Horseshoe Johnson base map after Hawkins 1998:Figure 6.2; Wegerzyn base map produced by William Kennedy.)

Only the Anderson and Madisonville sites have been excavated to an extent to allow for inspection of row patterning in burials. Both sites contain row patterning; however, the Madisonville pattern is most similar to SunWatch, which may be related to these being the only Fort Ancient sites where central postholes have been documented. As was the case at SunWatch, rows are generally oriented toward the central posthole, neighboring rows sometimes converge on each other, and some rows are in closer proximity to the central posthole. Burials outside of the circle are generally less structured in their placement, which is also consistent with the SunWatch pattern (see Figure 6.4).

Artifacts

Middle Mississippian–style pottery has been noted for Madisonville, State Line, SunWatch, and Turpin 1 (Table 6.3). The Turpin 1 site contains negative painting on pottery (Oehler 1973:Photo 10), pottery vessels with Ramey-like designs (Griffin 1943:Plate LXXXIV; Oehler 1973:Photo 8), and one vessel with "Cahokia" shoulders (Griffin 1943:Plate LXXXII). The State Line site contains numerous Middle Mississippian pottery attributes, including negative painting and painting (one was a cross-in-circle motif), Ramey-like designs, a water bottle, a plate, a human head adorno, and an owl rattle adorno, many of which appear to have been manufactured using nonlocal pastes (Vickery et al. 2000: Tables 8.6 and 8.7). Sand Ridge contains a "Middle Mississippian type water bottle" (Oehler 1973:Photo 61). Madisonville contains a pottery vessel in the shape of a human head, with a face similar to those represented on pottery vessels in Missouri (Drooker 1997:327), as well as another vessel reminiscent of a Middle Mississippian form (326). Campbell Island also contains a vessel resembling Middle Mississippian variants (Griffin 1943:Plate LXXXIX). To assess pottery similarities on a broader scale, the percentage of shell-tempered pottery was compared (see Table 6.3). The general pattern is that sites located in the upper parts of the Miami River valleys contain smaller amounts of shell-tempered pottery than those located in the lower parts of these river systems.

Marine shell artifacts are a common indicator of status in Middle Mississippian societies and were shown to function in this capacity at SunWatch. They are present at several other sites in the region (see Table 6.3). Engraved gorgets have been located at Anderson, Madisonville, and State Line. These depict a variety of Southern Cult motifs most common among neighboring Middle Mississippian societies to the south of Fort Ancient, including a cross-in-circle design (Taylor [Griffin 1943:Plate XLVII]), weeping-eye motifs, and rattlesnake depictions (Madisonville [Drooker 1997:163, 335]). The regional distribution of annular shell gorgets is suggestive of a strong western connection (Figure 8.20 and Figure 8.22). Whelk shells have been recovered from SunWatch and Taylor (Griffin 1943:Plate XLVIII) (conch shell columella beads are present at Turpin but are associated with a Late Woodland burial [Oehler 1973:40–41]). Marginella shells have been noted for Anderson, Bunnell Kame, Campbell Island, Madisonville, State Line, Taylor, and Turpin 1. Shell discs are present at Anderson, Campbell Island, Madisonville, Sand Ridge, State Line, Steele Dam, Taylor, Turpin, and Wood 73.

Lithic artifacts similar to Middle Mississippian examples include discoidals, limestone spatulates, "Ramey" knives, and smoking pipes (see Table 6.3).

Table 6.3. Middle Mississippian–Style Artifacts from Sample of Fort Ancient Sites

Site Name	Miss.-Style Pottery	Shell-Tempered Pottery	Miss.-Style Gorgets	Shell Discs	Marginella Shells	Large Marine Shells	Discoidals	Miss.-Style Pipes	Miss.-Style Lithics
Anderson		10%	X	X	X		X		
Blum									
Bunnell Kame		50%			X				
Campbell Island	X	80%		X	X	X			
Carroll-Oregonia		60%					X		
Clear Creek		100%							
Driving Range		90%							
Erp		<1%							
Guard		99%							X
Haag		<1%							
Hahn's Field		100%							
Hine		67%							
Horseshoe Johnson		58%							
Kemp		13%					X		
Madisonville	X	100%	X	X	X	X	X	X	X
Mill Grove									
Sand Ridge	X	53%		X			X		
Sandy Run		none							
Schomaker		100%							
South Fort		<1%							

State Line	X	86%	X	X	X		X	X	
Steel Plant									
Steele Dam		10%			X				
SunWatch	X	2%		X	X	X	X	X?	
Taylor		most	X	X	X	X			X
Thomas		<1%							
Turpin 1	X	52%		X	X	X	X	X	X
Turpin 2									
Turpin 3									
Waterworks		100%							
Watson									
Wegerzyn		<1%			X				
Wilson		none							
Wood 73		10%		X					

Note: See text for references. (Percentages of shell-tempered pottery was completed with data gathered by Ted Sunderhaus.)

Discoidals are present at several sites, including Anderson, Carroll-Oregonia, Kemp, Madisonville, State Line, SunWatch, and Turpin. Middle Mississippian–style lithic artifacts have been reported from Guard (Robert Genheimer, personal communication 2006), Taylor (Griffin 1943:Plate XLV), and Turpin 1 (limestone spatulate [Oehler 1973:Photo 25]). Middle Mississippian–style pipes have been recovered from a few sites. Frog effigy pipes have been located at State Line and Turpin 1 (Photo 29), and a crouching human pipe (with a hairstyle like those shown on pipes from Kincaid and the Illinois River valley) is present in the Turpin 1 assemblage (Drooker 1997:90). Turpin also contains a "Middle Mississippian shell tempered platform pipe" (Oehler 1973:Photo 10). Engraved weeping-eye motifs—common Southeastern Ceremonial Complex motifs—are depicted on pipes at Madisonville (Drooker 1997:335). The SunWatch "wolf/man" pipe may also depict a weeping-eye motif (Lileas 1988b:46), and the platform pipe buried with one of the two identified "leaders" is similar in form to one found at the Turpin 1 site (Oehler 1973:Photo 10).

Examining the Peer Model

The SunWatch pattern shares a series of Middle Mississippian–style characteristics with several Fort Ancient villages in southwest Ohio. The following sections evaluate key criteria associated with peer polity interaction, on both interregional and intraregional levels.

Highly Visible Structural Parallels

Structural parallels between Middle Mississippian and Fort Ancient villages include central postholes in a circular village layout with plazas of similar sizes and with uniquely built and larger structures in closer proximity to the site center. Additionally, burial rows are common and stone slabs are a prevalent component in the Middle Cumberland region. These criteria were met at SunWatch, and to varying degrees in other villages for which we have a reasonably complete site plan. Madisonville and Anderson are both very similar to SunWatch; both sites contained a similarly sized plaza (at some point in their occupation). Madisonville has a central posthole and many burials are positioned in rows. Anderson also has burial rows.

Previous Contact

Some of the earliest sites in southwestern Ohio contain the most distinct Middle Mississippian–style artifacts. State Line and Turpin contain Middle Mississippian–style pottery (Ramey-like, negative painting). Both sites contain wall trench houses. The basic Middle Fort Ancient village pattern, exemplified at SunWatch but clearly present at other sites, mirrors Middle Mississippian rules on a variety of levels. The clearest evidence of Middle Mississippian contact at SunWatch (i.e., the wall trench house) dates from the beginning of the Late Fort Ancient period, a time of marked increases in social complexity (see below).

Prestige Goods

Marine shell gorgets and pottery with Middle Mississippian motifs (cross-in-circle, weeping eye, Ramey Incised, negative painting), whelk shells, and shell discs (often manufactured from marine shell) were the most recognizable prestige goods in Fort Ancient villages in southwest Ohio. Whelk shells and shell discs were restricted to individuals of higher rank at SunWatch (recall that Burial Cluster 4 was restricted to adult males and children and Burial Cluster 5 included only one male, who was interred with the only complete whelk shell present in the assemblage [see Chapter 5]). Several of these same items are status markers in Middle Mississippian communities, signifying they were acting in similar ways in Fort Ancient communities. This trend increases in the Late Fort Ancient period.

Increase in Social Complexity

The arrival of people who built a Middle Mississippian–style house, associated with Middle Mississippian pottery characteristics (shell temper, negative painting), coincides with a series of changes toward increased social complexity at SunWatch. At this time, the leader/ritual precinct develops, and the majority of associated features are closer to the central posthole than is the case elsewhere in the village. The wall trench house is the closest structure to the central posthole. The highest-status burials, perhaps the best indicator of increased social complexity, date to this time period as well.

This development at SunWatch coincides with the beginning of the Late Fort Ancient period. Changes in terms of increased interaction and social complexity are clear throughout the Fort Ancient region at this time and have been recognized for some time, most notably in the adoption of similar pottery styles (Cowan 1987:9). It is very interesting that the development of village leadership at SunWatch is closely connected (temporally) with this major Fort Ancient transition. However, perhaps the clearest evidence is that revealed through an analysis of the Madisonville mortuary program, which showed a more formalized system of two hierarchical social levels, the upper one consisting of two individuals possessing cross-shaped artifacts of panregional symbolism "analogous to symbol badges worn by men of authority in contemporaneous Oneota and Mississippian groups" (Drooker 2000:257). Site diversification may increase through time, but we need systematic survey data to further assess this. It is clear that not all nonvillage sites are restricted to winter uses, leaving open the possibility that there were small-scale settlement hierarchies, with the village as the apical type in this emergent system of social complexity (Riordan 2000; Vickery et al. 2000). This would be similar to the Middle Mississippian Mouse Creek complex in eastern Tennessee (see Chapter 2).

Peers and Polities

Wall trench houses are located in several Fort Ancient villages that also contain a suite of other Middle Mississippian characteristics. Moreover, only one such structure is usually present in Fort Ancient villages, suggesting the presence of only a few individual trade partners. The only exception to this pattern is at the State Line site, where multiple wall trench houses have been excavated. Because this site is relatively early, it is possible that it acted as an entrepôt of sorts, from which Mississippian ideas regarding village structure and leadership style spread. The presence of several mounds around a possible plaza supports the conclusion that it was of higher rank in a settlement system, but more data are needed before reaching such a conclusion. It is particularly interesting that State Line is located in the southwesternmost concentration of sites in the study area, in closest proximity to the Prather Complex (see Figure 1.1 and Figure 6.1). Regional surveys in the vicinity of the Haag site indicate "a major population increase during the [early] Fort Ancient period" (Reidhead 1976:63). While this is a poorly known area, it appears to be on the lower side of the Middle Mississippian scale of complexity. The Prather site itself is a mound center that may not be that different from State Line. While it is speculative at this point, it is not unreasonable to suggest that State Line and Prather could be peers of a higher level.

The final consideration for the operation of a periphery peer polity system within the southwestern Ohio region pertains to the spacing of similar villages. Considering data presented in this chapter, there are six villages that are demonstrably similar to SunWatch in terms of containing a suite of Middle Mississippian–style attributes: Anderson, Campbell Island, Madisonville, State Line, Taylor, and Turpin (see Table 6.2 and Table 6.3). When the location of these villages is considered, it is apparent that they are relatively evenly spaced throughout the region (see Figure 6.1). Interestingly, three of these sites (Anderson, SunWatch, and Taylor) contain particularly high proportions of stone-covered graves (Drooker 1997:Table 4.6), signifying a particularly stronger connection between southwest Ohio Fort Ancient and Middle Mississippians from the Middle Cumberland region.

Conclusion

Middle Mississippian–style artifacts and architectural characteristics coincide in terms of their occurrence in Fort Ancient villages. These sites were utilized mostly between the periods of A.D. 1100 and 1500. Generally, Middle Mississippian–style artifacts and architectural characteristics are located in villages, not smaller sites. Middle Mississippian–style architectural characteristics (wall trench houses), are concentrated in the southern and western portions of the study area. Central postholes have been located only in circular villages containing wall trench houses, burial rows, and diagnostic Middle Mississippian–style artifacts (Madisonville and SunWatch). Middle Mississippian contacts occur early in the sequence of Fort Ancient development in southwest Ohio.

The general conclusion from this examination of the Fort Ancient settlement pattern in southwest Ohio is the following. Characteristics that were defined at SunWatch are present in several other villages. Sites located closer to Middle Mississippians have greater quantities of alleged trade items, and State Line has several mounds. My interpretation of this pattern is that interregional interactions were initiated at State Line and Turpin 1 in a periphery peer system. Looking more broadly, another possible point of initial contact is central Ohio, as sites like Baum and Gartner also contain many Middle Mississippian–related attributes, including a substructure mound at the Baum site (Griffin 1992) (this is the only substructure mound reported in the Fort Ancient region). Given this finding, this site could also be analogous to smaller Middle Mississippian mound centers (as could the State Line site), although it has never been proposed to be an upper-level site in a settlement hierarchy (Drooker 1997:72). Based on what was perceived as clear distinctions in material culture, Prufer and Shane (1970:259) have argued that this area was the point of origin of Fort Ancient from Middle Mississippian migrants. Of course, it is very likely that there were multiple points of contact, southwest Ohio being of a similar timing as central Ohio (contra Prufer and Shane 1970:257).

The main point of this study is not to isolate individual loci of "first" contacts, which peer polity models acknowledge is not possible (see Chapter 1), but to begin recognizing the spread of ideas that significantly contributed to Fort Ancient village structures. I do not view this process as a diffusion of "traits" from Middle Mississippians to Fort Ancient, but rather as a coevolutionary periphery peer process of social development that became a peer polity system within the region, which clearly increases in Late Fort Ancient times. Middle Mississippian and Fort Ancient villages formed together. The peer system that was so much a part of Late Fort Ancient interaction patterns developed during the Early/Middle Fort Ancient period and can be linked with significant interactions along Middle Mississippian peripheries. The relative strength of Middle Mississippian influences on western Middle Fort Ancient appears to be more from the south (Middle Cumberland) than from the west, based largely on the use of stone in grave construction, which is particularly prevalent in sites located near SunWatch (Anderson and Taylor) as well as at least one site in Kentucky (Fox Farm) (Drooker 1997:329; see I. Brown 1981:Figure 3 for distribution of stone box graves). In Late Fort Ancient times, there are a variety of stylistic similarities that continued to link these regions as well as points further south (e.g., Coosa) (Pollack and Henderson 1992).

Fort Ancient site distribution reaches its height precisely at a time when neighboring Middle Mississippian settlement distribution was at its maximum geographical extent. The period between A.D. 1200 and 1500, the Middle Mississippian "crest" (Griffin 1985:63), is precisely the time period in which Fort Ancient villages became commonplace and sites were located throughout the region (Pollack and Henderson 1992:284–285, 2000). This Fort Ancient development is accompanied by increased pottery decorations on jars, which are similar in some respects to Middle Mississippian examples such as line-filled triangle and scroll motifs (compare designs depicted in Figure 3.4 with Hilgeman [2000:98–126]). Furthermore, the intensification of mound use, an increase in the use of crushed shell for pottery temper, and the occurrence of wall trench houses at sites in the western part of the region attest to an increased Middle Mississippian influence at this time. During this time, site locations are most common in the western Fort Ancient area, closest to Angel and Prather phase Middle Mississippian groups. While it is difficult to determine with a high degree of accuracy, this pattern changes over the course of the Fort Ancient period: "over time, the center of gravity for Fort Ancient sites apparently shifted from west to east" (Drooker 1997:70).

The occurrence of wall trench houses may have increased in frequency toward the end of the Middle Fort Ancient period. However, this is based on a sample of two dated examples (Schomaker and SunWatch). Other wall trench houses, particularly those at sites that appear to be relatively early (Turpin and State Line), are critical to directly date. However, if in fact these are a relatively late occurrence, the key question becomes: Were the Middle Mississippians represented by the wall trench houses trade partners or refugees who moved upstream into Fort Ancient villages after the collapse of the Angel and Middle Cumberland chiefdoms? Interestingly, the Mouse Creek phase develops at approximately this time, a settlement system and village (Ledford Island) that bear perhaps the closest resemblance to the SunWatch case and Fort Ancient settlement pattern. Was it the "postclassic" simplified form of Middle Mississippian society that influenced Fort Ancient the most? While these possibilities each warrant further consideration, the conclusion is clear. Interactions between Fort Ancient and Middle Mississippians were substantial enough to lead both systems down similar paths.

7
A Model of Fort Ancient Village Development

This study has investigated the social structure and formation of the SunWatch site, a Fort Ancient village occupied during the crest of neighboring Middle Mississippian developments. The theoretical perspective incorporated multiple spatial scales, focusing on the emergence of corporate groups and village leaders within a broad geographical framework. A theoretical and methodological perspective was developed that could account for variation among architectural, mortuary, pit feature, and artifact attributes within the village. Findings were then examined against a regional data set to assess the extent of the pattern. This concluding chapter summarizes key findings, focusing on the formation and structure of corporate groups and the development of village leadership in relation to interactions between Fort Ancient and Middle Mississippians.

A Brief History of SunWatch

Examination of the concordance between radiocarbon dates, architectural rebuilding, diagnostic feature and artifact attributes, and pottery refits resulted in the determination of a consistent pattern of village formation consisting of three distinct stages of construction (Figure 7.1). The first stage of construction is concentrated in the northern and southern portions of the village, and the village was primarily used in the spring and summer months at this time. These areas of initial use are also apparent at other less intensively occupied Fort Ancient villages (e.g., Campbell Island [Shetrone 1926:3], Capitol View [Henderson 1992:Figure 5]). The earliest houses built in the northern part of SunWatch are located in two closely spaced pairs, while the three early houses in the southern part of the village are more evenly spaced (i.e., there are no clear house pairs). The pair of houses in the northwestern quadrant of the village may have been built slightly later than the other initial groups of houses. The first of two center poles and the large house in the western part of the village were also in use at this time (although this house may have been smaller at this time [Cook 2005:361–364]). The inner stockade encloses these houses. Seasonality data suggest that the second and third uses of the village were more

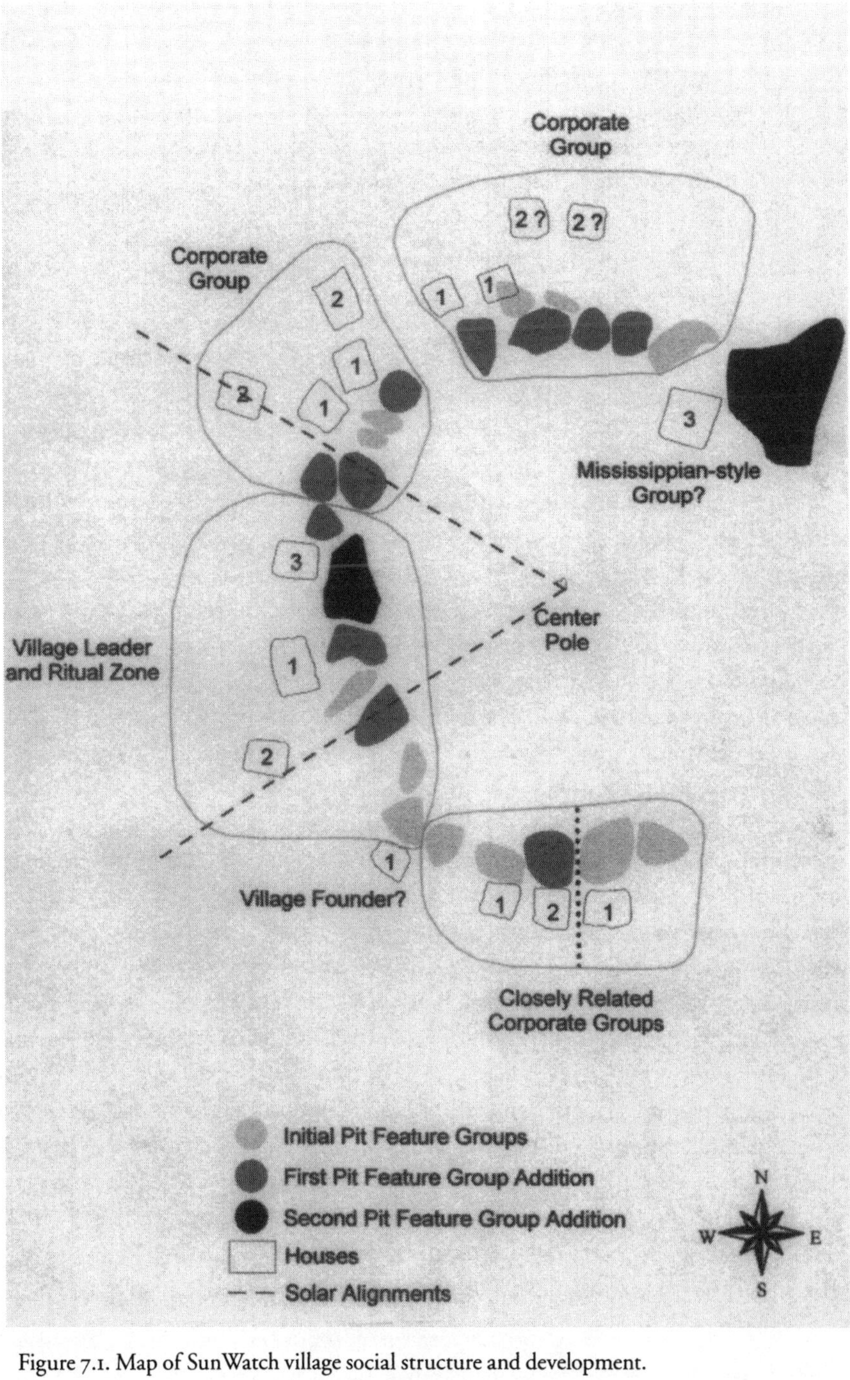

Figure 7.1. Map of SunWatch village social structure and development.

year-round. The second stage of construction is concentrated in the western and northern parts of the village. The third stage of construction includes the addition of the Middle Mississippian–style wall trench house and the red cedar house, which were integral in the development of villagewide leadership and ritual in the village. The outer stockade enclosed all houses within the site.

Corporate Group Development

Expectations of corporate groups as bounded sets of mortuary areas are met. The predominant form for burial groups is an arc-row pattern. Adults are generally buried closer to the village center and are more frequently covered with limestone slabs. I attribute these findings in part to Middle Mississippian influences.

Two to four household activity areas are directly associated with individual corporate groups (i.e., cemeteries were shared by multiple households) (see Figure 7.1). Growth of corporate groups is supported by concordance between burial row frequencies, architectural rebuilding, and temporally distinct artifact and feature indicators in household activity areas. When more than two households are associated with a corporate group, the oldest features are positioned in a central location from which subsequent households formed. In two cases, corporate groups were initiated by two closely spaced households, adhering well with findings at villages occupied for shorter time periods (e.g., Capitol View [Henderson 1992]). Pottery refits link newer houses with older ones, which are interpreted as having been built by corporate group founders. Pottery linkages between newer houses and the founding households suggest that these families cooperated closely with people living in the older structures, which is often the case in segmented social systems (Fortes 1953). Differences in the numbers of households comprising a corporate group appear to be related to early and late stages in the development cycle of extended families (Fortes 1949; Goody 1958, 1972; Tourtellot 1988).

Each of the residential zones was home to an individual corporate group or closely related corporate groups. The village leader and ritual area were clearly demarcated by closer proximity to the central posthole and solstice alignments, which were used in part to legitimize his power in the village. While this area developed late in the occupational sequence, it was likely planned from the beginning of the occupation, based on the relatively early radiocarbon date from the central posthole (see Figure 4.1). Based on pottery refits and a host of shared attributes, the house in the southwestern quadrant of the village was equally related to corporate groups in the southern and western zones. Early artifact and feature attributes corresponded with activity areas associated with this house, suggesting that this was one of the first houses built in the village. The village leader was most closely associated with a southern corporate group.

The identification of corporate groups and their development specifically expands our understanding of Fort Ancient residential behavior by revealing processes by which smaller villages become larger as a result of both internal growth and the joining of additional groups. While these processes have been previously mentioned as possibilities (Carskadden and Morton 2000; Drooker 1997:200–202, 206–209, 279–282; Henderson 1992), they have not been directly investigated. This finding also expands our understanding of corporate group development on a more general level, particularly with respect to the close relationship between mortuary and residential spaces.

Periphery Peers

Griffin (1992) once described the Fort Ancient as "having no class." Indeed this is true if we are comparing it to Middle Mississippian chiefdoms, in which inherited positions of rank are often clear. However, by examining the issue from a processual instead of a typological perspective and with a broader range of Middle Mississippian analogues, this study provides an alternate view of the problem by specifically identifying a case of village-level leadership akin to that expressed in Middle Mississippian villages. The following summary of SunWatch leadership and overall village structure shifts definitions of Fort Ancient away from those Middle Mississippian characteristics that are lacking to those that are present.

Middle Mississippian material culture, while a small component of the total assemblage, could not be in clearer contexts. Middle Mississippian–style artifacts (shell-tempered pottery, negative-painted designs) occurred later in the occupational sequence, and they were localized around a wall trench house (with associated burials), a red cedar house, and wolf and dog remains in burials (see Figure 4.11 and Figure 4.19). These findings further support a small-scale population influx, quite possibly associated with a local clan and stays in a men's house, coinciding with the growth of the political precinct of this Fort Ancient village. By identifying key elements of site structure and the particular context of Middle Mississippian–style features and artifacts, this study has shown that the relationship between local and nonlocal influences in the formation of Fort Ancient villages was dynamic. This includes the movement of individuals or small groups into Fort Ancient villages, which factored heavily into subsequent developments. This view contrasts with earlier conclusions that Fort Ancient developed from migrating Middle Mississippian groups in isolation of local populations (Prufer and Shane 1970:258–262) or that the influence of Middle Mississippian interactions on the development of Fort Ancient was insignificant (Pollack and Henderson 1992, 2000).

However, more than artifacts and a house indicate Middle Mississippian influences. By refocusing the problem away from the low occurrence of Middle Mississippian artifacts and the lack of rigid hierarchies, the presence of Middle Mississippian ideas has become clearer. It is important to think beyond specific material correlates in addressing the Mississippian transformation (Anderson 1997:259–260). This study provides a specific mechanism to account for the development of social systems, forcing us to rethink (again) what it means to be Mississippian and to allow a place in our definition for Fort Ancient societies that coevolved some key elements with their Middle Mississippian neighbors.

I begin my concluding comments with a view from the perspective of an inhabitant approaching either a Fort Ancient or Middle Mississippian village (Figure 7.2). If you swapped SunWatch, and presumably many other Fort Ancient villages, with a Middle Mississippian village, it would be difficult to recognize the difference in terms of the most visible elements. A Fort Ancient villager would feel quite at home in a Middle Mississippian village and vice versa. The patterning at SunWatch is consistent with the spatial and social structure of lower-order Middle Mississippian villages. The general spatial and theoretical model that best encapsulates the findings of this study depicts Fort Ancient villages as forming in periphery peer types of relations with other Fort Ancient villages and neighboring Middle Mississippian villages. It is a social landscape that grades from more to less complex systems; Fort Ancient settlements are equivalent to the lowest end of the range of Mississippian social complexity (see Figure 1.3).

SunWatch leaders were identified on the basis of several criteria. Beginning with the mortuary realm, cluster analysis isolated one individual with a supralocal symbol (the only complete whelk shell) and the most diverse artifact assemblage. A small cluster of 11 individuals, consisting only of adult males and children, possesses the only occurrences of perforated shell discs (aside from the village leader, who also possessed these). The two individuals with the greatest artifact diversity (Cluster 5 and a member of Cluster 4) were further shown to be located near the heaviest concentrations of debitage and chipped-stone tool-making artifacts, suggesting a linkage between leadership and craft production, which has been noted in rural Middle Mississippian contexts (e.g., Goldstein 1980:135). A series of additional connections between the villagewide leader and kin groups in the southern part of the village suggests that asymmetry between formerly egalitarian groups had developed, which adheres to the general evolutionary model (Knight 1990; Marcus and Flannery 1996:239; also see Chapter 1). Bone collagen samples from these two individuals produced radiocarbon dates in the late Middle to early Late Fort Ancient period (ca. A.D.

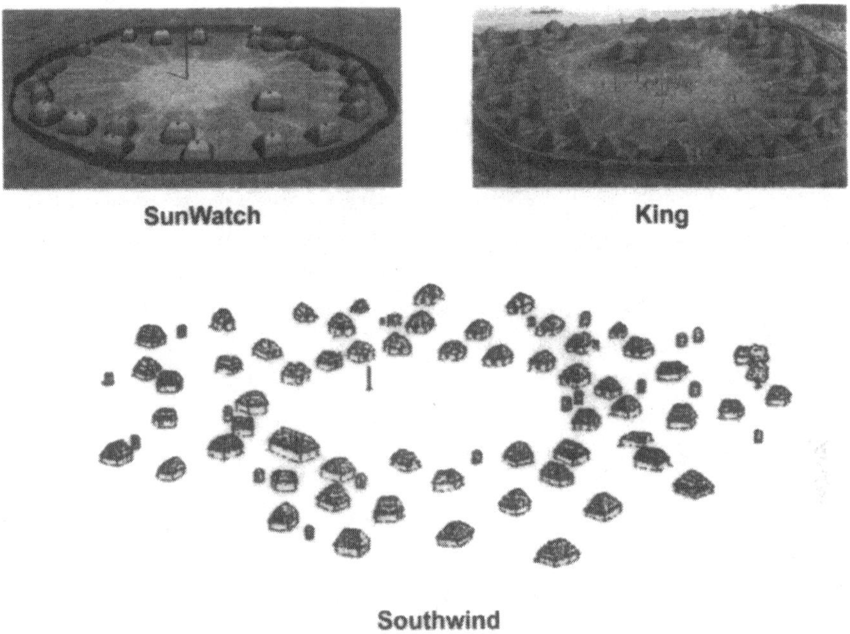

Figure 7.2. Reconstructed views of the SunWatch site and two Middle Mississippian villages, one to the south of Fort Ancient (King) and one to the west (Southwind). (King site painting by Kenneth Townsend; SunWatch computer rendering by Jeff Door and Robert Cook; Southwind site drawing by Ellen Sieber and Cheryl Munson.)

1394 to 1513), indicating that power emerged later in the village occupation, at a time of demonstrated Middle Mississippian contact and during a point of substantial change in Fort Ancient society.

Two areas of the site are positioned closer to the central posthole, adhering to general rules associated with Middle Mississippian village design. The same areas contain unique architecture, and one area is clearly associated with all major solar alignments and a potential case of restricted access to storage, all of which have been noted for some Middle Mississippian leader contexts. The most pronounced burial rows and groups are also associated with solar alignments. The SunWatch indicators of leadership clearly share a number of elements with Middle Mississippian examples, coevolving at a time of demonstrated local population growth. The integration of multiple social groups and the emergence of social complexity fit well with existing models of Fort Ancient evolution (Pollack and Henderson 1992, 2000). However, the explicit Middle Mississippian connection expands the view to include a substantial role for interregional interaction in this development.

A local leader could have used long-distance exchange relationships with

Middle Mississippians to gain status and power. Ethnographic and archaeological research has documented the development and manipulation of long-distance trade networks by individuals to generate power, status, and leadership positions in many transegalitarian societies (e.g., Blanton et al. 1996; Chagnon 1968; Cochrane 1970; Douglas 1967; Hayden 1995; Helms 1988, 1993; Leach and Leach 1983; Peregrine 1992; Renfrew 1986). SunWatch leadership could have been predicated on personal connections with distant Middle Mississippians. However, these long distance ties from SunWatch to Middle Mississippian villages were likely mediated through other Fort Ancient villages located in southwest Ohio.

A Ceremonial Context

Much of what is considered to be "Mississippian" may well be in the ideology that undoubtedly spread across much of the eastern United States after Cahokia's "big bang in the bottom" (Pauketat and Emerson 1997:31). The SunWatch case clearly supports a relatively late interaction with Middle Mississippians, during a "postclassic" time period for many Middle Mississippian groups. One of the more intriguing aspects associated with this interaction may pertain to Green Corn ceremonialism. While this was not an explicit component in the research project, there is reason to suggest that this development coincided with Middle Mississippian interactions. At least one other Fort Ancient village (Blain village, located in central Ohio) contains evidence for this ceremony as well, in addition to Middle Mississippian–style artifacts (Prufer and Shane 1970:256). This suggests that this may form a component of Fort Ancient sites more generally.

As discussed in Chapter 2, there is evidence at SunWatch for Green Corn ceremonialism (Cook 2004; Harold 1985; Heilman and Hoefer 1981; Robertson 1980), to which I would add negative-painted pottery (after Hilgeman 1991). The present study's focus on internal site chronology has inadvertently added a temporal dimension to our understanding of the spread of Green Corn ceremonialism into the village. It has long been suggested that a few features near the red cedar house contained evidence for this renewal ceremony in the form of numerous broken artifacts and abundant quantities of burned corn (Heilman and Hoefer 1981; Robertson 1980:57–58; see Chapter 1). One of the key features is a large pit (19e/74, which is the most recent of a series of overlapping pit features, including 19w/74 and 19ww/74) located along the equinox alignment (see Figure 1.5). I suggest that Green Corn ceremonialism developed later in the site use, as the median radiocarbon date obtained for Feature 19ww/74 is A.D. 1359 (see Figure 4.1). Feature 19e/74 would have been filled after use of this pit, in the general time frame in which village leadership developed.

The growing case for this renewal ceremony being part of Fort Ancient life warrants specific consideration of models that could account for its spread to SunWatch. Emerson (1997:264) and Pauketat and Emerson (1991) have suggested that during Green Corn renewal and fertility ceremonies elites distributed Ramey Incised pottery vessels. The practice of such events in rural contexts is a result of elite use of the fertility cult to further centralize power by consolidating rural populations. Only through the brokerage of the elite could commoners have access to spiritual or earthly sustenance (Emerson 1997:261).

Knight (1986, 1997) casts the spread of elite pottery in a different light by identifying a marked shift in the spatial contexts of these wares. Elite iconography was initially restricted to mound centers, but as Middle Mississippian systems reached the height of their complexity, these materials spread to smaller settlements, a shift described as "communalization" of cult symbolism (1986:682–683): "pottery . . . probably made only at the regional center . . . ends up in patently non-elite contexts extending to the most remote farmsteads of the chiefdom (and beyond) . . . the abstruse symbolism of the elite now became, to some degree, the abstruse symbolism of everybody" (1997:240). Chiefly iconography became transferred to function as common wealth items (246). In two different Middle Mississippian contexts (Cahokia and Moundville), the far-flung nature of elite iconography occurs for about a 150-year interval after the apex of political consolidation (ca. A.D. 1200–1350 at Cahokia and ca. A.D. 1400–1550 at Moundville). This shift is accompanied by a fundamental change in the use of regional centers, from towns with numerous residents to places focused on public and ceremonial activity. The basic pattern is the decentralization of authority while maintaining the ceremonial importance of primary centers (241).

Whether or not one concludes that the Green Corn ceremony was used by elites in chiefdoms to ideologically control commoners in outlying communities, the situation for Fort Ancient was different. However, at SunWatch evidence for Green Corn ceremonialism occurs at a time of marked Middle Mississippian influence. Middle Mississippian–style pottery others have associated with this ceremony has been identified at SunWatch and several other southwest Ohio sites (see Chapter 6). In the larger picture, this is consistent with the timing of the "communalization" of the fertility cult (Knight 1986:682–683). Periphery peer interactions appear to have been at least partially conducted within the context of this ceremony, specifically linking Fort Ancient into the Middle Mississippian world on the basis of a shared ideology, a common element in coevolving systems (Schortman and Urban 1998; also see Chapter 1). Certainly, the use of central posts attests to further ideological connections. These findings also suggest that perhaps a different process was occurring for

Fort Ancient as compared with Oneota groups. SunWatch does not exhibit something markedly different from those with whom they interacted (contra Emerson 1999); in fact, the case seems to be quite the opposite.

Interestingly, the complete negative-painted vessel at SunWatch also contains a guilloche motif and is tempered with both grit and shell (see Figure 3.3). Furthermore, it is located directly in front of the red cedar house, close to a dog burial (see Figure 5.5). The combination of Middle Mississippian–influenced characteristics with presumably local ones in a ritual context hints at the syncretic nature of coevolving systems.

Future Research

There are several avenues of future research that have been generated by this study. The most obvious gap in information is the paucity of village-level data for both Middle Mississippian and Fort Ancient. This study has shown the potential of what can be accomplished in terms of the diachronic dimension of social behavior, setting up a rich context for examining a variety of further questions. A particularly interesting study would assess genetic relationships between potential kin groups and for individuals I have suggested were more "connected" with Middle Mississippians. There are also many important questions pertaining to changes in foodways and technology within a defined set of social groups. In other words, the SunWatch case provides a wealth of bioarchaeological research opportunities.

The most pressing need within the Fort Ancient region is to begin systematically investigating the issue of settlement hierarchy, which has been hinted at, mistakenly identified, and then abandoned as a worthwhile research pursuit. It would be particularly useful for such investigations to initially focus on areas surrounding sites that in fact could be small mound centers and that contain the highest concentration of Middle Mississippian attributes (e.g., State Line). It is particularly interesting that State Line is located in the southwesternmost concentration of Fort Ancient sites in the study area, in closest proximity to the Prather Complex (see Figure 1.1 and Figure 6.1). While it is not unreasonable to suggest that they could be peers of a higher level, we must not forget that villages can also be the center of smaller-scale settlement hierarchies, such as is the case for Mouse Creek. With this said, the study of a series of villages would likely yield a better understanding of the associated settlement system, given the higher occurrence of Middle Mississippian–style attributes (Anderson, Campbell Island, Madisonville, SunWatch, Taylor, Turpin). Dating issues are a key problem for such a study. The present study should aid in this capacity around SunWatch (and perhaps more broadly), but similar diachronic analyses should probably precede regional work around other such "centers."

One of the key findings of this study has been to isolate the productivity of pursuing two issues of mobility that need to be further considered on a regional scale: (1) individuals or small groups moving between villages; and (2) movement and reoccupation of the village as a whole. Individuals moving in may have consisted of marriage partners (possibly the makers of some of the shell-tempered pottery) and visitors staying with fellow clan members or in the village sodality. Issues of village mobility are suggested by the bimodal distribution of radiocarbon dates and associated diagnostic attributes. On this basis, SunWatch should serve as a useful model for interpreting other Fort Ancient sites, as other sites contain similar bimodality in radiocarbon sequences (Carr and Haas 1996; Cowan et al. 1990; Harper 2000), as well as the general suite of pit feature and artifact attributes explored here. Reoccupation and the joining of individuals and small groups of people at Fort Ancient villages are undoubtedly part of a much larger pattern.

Not only do we have limited knowledge of other Fort Ancient and Middle Mississippian site plans, but we are also unable to answer the big question that readers should have been asking throughout the study: What elements of SunWatch are attributable to local Late Woodland groups? Unfortunately, at this point we cannot answer this critical question as we have little detailed information of the Late Woodland period in this portion of Ohio, particularly with respect to chronology and settlement data (Seeman and Dancey 2000: 603). We desperately need to remedy this deficiency. My suspicion is that some elements I have described as "Middle Mississippian–style" have deeper roots and/or can be connected with local influences. For example, central postholes and renewal ceremonies are present from earlier times in the vicinity of Cahokia (Kelly1990b), and whelk shells have been traded among important people in the region for millennia. However, I suggest that the search for the origin of individual traits should not be the focus of investigating problems of interregional patterns of mutual influence. The geographical messiness and time-depth interregional interaction may play a substantial role in the problem of defining archaeological "cultures" to begin with.

This study should be viewed as a starting point is addressing a complicated and multidimensional problem. Conclusions reached will undoubtedly change as we, hopefully, acquire additional broader-scale excavation data and systematically collected regional data. The fact that SunWatch is far removed from neighboring Middle Mississippians, while at the same time exhibiting such a series of distinct similarities, makes it all the more intriguing and demands further exploration.

References Cited

Adams, R. N.

1975 *Energy and Structure: A Theory of Social Power.* University of Texas Press, Austin.

Allen, W. L., and J. B. Richardson

1971 The Reconstruction of Kinship from Archaeological Data: the Concept, the Methods, and the Feasibility. *American Antiquity* 36:41–53.

Allman, John C.

1959 An Interesting Bluff-Top Enclosure with Semi-Lunar Wall and Ditch. *Ohio Archaeologist* 9:54–55.

1960 The Erp Bluff-Top Site. *Ohio Archaeologist* 10:60–66.

1968 The Incinerator Village Site. *Ohio Archaeologist* 18:50–56.

Anderson, David G.

1994 *The Savannah River Chiefdoms.* University of Alabama Press, Tuscaloosa.

1997 The Role of Cahokia in the Evolution of Southeastern Mississippian Society. In *Cahokia: Domination and Ideology in the Mississippian World,* edited by T. R. Pauketat and T. E. Emerson, pp. 248–268. University of Nebraska Press, Lincoln.

Aveni, Anthony F.

2003 Archaeoastronomy in the Ancient Americas. *Journal of Archaeological Research* 11:149–192.

Bartram, William

1853 [1789] Observations on the Creek and Cherokee Indians. *Transactions of the American Ethnological Society* 3:1–81.

Benchley, Elizabeth

1970 Mississippian Calendrics: Some Suggestions. Paper presented at the annual meeting of the American Anthropological Association, San Diego.

Berryman, Hugh E.

1981 *The Averbuch Skeletal Series: A Study of Biological and Social Stress at a Late Mississippian Period Site from Middle Tennessee.* Ph.D. dissertation, Department of Anthropology, University of Tennessee, Knoxville. University Microfilms, Ann Arbor, Michigan.

Binford, Lewis H.

1962 Archaeology and Anthropology. *American Antiquity* 28:217–225.

1971 Mortuary Practices: Their Study and Their Potential. In *Approaches to the Social Dimensions of Mortuary Practices,* edited by James A. Brown, pp. 6–

29. Memoirs of the Society for American Archaeology No. 25. Washington, D.C.

Black, Glenn A.

1934 Archaeological Survey of Dearborn and Ohio Counties. *Indiana History Bulletin* 11(7).

1967 *Angel Site: An Archaeological, Historical, and Ethnological Study.* Indiana Historical Society, Indianapolis.

Blanton, Richard E., Gary M. Feinman, Stephen A. Kowalewski, and Peter N. Peregrine

1996 A Dual-Processual Theory for the Evolution of Mesoamerican Civilization. *Current Anthropology* 37:1–14.

Blitz, John H.

1999 Mississippian Chiefdoms and the Fission-Fusion Process. *American Antiquity* 64:577–592.

Blitz, John H., and Karl G. Lorenz

2006 *The Chattahoochee Chiefdoms.* University of Alabama Press, Tuscaloosa.

Bourdieu, Pierre

1977 *Outline of a Theory of Practice.* Cambridge University Press, Cambridge.

Boyd, C. C., Jr., and D. C. Boyd

1991 A Multidimensional Investigation of Biocultural Relationships among Three Late Prehistoric Societies in Tennessee. *American Antiquity* 56:75–88.

Bradbury, Andrew P., and Michael D. Richmond

2004 A Preliminary Examination of Quantitative Methods for Classifying Small Triangular Points from Late Prehistoric Sites: A Case Study from the Ohio River Valley. *Midcontinental Journal of Archaeology* 29:43–62.

Brose, David S.

1982 The Archaeological Investigation of a Fort Ancient Community Near Ohio Brush Creek, Adams County, Ohio. *Kirtlandia* 34.

Brose, David S., and Nancy M. White

1983 Recent Data on Fort Ancient Occupation in the Ceasar Creek Valley, Southwestern Ohio. *West Virginia Archaeologist* 35:3–26.

Broster, John B.

1972 The Ganier Site: A Late Mississippian Village on the Cumberland River. In *The Middle Cumberland Culture,* edited by R. B. Ferguson, pp. 51–78. Vanderbilt University Publications in Anthropology No. 3. Nashville, Tennessee.

Brown, Ian

1981 A Study of Stone Box Graves in Eastern North America. *Tennessee Anthropologist* 6:1–26.

Brown, James A.

1971 Introduction. In *Approaches to the Social Dimensions of Mortuary Practices,* edited by James A. Brown, pp. 1–5. Memoirs of the Society for American Archaeology No. 25. Washington, D.C.

1981 The Search for Rank in Prehistoric Burials. In *The Archaeology of Death,* edited by Robert Chapman, Ian Kinnes, and Klavs Randsborg, pp. 25–38. Cambridge University Press, New York.

1982 What Kind of Economy Did the Oneota Have? In *Oneota Studies,* edited by Guy E. Gibbon, pp. 107–112. University of Minnesota Publications in Anthropology No. 1. Minneapolis.

Brown, James A., Richard A. Kerber, and Howard D. Winters

1990 Trade and the Evolution of Exchange Relations at the Beginning of the Mississippian Period. In *The Mississippian Emergence,* edited by Bruce D. Smith, pp. 251–280. Smithsonian Institution Press, Washington, D.C.

Callahan, Errett

1979 The Basics of Biface Knapping in the Eastern Fluted Point Tradition: A Manual for Flintknappers and Lithic Analysts. *Archaeology of Eastern North America* 7:1–180.

Callendar, Charles

1978 Great Lakes-Riverine Sociopolitical Organization. In *Handbook of North American Indians: Northeast,* edited by Bruce G. Trigger, pp. 610–621. Smithsonian Institution Press, Washington, D. C.

Cameron, Catherine M.

1991 Structure Abandonment in Villages. *Archaeological Method and Theory* 3:155–191.

Carr, Christopher

1985 *For Concordance in Archaeological Analysis.* Waveland Press, Prospect Heights, Illinois.

Carr, Christopher, and Herbert Haas

1996 Beta-Count and AMS Radiocarbon Dates of Woodland and Fort Ancient Occupations in Ohio, 1350 B.C.–A.D. 1650. *West Virginia Archaeologist* 48:19–53.

Carskadden, James

1992 Possible Summer and Winter Houses at the Fort Ancient Philo II Site. *West Virginia Archaeologist* 26:24–28.

Carskadden, James, and James Morton

2000 Fort Ancient in the Central Muskingum Valley of Eastern Ohio: A View from the Philo II Site. In *Cultures Before Contact: The Late Prehistory of Ohio and Surrounding Regions,* edited by Robert A. Genheimer, pp. 158–193. Ohio Archaeological Council, Columbus.

Chagnon, Napolean A.

1968 *Yanomamo: The Fierce People.* Holt, Rinehart, and Winston, New York.

Chang, Kwang-Chih

1958 Study of the Neolithic Social Grouping: Examples from the New World. *American Anthropologist* 60:298–334.

Church, Flora

1987 *An Enquiry into the Transition from Late Woodland to Late Prehistoric Cultures in the Central Scioto Valley, Ohio, circa A.D. 500 to A.D. 1250.* Ph.D. dissertation, Department of Anthropology, Ohio State University, Columbus. University Microfilms, Ann Arbor, Michigan.

Clay, R. Berle

1976 Tactics, Strategy, and Operations: The Mississippian System Responds to Its Environment. *Midcontinental Journal of Archaeology* 1:137–162.

Cochrane, Glynn
1970 *Big Men and Cargo Cults.* Clarendon, Oxford.
Collins, James M.
1997 Cahokia Settlement and Social Structures as Viewed from the ICT-II. In *Cahokia: Domination and Ideology in the Mississippian World,* edited by Timothy R. Pauketat and Thomas E. Emerson, pp. 124–140. University of Nebraska Press, Lincoln.
Conrad, Lawrence A.
1991 The Mississippian Cultures of the Central Illinois River Valley. In *Cahokia and the Hinterlands: Middle Mississippian Cultures of the Midwest,* edited by Thomas E. Emerson and R. Barry Lewis, pp. 119–156. University of Illinois Press, Urbana-Champaign.
Cook, Robert A.
2004 *Upper Mississippian Village Structure and Formation: Spatial Analysis of SunWatch, a Fort Ancient Site in Southwest Ohio.* Ph.D. dissertation, Department of Anthropology, Michigan State University, Lansing. University Microfilms, Ann Arbor, Michigan.
2005 Reconstructing Perishable Architecture: Prospects and Limitations of a Fort Ancient Example. *North American Archaeologist* 26:357–388.
2007 Single Component Sites with Long Sequences of Radiocarbon Dates: The SunWatch Site and Middle Fort Ancient Village Growth. *American Antiquity* 72:439–460.
Cook, Robert A., and Lane F. Fargher
2007 Fort Ancient/Mississippian Interaction and Shell-Tempered Pottery at the SunWatch Site. *Journal of Field Archaeology* 32:1–12.
Cook, Robert A., and William E. Kennedy
2005 Preliminary Results of the 2005 Ohio State University/Dayton Society of Natural History Summer Archaeological Field Program. Paper presented at the Midwest Archaeological Conference, Dayton, Ohio.
Cook, Robert A., and Leah Merz
2000 The Occupational Complexity of a Single-Component Fort Ancient Village: Using G.I.S. to Examine the Formation of the SunWatch Site. Paper presented at the joint Midwest Archaeological Conference/Plains Anthropological Conference, St. Paul, Minnesota.
Cook, Robert A., and Theodore S. Sunderhaus
1999 Cultural Interaction within a Fort Ancient Village: Spatial Analysis of the Incinerator Site Ceramic Assemblage. Paper presented at annual meeting of the Society for American Archaeology, Chicago.
Cooper, Daniel C.
1800 Field notes, general land office survey. Township 1, Range 6, East of the Meridian, Vol. 3, and Congress Lands between the Miami Rivers, Vol. 3. Manuscript on file, Office of the State Auditor, Columbus, Ohio.
Coupland, Gary, and E. B. Banning
1996 Introduction: The Archaeology of Big Houses. In *People Who Lived in Big Houses: Archaeological Perspectives on Large Domestic Structures,* edited by

Gary Coupland and E. B. Banning, pp. 1–9. Prehistory Press, Madison, Wisconsin.

Cowan, C. Wesley

1986 *Fort Ancient Chronology and Settlement Evaluation in the Great Miami Valley,* vol. II: *Excavations and Chronology.* Ohio Historic Preservation Office, Columbus.

1987 *First Farmers of the Middle Ohio Valley: Fort Ancient Societies, A.D. 1000–1670.* Cincinnati Museum of Natural History, Cincinnati.

1988 From Pithouse to Longhouse, from Community to Chaos: Late Prehistoric and Proto-historic Developments in the Middle Ohio Valley. Paper presented at the Midwest Archaeological Conference, Urbana-Champaign, Illinois.

1992 The Dawn of History and the Demise of the Fort Ancient Cultures of the Central Ohio Valley. Paper presented at the annual meeting of the Society for American Archaeology, Pittsburgh.

Cowan, C. Wesley, Sandra Dunavan, John P. Nass, Jr., and Susan Scott

1990 The Schomaker Site: A Middle Period Fort Ancient Town on the Great Miami River, Hamilton County, Ohio. *West Virginia Archaeologist* 42:11–35.

Creamer, Winifred, and Jonathan Haas

1985 Tribes versus Chiefdoms in Lower Central America. *American Antiquity* 50:738–754.

Crumley, Carole L.

1979 Three Locational Models: An Epistemological Assessment of Anthropology and Archaeology. *Advances in Archaeological Method and Theory* 2:141–173.

Dancey, William S.

1992 Village Origins in Central Ohio: The Results and Implications of Recent Middle and Late Woodland Research. In *Cultural Variability in Context: Woodland Settlements of the Mid-Ohio Valley,* edited by Mark F. Seeman, pp. 24–29. Midcontinental Journal of Archaeology Special Paper No. 7. Kent State University Press, Kent, Ohio.

1998 The Value of Surface Archaeological Data in Exploring the Dynamics of Community Evolution in the Middle Ohio Valley. In *Surface Archaeology,* edited by Alan P. Sullivan, pp. 3–19. University of New Mexico Press, Albuquerque.

Deetz, James

1965 *The Dynamics of Stylistic Change in Arikara Ceramics.* Illinois Studies in Anthropology No. 4. University of Illinois Press, Urbana.

Dincauze, Dena F., and Robert J. Hasenstab

1989 Explaining the Iroquois: Tribalization on a Prehistoric Periphery. In *Centre and Periphery,* edited by Tim C. Champion, pp. 67–87. Unwin Hyman, London.

Douglas, Mary

1967 Primitive Rationing: A Study in Controlled Exchange. In *Themes in Economic Anthropology,* edited by Raymond Firth, pp. 119–147. Tavistock, London.

Drooker, Penelope B.

1997 *The View from Madisonville: Protohistoric Western Fort Ancient Interaction Pat-*

terns. Museum of Anthropology, Memoirs No. 31. University of Michigan, Ann Arbor.

2000 Madisonville Focus Revisited: Reexcavating Southwestern Ohio Fort Ancient from Museum Collections. In *Cultures Before Contact: The Late Prehistory of Ohio and Surrounding Regions,* edited by Robert A. Genheimer, pp. 228–270. Ohio Archaeological Council, Columbus.

Drooker, Penelope B., and C. Wesley Cowan

2001 Transformation of the Fort Ancient Cultures of the Central Ohio Valley. In *Societies in Eclipse: Archaeology of the Eastern Woodlands Indians, A.D. 1400–1700,* edited by David S. Brose, C. Wesley Cowan, and Robert C. Mainfort, pp. 83–106. Smithsonian Institution Press, Washington, D.C.

Dunnell, Robert C.

1961 A General Survey of Fort Ancient in the Kentucky–West Virginia Area. Manuscript on file, Department of Anthropology, University of Kentucky, Lexington.

1971 *Systematics in Prehistory.* Free Press, New York.

Eisenberg, Leslie E.

1991 Mississippian Cultural Terminations in Middle Tennessee: What the Bio-archaeological Evidence Can Tell Us. In *What Mean These Bones? Studies in Southeastern Bioarchaeology,* edited by Mary Lucas Powell, Patricia S. Bridges, and Ann Marie Wagner Mires, pp. 70–88. University of Alabama Press, Tuscaloosa.

Emerson, Thomas E.

1988 The Mississippian Dispersed Village as a Social and Environmental Adaptive Strategy. Paper presented at the International Congress of Americanists, Amsterdam.

1997 *Cahokia and the Archaeology of Power.* University of Alabama Press, Tuscaloosa.

1999 The Langford Tradition and the Process of Tribalization on the Middle Mississippian Borders. *Midcontinental Journal of Archaeology* 24:3–56.

Emery, F. E., and E. L. Trist

1965 The Causal Texture of Organizational Environments. *Human Relations* 18:21–32.

Essenpreis, Patricia S.

1978 Fort Ancient Settlement: Differential Response at a Mississippian–Late Woodland Interface. In *Mississippian Settlement Patterns,* edited by Bruce D. Smith, pp. 143–167. Academic Press, New York.

1982 *The Anderson Village Site: Redefining the Anderson Phase of the Fort Ancient Tradition of the Middle Ohio Valley.* Ph.D. dissertation, Department of Anthropology, Harvard University, Cambridge, Massachusetts. University Microfilms, Ann Arbor, Michigan.

1988 An Introduction to the Fort Ancient Cultural Complexes of the Middle Ohio Valley. In *A History of 17 Years of Excavation and Reconstruction: A Chronicle of 12th Century Human Values and the Built Environment,* edited by James M. Heilman, Malinda C. Lileas, and Christopher A. Turnbow, pp. 1–22. Dayton Museum of Natural History, Dayton, Ohio.

Evans-Eargle, Sarah J.
1998 *Mortuary Data as Indicators of Social Organization at the Incinerator Site (33MY57).* M.A. thesis, Department of Anthropology, University of South Carolina, Columbia. University Microfilms, Ann Arbor, Michigan.

Ferguson, Robert B.
1972 The Arnold Village Site Excavations of 1965–1966. In *The Middle Cumberland Culture,* edited by Robert B. Ferguson, pp. 1–50. Vanderbilt University Publications in Anthropology No. 3. Nashville, Tennessee.

Flannery, Kent V.
1968 The Olmec and the Valley of Oaxaca: A Model for Interregional Interaction in Formative Times. In *Dumbarton Oaks Conference on the Olmec,* edited by E. P. Benson, pp. 79–110. Dumbarton Oaks, Washington, D.C.
1972 The Cultural Evolution of Civilizations. *Annual Review of Ecology and Systematics* 3:399–426.

Foerste, Auguste A.
1885 Ancient Relics at Dayton, Ohio. In *Annual Report of the Smithsonian Institution (1883),* pp. 838–844. Washington, D.C.

Fortes, Meyer
1949 *The Web of Kinship among the Tallensi.* Oxford University Press, London.
1953 The Structure of Unilineal Descent Groups. *American Anthropologist* 55:17–41.
1958 Introduction. In *The Developmental Cycle in Domestic Groups,* edited by Jack Goody, pp. 1–14. Cambridge University Press, Cambridge.

Fowler, Melvin L.
1974 *Cahokia: Ancient Capital of the Midwest.* Addison-Wesley, Boston.

Fried, Morton H.
1967 *The Evolution of Political Society: An Essay in Political Anthropology.* Random House, New York.
1983 Tribe to State or State to Tribe in Ancient China? In *The Origins of Chinese Civilization,* edited by David N. Keightley, pp. 467–493. University of California Press, Berkeley.

Gibbon, Guy E.
1982 Oneota Origins Revisited. In *Oneota Studies,* edited by G. E. Gibbon, pp. 85–89. University of Minnesota Publications in Anthropology No. 1. Minneapolis.
1995 Oneota at the Periphery: Trade, Political Power, and Ethnicity in Northern Minnesota and on the Northeastern Plains in the Late Prehistoric Period. In *Oneota Archaeology: Past, Present, and Future,* edited by William Green, pp. 175–199. Report No. 20. University of Iowa, Office of the State Archaeologist, Iowa City.

Giddens, Anthony
1984 *The Constitution of Society: Outline of the Theory of Structuration.* University of California Press, Berkeley.

Giesen, Myra J.
1992 *Late Prehistoric Populations in the Ohio Area: Biological Affinities and Stress In-*

dicators. Ph.D. dissertation, Department of Anthropology, Ohio State University, Columbus. University Microfilms, Ann Arbor, Michigan.

Goldstein, Lynne G.

1980 *Mississippian Mortuary Practices.* Scientific Papers No. 4. Northwestern University Archeological Program, Kampsville, Illinois.

1991 The Implications of Aztalan's Location. In *New Perspectives on Cahokia: Views from the Periphery,* edited by James B. Stoltman, pp. 209–228. Prehistory Press, Madison, Wisconsin.

Goldstein, Lynne G., and John D. Richards

1991 Ancient Aztalan: The Cultural and Ecological Context of a Late Prehistoric Site in the Midwest. In *Cahokia and the Hinterlands: Middle Mississippian Cultures of the Midwest,* edited by Thomas E. Emerson and R. Barry Lewis, pp. 193–206. University of Illinois Press, Urbana-Champaign.

Goodenough, Ward H.

1956 Residence Rules. *Southwestern Journal of Anthropology* 12:22–37.

1965 Rethinking "Status" and "Role": Toward a General Model of the Cultural Organization of Social Relationships. In *The Relevance of Models for Social Anthropology,* edited by Michael Banton, pp. 1–24. Tavistock, London.

Goody, Jack

1958 The Fission of Domestic Groups among the LoDagaba. In *The Developmental Cycle in Domestic Groups,* edited by Jack Goody, pp. 53–91. Cambridge University Press, Cambridge.

1972 The Evolution of the Family. In *Household and Family in Past Time,* edited by Peter Laslett and Richard Wall, pp. 103–124. Cambridge University Press, Cambridge.

Goss, Arthur F.

1988 Astronomical Alignments at the Incinerator Site. In *A History of 17 Years of Excavation and Reconstruction: A Chronicle of 12th Century Human Values and the Built Environment,* edited by James M. Heilman, Malinda C. Lileas, and Christopher A. Turnbow, pp. 314–335. Dayton Museum of Natural History, Dayton, Ohio.

Graybill, Jeffrey R.

1981 The Eastern Periphery of Fort Ancient (A.D. 1050–1650): A Diachronic Approach to Settlement Variability. Ph.D. dissertation, Department of Anthropology, University of Washington, Seattle. University Microfilms, Ann Arbor, Michigan.

Green, Thomas J., and Cheryl A. Munson

1978 Mississippian Settlement Patterns in Southwestern Indiana. In *Mississippian Settlement Patterns,* edited by Bruce D. Smith, pp. 293–330. Academic Press, New York.

Griffin, James B.

1943 *The Fort Ancient Aspect: Its Cultural and Chronological Position in Mississippi Valley Archaeology.* University of Michigan, Museum of Anthropology Anthropological Papers No. 28. Ann Arbor.

1978 Late Prehistory of the Ohio Valley. In *Handbook of North American Indians: Northeast,* edited by Bruce G. Trigger, pp. 547–559. Smithsonian Institution Press, Washington, D.C.

1985 Changing Concepts of the Prehistoric Mississippian Cultures of the Eastern United States. In *Alabama and the Borderlands: From Prehistory to Statehood,* edited by Reid R. Badger and Lawrence A. Clayton, pp. 40–63. University of Alabama Press, Tuscaloosa.

1992 Fort Ancient Has No Class: The Absence of an Elite Group in Mississippian Societies in the Central Ohio Valley. *In Lords of the Southeast: Social Inequality and the Native Elites of Southeastern North America,* edited by Alex W. Barker and Timothy R. Pauketat, pp. 53–59. Archaeological Papers of the American Anthropological Association No. 3. Washington, D.C.

1993 Cahokia Interaction with Contemporary Southeastern and Eastern Societies. *Midcontinental Journal of Archaeology* 18:3–17.

Hall, Robert L.

1991 Cahokia Identity and Interaction Models of Cahokia Mississippian. In *Cahokia and the Hinterlands: Middle Mississippian Cultures of the Midwest,* edited by Thomas E. Emerson and R. Barry Lewis, pp. 3–34. University of Illinois Press, Urbana-Champaign.

Hally, David J.

1975 Introduction to the Symposium: The King Site and Its Investigation. *Southeastern Archaeological Conference Bulletin* 18:48–54.

1988 Archaeology and Settlement Plan of the King Site. In *The King Site: Continuity and Contact in Sixteenth-Century Georgia,* edited by Robert Blakely, pp. 3–16. University of Georgia Press, Athens.

2004 Mortuary Patterns at a Sixteenth-Century Town in Northwestern Georgia. *Southeastern Archaeology* 23:166–177.

Hally, David J., and Hypatia Kelly

1998 The Nature of Mississippian Towns in Georgia: The King Site Example. In *Mississippian Towns and Sacred Spaces: Searching for an Architectural Grammar,* edited by R. Barry Lewis and Charles Stout, pp. 49–63. University of Alabama Press, Tuscaloosa.

Hally, David J., Marvin T. Smith, and James B. Langford, Jr.

1990 The Archaeological Reality of de Soto's Coosa. In *Columbian Consequences: Archaeological and Historical Perspectives on the Spanish Borderlands East,* vol. 2, edited by David H. Thomas, pp. 121–138. Smithsonian Institution, Washington D.C.

Hammerstedt, Scott W.

2005 Mississippian Status in Western Kentucky: Evidence from the Annis Mound. *Southeastern Archaeology* 24:11–27.

Harn, Alan D.

1971 *The Prehistory of Dickson Mounds: A Preliminary Report.* Illinois State Museum, Springfield.

Harold, Jeanne

1985 *An Analysis of House #II/78, the Incinerator Site (33-MY-57), Montgomery*

County, Ohio. M.A. thesis, Department of Anthropology, Kent State University, Kent, Ohio. University Microfilms, Ann Arbor, Michigan.

Harper, Brett

2000 New Perspectives on South Fort Village, a Late Prehistoric Site within the Fort Ancient State Memorial, Warren County, Ohio. In *Cultures Before Contact: The Late Prehistory of Ohio and Surrounding Regions,* edited by Robert A. Genheimer, pp. 330–366. Ohio Archaeological Council, Columbus.

Hart, John P.

1993 Monongahela Subsistence-Settlement Change: The Late Prehistoric Period in the Lower Upper Ohio River Valley. *Journal of World Prehistory* 7:71–120.

Hart, John P., and H. J. Brumbach

2003 The Death of Owasco. *American Antiquity* 68:737–752.

Hatch, J. W., and C. M. Stevenson

1980 A Functional Analysis of the Fisher Farm Features. In *The Fisher Farm Site,* edited by J. W. Hatch, pp. 140–170. Occasional Papers No. 12. Department of Anthropology, Pennsylvania State University, University Park.

Haviland, William A.

1988 Musical Hammocks at Tikal: Problems with Reconstructing Household Composition. In *Household and Community in the Mesoamerican Past,* edited by Richard R. Wilk and Wendy Ashmore, pp. 121–134. University of New Mexico Press, Albuquerque.

Haviland, William A., Harold E. L. Prins, Dana Walrath, and Bunny McBride

2005 *Cultural Anthropology: The Human Challenge.* 11th ed. Thomson Wadsworth, Belmont, California.

Hawkins, Rebecca A.

1998 Coming Full Circle: Plowzone Assemblages and the Interpretation of Fort Ancient Settlement Structure. In *Surface Archaeology,* edited by Alan P. Sullivan, pp. 91–109. University of New Mexico Press, Albuquerque.

Hayden, Brian

1995 Pathways to Power: Principles for Creating Socioeconomic Inequalities. In *Foundations of Social Inequality,* edited by T. Douglas Price and Gary M. Feinman, pp. 15–85. Plenum, New York.

Heilman, James M.

1988a Archaeological Methodology at 33My57. In *A History of 17 Years of Excavation and Reconstruction: A Chronicle of 12th Century Human Values and the Built Environment,* edited by James M. Heilman, Malinda C. Lileas, and Christopher A. Turnbow, pp. 55–62. Dayton Museum of Natural History, Dayton, Ohio.

1988b Ceramics as Indicators of Social Organization. In *A History of 17 Years of Excavation and Reconstruction: A Chronicle of 12th Century Human Values and the Built Environment,* edited by James M. Heilman, Malinda C. Lileas, and Christopher A. Turnbow, pp. 242–260. Dayton Museum of Natural History, Dayton, Ohio.

Heilman, James M., and Roger Hoefer

1981 Possible Astronomical Alignments in a Fort Ancient Settlement at the Incinerator Site in Dayton, Ohio. In *Archaeoastronomy in the Americas,* edited by Ray Williamson, pp. 157–171. Ballena Press, Menlo Park, California.

Helms, Mary W.

1988 *Ulysses' Sail: An Ethnographic Odyssey of Power, Knowledge, and Geographical Distance.* Princeton University Press, Princeton, New Jersey.

1993 *Craft and the Kingly Ideal: Art, Trade, and Power.* University of Texas Press, Austin.

Henderson, A. Gwynn

1992 Capitol View: An Early Madisonville Horizon Settlement in Franklin County, Kentucky. In *Current Archaeological Research in Kentucky,* vol. 2, edited by David Pollack and A. Gwynn Henderson, pp. 223–240. Kentucky Heritage Council, Frankfort.

1992 (editor) *Fort Ancient Cultural Dynamics in the Middle Ohio Valley.* Prehistory Press, Madison, Wisconsin.

1998 *Middle Fort Ancient Villages and Organizational Complexity in Kentucky.* Ph.D. dissertation, Department of Anthropology, University of Kentucky, Lexington. University Microfilms, Ann Arbor, Michigan.

Henderson, A. Gwynn, and David Pollack

2001 Fort Ancient. In *Encyclopedia of Prehistory,* vol. 6, edited by Peter N. Peregrine and Melvin Ember, pp. 174–194. Kluwer Academic/Plenum Publishers, New York.

Henderson, A. Gwynn, David Pollack, and Christopher A. Turnbow

1992 Chronology and Cultural Patterns. In *Fort Ancient Cultural Dynamics in the Middle Ohio Valley,* edited by A. Gwynn Henderson, pp. 253–279. Prehistory Press, Madison, Wisconsin.

Henderson, A. Gwynn, and Christopher A. Turnbow

1992 Previous Fort Ancient Chronologies. In *Fort Ancient Cultural Dynamics in the Middle Ohio Valley,* edited by A. Gwynn Henderson, pp. 9–18. Prehistory Press, Madison, Wisconsin.

Hendon, Julie A.

2000 Having and Holding: Storage, Memory, Knowledge, and Social Relations. *American Anthropologist* 102:42–53.

Hilgeman, Sheri L.

1991 Angel Negative Painted Design Structure. *Midcontinental Journal of Archaeology* 16:3–33.

2000 *Pottery and Chronology at Angel.* University of Alabama Press, Tuscaloosa.

Hill, James N.

1968 Broken K Pueblo: Patterns of Form and Function. In *New Perspectives in Archeology,* edited by Sally R. Binford and Lewis R. Binford, pp. 103–142. Aldine, Chicago.

Hollinger, R. Eric

2005 *Conflict and Culture Change in the Late Prehistoric and Early Historic American Midcontinent.* Ph.D. dissertation, Department of Anthropology, University of Illinois, Urbana-Champaign. University Microfilms, Ann Arbor, Michigan.

Holmes, William H.

1886 Ancient Pottery of the Mississippi Valley. In *Bureau of American Ethnology 4th Annual Report, 1882–83*, pp. 367–436. Government Printing Office, Washington, D.C.

1903 Aboriginal Pottery of the Eastern United States. *Bureau of American Ethnology Twentieth Annual Report No. 20*. Smithsonian Institution, Washington D.C.

Hudson, Charles

1976 *The Southeastern Indians.* University of Tennessee Press, Knoxville.

Johnson, Allen W., and Timothy K. Earle

2000 *The Evolution of Human Societies: From Foraging Group to Agrarian State.* 2nd. ed. Stanford University Press, Stanford, California.

Johnson, Gregory

1982 Organizational Structure and Scalar Stress. In *Theory and Explanation in Archaeology: The Southampton Conference,* edited by Colin Renfrew, Michael J. Rowlands, and Barbara A. Segraves, pp. 389–423. Academic Press, New York.

Keesing, Roger M.

1975 *Kin Groups and Social Structure.* Harcourt Brace Jovanovich, New York.

Kelly, John E.

1990a The Emergence of Mississippian Culture in the American Bottom. In *The Mississippian Emergence,* edited by Bruce D. Smith, pp. 113–152. Smithsonian Institution Press, Washington, D.C.

1990b Range Site Community Patterns and the Mississippian Emergence. In *The Mississippian Emergence,* edited by Bruce D. Smith, pp. 67–112. Smithsonian Institution Press, Washington, D.C.

Kelly, Robert L.

1989 Mobility/Sedentism: Concepts, Archaeological Measures, and Effects. *Annual Review of Anthropology* 21:43–66.

Knick, Steven G., III

1977 Paleopathological Evidence of Familial Relationships in a Prehistoric Population. Paper presented at the annual meeting of the American Association of Physical Anthropologists, Seattle, Washington.

Knight, Vernon J.

1986 The Institutional Organization of Mississippian Religion. *American Antiquity* 51:675–687.

1990 Social Organization and the Evolution of Hierarchy in Southeastern Chiefdoms. *Journal of Anthropological Research* 46:1–23.

1997 Some Developmental Parallels between Cahokia and Moundville. In *Cahokia: Domination and Ideology in the Mississippian World,* edited by Timothy R. Pauketat and Thomas E. Emerson, pp. 229–247. University of Nebraska Press, Lincoln.

2006 Moundville as a Diagrammatic Ceremonial Center. In *Archaeology of the Moundville Chiefdom,* edited by Vernon J. Knight and Vincas Steponaitis, pp. 44–62. Smithsonian Institution, Washington, D.C.

Kreinbrink, Jeanine, Thomas King, K. Huebchen, P. Hartman, S. Roberts, and Laura Clifford

1993 *Prehistoric Discoveries at the Driving Range Site 33Ha586, Newtown, Ohio.* Ohio Historic Preservation Office, Columbus.

Leach, Jerry W., and Edmond R. Leach (editors)

1983 *The Kula: New Perspectives on Massim Exchange.* Cambridge University Press, Cambridge.

Lewis, R. Barry, Charles Stout, and Cameron B. Wesson

1998 The Design of Mississippian Towns. In *Mississippian Towns and Sacred Spaces: Searching for an Architectural Grammar,* edited by R. Barry Lewis and Charles Stout, pp. 1–21. University of Alabama Press, Tuscaloosa.

Lewis, Thomas M. N., and Madeline Kneberg

1946 *Hiwassee Island: An Archaeological Account of Four Tennessee Indian Peoples.* University of Tennessee Press, Knoxville.

Lightfoot, Kent G., and Gary Feinman

1982 Social Differentiation and Leadership Development in Early Pithouse Villages in the Mogollon Region of the American Southwest. *American Antiquity* 47:64–86.

Lightfoot, Kent G., and Antoinette Martinez

1995 Frontiers and Boundaries in Archaeological Perspective. *Annual Review of Anthropology* 24:471–492.

Lightfoot, Kent G., Antoinette Martinez, and A. M. Schiff

1998 Daily Practice and Material Culture in Pluralistic Social Settings: An Archaeological Study of Culture Change and Persistence from Fort Ross, California. *American Antiquity* 63:199–222.

Lileas, Malinda C.

1988a Early Development of the Incinerator Site. In *A History of 17 Years of Excavation and Reconstruction: A Chronicle of 12th Century Human Values and the Built Environment,* edited by James M. Heilman, Malinda C. Lileas, and Christopher A. Turnbow, pp. 25–35. Dayton Museum of Natural History, Dayton, Ohio.

1988b History of the Dayton Museum of Natural History's Involvement with the Incinerator Site. In *A History of 17 Years of Excavation and Reconstruction: A Chronicle of 12th Century Human Values and the Built Environment,* edited by James M. Heilman, Malinda C. Lileas, and Christopher A. Turnbow, pp. 36–54. Dayton Museum of Natural History, Dayton, Ohio.

Linton, Ralph

1936 *The Study of Man.* Appleton-Century, New York.

Litfin, James C., Patricia C. Jackson, and Kent D. Vickery

1993 A Chronological Seriation Approach to Fort Ancient Triangular Arrowpoints in the Central Ohio Valley. Paper presented at the 58th Annual Meeting of the Society for American Archaeology. St. Louis, Missouri.

Longacre, William A.

1970 *Archaeology as Anthropology: A Case Study.* Anthropological Papers No. 17. University of Arizona Press, Tucson.

McIntosh, R. J.
1976 Square Huts in Round Concepts. *Archaeology* 29:92–101.
McKern, William C.
1939 The Midwestern Taxonomic Method as an Aid to Archaeological Culture Study. *American Antiquity* 4:301–313.
Marcus, Joyce, and Kent Flannery
1996 *Zapotec Civilization: How Urban Society Evolved in Mexico's Oaxaca Valley.* Thames and Hudson, New York.
Mayer-Oakes, William J.
1955 *Prehistory of the Upper Ohio Valley: An Introductory Archaeological Study.* Annals of Carnegie Museum Vol. 34. Anthropological Series No. 2. Carnegie Museum, Pittsburgh.
Mehrer, Mark W.
1995 *Cahokia's Countryside: Household Archaeology, Settlement Patterns, and Social Power.* Northern Illinois University Press, DeKalb.
Mehrer, Mark W., and James M. Collins
1995 Household Archaeology at Cahokia and in Its Hinterlands. In *Mississippian Communities and Households,* edited by J. Daniel Rogers and Bruce D. Smith, pp. 32–57. University of Alabama Press, Tuscaloosa.
Metz, Charles L.
1878 The Prehistoric Monuments of the Little Miami Valley. *Journal of the Cincinnati Society of Natural History* 1:119–128.
1881 The Prehistoric Monuments of Anderson Township, Hamilton County, Ohio. *Journal of the Cincinnati Society of Natural History* 4:293–305.
1885 Explorations in the "Hahn Field." Field notes on file, Harvard University Peabody Museum Collections Department, Accession File No. 86–46. Cambridge, Massachusetts.
Miller, Orloff
1997 *Phase III Mitigation Investigations at the Turpin Archaeological District, for Cinergy Corp State Route 32 Pipeline Project, Hamilton County, Ohio.* Prepared for Cinergy Corp. Ohio Historic Preservation Office, Columbus.
Mills, William C.
1904 Explorations of the Gartner Mound and Village Site. *Ohio State Archaeological and Historical Society, Publications* 13:128–189.
1906 Explorations of the Baum Prehistoric Village Site. *Ohio Archaeology and Historical Quarterly* 15:45–136.
Milner, George R.
1984 Social and Temporal Implications of Variation among American Bottom Mississippian Cemeteries. *American Antiquity* 49:468–488.
1998 *The Cahokia Chiefdom: The Archaeology of a Mississippian Society.* Smithsonian Institution Press, Washington, D.C.
Milner, George R., Thomas E. Emerson, Mark W. Mehrer, J. A. Williams, and Duane Esaray
1984 Mississippian and Oneota Period. In *American Bottom Archaeology,* edited by Charles J. Bareis and James W. Porter, pp. 158–186. University of Illinois Press, Urbana-Champaign.

Milner, George R., and Sissel Schroeder
1999 Mississippian Sociopolitical Systems. In *Great Towns and Regional Polities in the American Southwest and Southeast,* edited by Jill E. Neitzel, pp. 95–107. University of New Mexico Press, Albuquerque.

Mistovich, Timothy S.
1995 Toward an Explanation of Variation in Moundville Phase Households in the Black Warrior Valley, Alabama. In *Mississippian Communities and Households,* edited by J. Daniel Rogers and Bruce D. Smith, pp. 156–180. University of Alabama Press, Tuscaloosa.

Moorehead, William K.
1887 Graves at Fort Ancient. *American Antiquarian Oriental Journal* 9:293–300.
1890 *Fort Ancient, the Great Prehistoric Earthwork of Warren County, Ohio.* Robert Clarke, Cincinnati, Ohio.
1892 *Primitive Man in Ohio.* G.P. Putnam's Sons, New York.
1902 *The Field Diary of an Archaeological Collector.* Andover, Massachusetts (privately printed).
1908 *Fort Ancient, the Great Prehistoric Earthwork of Warren County, Ohio.* Phillips Academy, Andover, Massachusetts.

Morse, Daniel F., and Phyllis A. Morse
1983 *Archaeology of the Central Mississippi Valley.* Academic Press, New York.

Muller, Jon
1997 *Mississippian Political Economy.* Plenum Press, New York.

Muller, Jon, and Jeannette E. Stephens
1991 Mississippian Sociocultural Adaptations. In *Cahokia and the Hinterlands: Middle Mississippian Cultures of the Midwest,* edited by Thomas E. Emerson and R. Barry Lewis, pp. 297–310. University of Illinois Press, Urbana-Champaign.

Munson, Cheryl A. (editor)
1994 *Archaeological Investigations at the Southwind Site, a Mississippian Community in Posey County, Indiana.* Prepared for Indiana Department of Natural Resources, Division of Historic Preservation and Archaeology, Indianapolis.

Munson, Cheryl A., and Robert G. McCullough
2004 *Archaeological Investigations at the Prather Site, Clark County, Indiana: The 2003 Baseline Archaeological Survey.* Prepared for Indiana Department of Natural Resources, Division of Historic Preservation and Archaeology, Indianapolis, and the National Park Service, U.S. Department of Interior. Washington, D.C.

Nass, John P., Jr.
1987 *Use-Wear Analysis and Household Archaeology: A Study of the Activity Structure of the Incinerator Site, an Anderson Phase Fort Ancient Community in Southwestern Ohio.* Ph.D. dissertation, Department of Anthropology, Ohio State University, Columbus. University Microfilms, Ann Arbor, Michigan.
1989 Household Archaeology and Functional Analysis as Procedures for Studying Fort Ancient Communities in the Ohio Valley. *Pennsylvania Archaeologist* 59:1–13.

Nass, John P., Jr., and Richard W. Yerkes

1995 Social Differentiation in Mississippian and Fort Ancient Communities. In *Mississippian Communities and Households,* edited by J. Daniel Rogers and Bruce D. Smith, pp. 58–80. University of Alabama Press, Tuscaloosa.

Nickerson, W. B.

1885 Log Book of Archaeological Notes of Hamilton County, 1885. 2 vols. Manuscript on file, Cincinnati Historical Society.

Odell, George H.

2003 *Lithic Analysis.* Springer, New York.

Oehler, Charles

1973 *Turpin Indians: A Revised Report of the Findings of the Cincinnati Museum of Natural History's Archaeological Exploration of the Turpin Site, Hamilton County, Ohio 1946 to 1949.* Cincinnati Museum of Natural History Popular Publication Series No. 1. Cincinnati.

Oetelaar, Gerald A.

1993 Identifying Site Structure in the Archaeological Record: An Illinois Mississippian Example. *American Antiquity* 58:662–687.

Orton, Clive, Paul Tyers, and Alan Vince

1993 *Pottery in Archaeology.* Cambridge University Press, Cambridge.

O'Shea, John M.

1984 *Mortuary Variability: An Archaeological Investigation.* Academic Press, New York.

Pauketat, Timothy R., and Thomas E. Emerson

1991 The Ideology of Authority and the Power of the Pot. *American Anthropologist* 93:919–941.

1997 Introduction: Domination and Ideology in the Mississippian World. In *Cahokia: Domination and Ideology in the Mississippian World,* edited by Timothy R. Pauketat and Thomas E. Emerson, pp. 1–29. University of Nebraska Press, Lincoln.

Peebles, Christopher S.

1971 Moundville and Surrounding Sites: Some Structural Considerations of Mortuary Practices II. In *Approaches to the Social Dimensions of Mortuary Practices,* edited by James A. Brown, pp. 68–91. Memoirs of the Society for American Archaeology No. 25. Washington, D.C.

1978 Determinants of Settlement Size and Location in the Moundville Phase. In *Mississippian Settlement Patterns,* edited by Bruce D. Smith, pp. 369–416. Academic Press, New York.

Peebles, Christopher S., and Susan M. Kus

1977 Some Archaeological Correlates of Ranked Societies. *American Antiquity* 42:421–448.

Peregrine, Peter

1992 *Mississippian Evolution: A World-System Perspective.* Prehistory Press, Madison, Wisconsin.

Phillips, Philip and James A. Brown

1978 *Pre-Columbian Shell Engravings from the Craig Mound at Spiro, Oklahoma.*

Peabody Museum of Archaeology and Ethnology, Harvard University, Cambridge, Massachusetts.

Phillips, Philip, James A. Ford, and James B. Griffin

1951 *Archaeological Survey of the Lower Mississippi Valley.* Papers of the Peabody Museum of Archaeology and Ethnology No. 60. Harvard University, Cambridge, Massachusetts.

Pickard, William H.

1996 1990 Excavations at Capitolium Mound (33Wn13), Marietta, Washington County, Ohio: A Working Evaluation. In *A View from the Core: A Synthesis of Ohio Hopewell Archaeology,* edited by Paul J. Pacheco, pp. 274–285. Ohio Archaeological Council, Columbus.

Polhemus, Richard R.

1987 (editor) *The Toqua Site: A Late Mississippian Dallas Phase Town.* 2 vols. Report of Investigations 41. Department of Anthropology, University of Tennessee, Knoxville.

1990 Dallas Phase Architecture and Sociopolitical Structure. In *Lamar Archaeology: Mississippian Chiefdoms in the Deep South,* edited by Mark Williams and Gary Shapiro, pp. 125–138. University of Alabama Press, Tuscaloosa.

Pollack, David

2004 *Caborn-Welborn.* University of Alabama Press, Tuscaloosa.

Pollack, David, and A. Gwynn Henderson

1992 Toward a Model of Fort Ancient Society. In *Fort Ancient Cultural Dynamics in the Middle Ohio Valley,* edited by A. Gwynn Henderson, pp. 281–294. Prehistory Press, Madison, Wisconsin.

2000 Insights into Fort Ancient Culture Change: A View from South of the Ohio River. In *Cultures Before Contact: The Late Prehistory of Ohio and Surrounding Regions,* edited by Robert A. Genheimer, pp. 194–215. Ohio Archaeological Council, Columbus.

Pollack, David, A. Gwynn Henderson, and Christopher T. Begley

2002 Fort Ancient/Mississippian Interaction on the Northeastern Periphery. *Southeastern Archaeology* 21:206–220

Prufer, Olaf H., and Orrin C. Shane

1970 *Blain Village and the Fort Ancient Tradition in Ohio.* Kent State University Press, Kent, Ohio.

Purtill, Matthew P.

1999 Evidence for a Late Fort Ancient Fall/Winter Occupation in Southwestern Ohio. *North American Archaeologist* 20:105–133.

Putnam, Frederick W.

1886 Report of the Curator. In *Peabody Museum, 18th Annual Report.*

Railey, James A.

1992 Chipped Stone Artifacts. In *Fort Ancient Cultural Dynamics in the Middle Ohio Valley,* edited by. A. Gwynn Henderson, pp. 137–169. Prehistory Press, Madison, Wisconsin.

Redmond, Brian G., and Robert G. McCullough

2000 The Late Woodland to Late Prehistoric Occupations of Central Indiana. In

Late Woodland Societies: Tradition and Transformation across the Midcontinent, edited by Thomas E. Emerson, Dale L. McElrath, and Andrew C. Fortier, pp. 643–683. University of Nebraska Press, Lincoln.

Reidhead, Van A.

1976 *Optimization and Food Procurement at the Prehistoric Leonard Haag Site, Southeastern Indiana: A Linear Programming Approach.* Ph.D. dissertation, Department of Anthropology, Indiana University, Bloomington. University Microfilms, Ann Arbor, Michigan.

Reidhead, Van A., and William F. Limp

1974 The Haag Site (12D19): A Preliminary Report. *Indiana Archaeological Bulletin* 1:4–19.

Reimer, P. J., M. G. L. Baillie, E. Bard, A. Bayliss, J. W. Beck, C. Bertrand, P. G. Blackwell, C. E. Buck, G. Burr, K. B. Cutler, P. E. Damon, R. L. Edwards, R. G. Fairbanks, M. Friedrich, T. P. Guilderson, K. A. Hughen, B. Kromer, F. G. McCormac, S. Manning, C. Bronk Ramsey, R. W. Reimer, S. Remmele, J. R. Southon, M. Stuiver, S. Talamo, F. W. Taylor, J. van der Plicht, and C. E. Weyhenmeyer

2004 *Radiocarbon* 46:1029–1058.

Renfrew, Colin

1986 Introduction: Peer Polity Interaction and Socio-Political Change. In *Peer Polity Interaction and Socio-Political Change,* edited by Colin Renfrew and John F. Cherry, pp. 1–18. Cambridge University Press, Cambridge.

Rice, Prudence M.

1998 Contexts of Contact and Change: Peripheries, Frontiers, and Boundaries. In *Interaction, Culture Change, and Archaeology,* edited by John G. Cusick, pp. 44–66. Occasional Paper No. 25. Center for Archaeological Investigations, Southern Illinois University, Carbondale.

Riggs, Rodney E.

1977 *The Turpin Site Ft. Ancient Burial Mound and Surrounding Burial Pattern (33HA19): A Biological Comparison Using Non-metric Traits of the Cranial and Post-Cranial Skeleton.* M.A. thesis, Department of Anthropology, University of Cincinnati. University Microfilms, Ann Arbor, Michigan.

1986 New Stratigraphic Sequences from the Lower Little Miami Valley. *West Virginia Archaeologist* 38:1–21.

1998 *Ceramics, Chronology, and Cultural Change in the Lower Little Miami River Valley, Southwestern Ohio, circa 100 B.C. to circa A.D. 1650.* Ph.D. dissertation, Department of Anthropology, University of Wisconsin, Madison. University Microfilms, Ann Arbor, Michigan.

Riordan, Robert

2000 Peas in a Pod? Diversity at Small Late Prehistoric Components in Southwest Ohio. In *Cultures Before Contact: The Late Prehistory of Ohio and Surrounding Regions,* edited by Robert A. Genheimer, pp. 404–424. Ohio Archaeological Council, Columbus.

Robertson, James A.

1980 Chipped Stone and Socio-Cultural Interpretations. Unpublished M.A. thesis, Department of Anthropology, University of Illinois, Chicago.

1984 Chipped Stone and Functional Interpretations: A Fort Ancient Example. *Midcontinental Journal of Archaeology* 9:251–267.

Rogers, J. Daniel

1995 The Archaeological Analysis of Domestic Organization. In *Mississippian Communities and Households,* edited by J. Daniel Rogers and Bruce D. Smith, pp. 7–31. University of Alabama Press, Tuscaloosa.

Rothschild, Nan A.

1979 Mortuary Behavior and Social Organization at Indian Knoll and Dickson Mounds. *American Antiquity* 44:658–675.

Sahlins, Marshall D.

1968 *Tribesmen.* Prentice-Hall, Englewood Cliffs, New Jersey.

Sanders, William T.

1956 The Central Mexican Symbiotic Region: A Study in Prehistoric Settlement Patterns. In *Prehistoric Settlement Patterns in the New World,* edited by Gordon R. Willey, pp. 115–127. Viking Fund Publications in Anthropology No. 23. New York.

Saxe, Arthur A.

1970 Social Dimensions of Mortuary Practices. Unpublished Ph.D. dissertation, Department of Anthropology, University of Michigan, Ann Arbor.

Schiffer, Michael B.

1987 *Formation Processes of the Archaeological Record.* University of New Mexico Press, Albuquerque.

Schortman, Edward M., and Patricia A. Urban

1987 Modeling Interregional Interaction in Prehistory. *Advances in Archaeological Method and Theory* 11:37–95.

1998 Culture Contact Structure and Process. In *Interaction, Culture Change, and Archaeology,* edited by John G. Cusick, pp. 102–125. Occasional Paper No. 25. Center for Archaeological Investigations, Southern Illinois University, Carbondale.

Schroeder, Sissel

2004 Current Research on Late Precontact Societies of the Midcontinental United States. *Journal of Archaeological Research* 12:311–372.

Schroedl, Gerald F.

1980 Structures and Village Patterns at the Historic Overhill Cherokee Towns of Chota and Tanasee. Paper presented at the annual meeting of the Society for American Archaeology, New Orleans.

1998 Mississippian Towns in the Eastern Tennessee Valley. In *Mississippian Towns and Sacred Spaces: Searching for an Architectural Grammar,* edited by R. Barry Lewis and Charles Stout, pp. 64–92. University of Alabama Press, Tuscaloosa.

Schurr, Mark R., and Margaret J. Schoeninger

1995 Associations between Agricultural Intensification and Social Complexity: An Example from the Prehistoric Ohio Valley. *Journal of Anthropological Archaeology* 14:315–339.

Scott, Gary T., and Richard R. Polhemus

1987 Mortuary Patterning. In *The Toqua Site: A Late Mississippian Dallas Phase*

Town, edited by Richard R. Polhemus, pp. 378–432. Report of Investigations 41. University of Tennessee, Knoxville, Department of Anthropology and Publications in Anthropology 44. Tennessee Valley Authority.

Seeman, Mark F., and William S. Dancey

2000 The Late Woodland Period in Southern Ohio: Basic Issues and Prospects. In *Late Woodland Societies: Tradition and Transformation across the Midcontinent,* edited by Thomas E. Emerson, Dale L. McElrath, and Andrew C. Fortier, pp. 583–611. University of Nebraska Press, Lincoln.

Service, Elman R.

1962 *Primitive Social Organization: An Evolutionary Perspective.* Random House, New York.

1975 *Origins of the State and Civilization: The Process of Cultural Evolution.* Norton, New York.

Shane, Orrin C.

1988 An Interim Summary Report of the Vertebrate Faunal Remains from the Incinerator Site. In *A History of 17 Years of Excavation and Reconstruction: A Chronicle of 12th Century Human Values and the Built Environment,* edited by James M. Heilman, Malinda C. Lileas, and Christopher A. Turnbow, pp. 157–213. Dayton Museum of Natural History, Dayton, Ohio.

Shane, Orrin C., and Gail E. Wagner

1993 Seasonality and Diet at a Fort Ancient Site. Paper presented at the annual meeting of the Society for Ethnobiology, Boston.

Sharp, William E., and Christopher A. Turnbow

1987 The Muir Site: An Upland Fort Ancient Community in the Inner Bluegrass Region of Kentucky. In *Current Archaeological Research in Kentucky,* vol.1, edited by David Pollack, pp. 137–153. Kentucky Heritage Council, Frankfort.

Shennan, Stephen

1988 *Quantifying Archaeology.* Academic Press, San Diego.

Shepherd, Mimi

1992 The Allman Collection: Pottery Analysis. Manuscript on file, Boonshoft Museum of Discovery, Department of Anthropology, Dayton, Ohio.

Shetrone, Henry C.

1926 The Campbell Island Village Site and the Hine Mound and Village Site. In *Certain Mounds and Village Sites in Ohio,* edited by W. C. Mills, pp.437–467. F. J. Heer, Columbus, Ohio.

1930 Field Work in Ohio during 1929. *American Anthropologist* 32:366–367.

Siegel, Peter E.

1982 *A Feature Analysis of a Late Woodland Bluff-Top Encampment Located in the Central Mississippi Valley.* M.A. thesis, Department of Anthropology, State University of New York, Binghampton. University Microfilms, Ann Arbor, Michigan.

Smith, Bruce D.

1978 Variation in Mississippian Settlement Patterns. In *Mississippian Settlement Patterns,* edited by Bruce D. Smith, pp. 479–503. Academic Press, New York.

1984 Mississippian Expansion: Tracking the Historical Development of an Explanatory Model. *Southeastern Archaeology* 3:13–32.

1985 Mississippian Patterns of Settlement and Subsistence. In *Alabama and the Borderlands: From Prehistory to Statehood,* edited by Reid R. Badger and Lawrence A. Clayton, pp. 40–63. University of Alabama Press, Tuscaloosa.

1986 A Comparison of the Exploitation of Animal Species by Middle Mississippi and Fort Ancient Groups. *Southeastern Archaeological Conference Newsletter* 28:19–22.

1992 Mississippian Elites and Solar Alignments: A Reflection of Managerial Necessity, or Levers of Social Inequality? In *Lords of the Southeast: Social Inequality and the Native Elites of Southeastern North America,* edited by Alex W. Barker and Timothy R. Pauketat, pp. 11–30. Archeological Papers of the American Anthropological Association No. 3. Washington, D.C.

Smith, Charles

n.d. Field notes on file, Anthropology Department, Dayton Society of Natural History, Dayton, Ohio.

Smith, Harlan I.

1910 The Prehistoric Ethnology of a Kentucky Site. *American Museum of Natural History, Anthropological Papers* No. 6, Part 2.

Smith, Marvin T.

2000 *Coosa: The Rise and Fall of a Southeastern Mississippian Chiefdom.* University Press of Florida, Gainesville.

Speck, Frank G.

1931 *A Study of the Delaware Indian Big House Ceremony,* vol. 2. Publications of the Pennsylvania Historical Commission. Harrisburg.

Spencer, Charles S.

1997 Evolutionary Approaches in Archaeology. *Journal of Archaeological Research* 5:209–264.

Stanislawski, Michael B.

1978 If Pots Were Mortal. In *Explorations in Ethnoarchaeology,* edited by R. A. Gould, pp. 201–227. University of New Mexico Press, Albuquerque.

Starr, S. Frederick

1960 The Archaeology of Hamilton County, Ohio. *Journal of the Cincinnati Museum of Natural History* 23:1–130.

Stein, Gil J.

2002 From Passive Periphery to Active Agents: Emerging Perspectives in the Archaeology of Interregional Interaction. *American Anthropologist* 104:903–916.

Steponaitis, Vincas

1983 *Ceramics, Chronology, and Community Patterns: An Archaeological Study at Moundville.* Academic Press, New York.

Stuckey, Ronald L.

1981 Origin and Development of the Concept of the Prairie Peninsula. In *The Prairie Peninsula: In the "Shadow" of Transeau,* edited by Ronald L. Stuckey and Karen J. Reese, pp. 4–23. Ohio Biological Survey Biological Notes No. 15. Columbus.

Sullivan, Lynne P.

1987 The Mouse Creek Phase Household. *Southeastern Archaeology* 6:16–29.

1995 Mississippian Household and Community Organization in Eastern Tennessee. In *Mississippian Communities and Households,* edited by J. Daniel Rogers and Bruce D. Smith, pp. 99–123. University of Alabama Press, Tuscaloosa.

Tixier, Jacques

1963 *Typologie de l'epipaleolithique du Maghreb.* Mémoires du Centre de Recherches Anthropologiques Prehistoriques et Ethnographiques II. Paris.

Tourtellot, Gary

1988 Developmental Cycles of Households and Houses at Seibal. In *Household and Community in the Mesoamerican Past,* edited by Richard R. Wilk and Wendy Ashmore, pp. 97–120. University of New Mexico Press, Albuquerque.

Transeau, Edgar N.

1935 The Prairie Peninsula. *Ecology* 16:423–437.

Turnbow, Christopher A.

1989 Radiocarbon Determinations of the SunWatch Site (33My57), Montgomery County, Ohio. Manuscript on file, Department of Anthropology, Boonshoft Museum of Discovery, Dayton, Ohio.

Turnbow, Christopher A., and A. Gwynn Henderson

1992 Ceramic Analysis. In *Fort Ancient Cultural Dynamics in the Middle Ohio Valley,* edited by A. Gwynn Henderson, pp. 113–135. Prehistory Press, Madison, Wisconsin.

Turnbow, Christopher A., and Cynthia E. Jobe

1984 The Goolman Site: A Late Fort Ancient Winter Encampment in Clark County, Kentucky. In *Late Prehistoric Research in Kentucky,* edited by David Pollack, Charles D. Hockensmith, and Thomas N. Sanders, pp. 25–48. Kentucky Heritage Council, Frankfort.

Turnbow, Christopher A., Cynthia E. Jobe, Nancy O'Malley, Dee Ann Wymer, Michelle Seme, and Irvin Rovner

1983 *Archaeological Investigations of the Goolman, Devary, and Stone Sites in Clark County, Kentucky.* Archaeological Report No. 78. Department of Anthropology, University of Kentucky, Lexington.

Upham, Steadman

1990 Decoupling the Process of Political Evolution. In *The Evolution of Political Systems: Sociopolitics in Small-Scale Sedentary Societies,* edited by Steadman Upham, pp. 1–17. Cambridge University Press, Cambridge.

Varner, John, and Jeannette Varner (translators and editors)

1951 *The Florida of the Inca,* by Garcilaso de la Vega. University of Texas Press, Austin.

Vickery, Kent D., Theodore S. Sunderhaus, and Robert A. Genheimer

2000 Preliminary Report on Excavations at the Fort Ancient State Line Site, 33 Ha 58, in the Central Ohio Valley. In *Cultures Before Contact: The Late Prehistory of Ohio and Surrounding Regions,* edited by Robert A. Genheimer, pp. 272–328. Ohio Archaeological Council, Columbus.

Wagner, Gail E.

1979 Wood in a 1200 A.D. Stockaded Village. Paper presented at the annual meeting of the Society for Economic Botany, Raleigh, North Carolina.

1996 Feast or Famine? Seasonal Diet at a Fort Ancient Community. In *Case Studies in Environmental Archaeology,* edited by Elizabeth J. Reitz, Lee A. Newsom, and Sylvia J. Scudder, pp. 319–337. Plenum Press, New York.

Ward, Trawick

1965 Correlation of Mississippian Sites and Soil Types. *Southeastern Archaeological Conference Bulletin* 3:42–48.

Warrick, Gary A.

1988 Estimating Ontario Iroquoian Village Duration. *Man in the Northeast* 36:21–60.

Webb, Paul A. (editor)

1992 *The Petitt Site (11-Ax-253), Alexander County, Illinois.* Research Papers No. 8. Southern Illinois University at Carbondale, Center for Archaeological Investigations.

Wesson, Cameron B.

1999 Chiefly Power and Food Storage in Southeastern North America. *World Archaeology* 31:145–164.

Wilk, Richard, and Robert Netting

1984 Households: Changing Form and Function. In *Households: Comparative and Historical Studies of the Domestic Group,* edited by Robert Netting, Richard Wilk, and Eric Arnould, pp. 1–28. University of California Press, Berkeley.

Winter, Marcus C.

1976 The Archaeological Household Cluster in the Valley of Oaxaca. In *The Early Mesoamerican Village,* edited by Kent V. Flannery, pp. 25–30. Academic Press, New York.

Witthoft, John

1949 *Green Corn Ceremonialism in the Eastern Woodlands.* Occasional Contributions from the Museum of Anthropology of the University of Michigan No. 13. Ann Arbor.

Wittry, Warren L.

1969 The American Woodhenge. In *Cahokia Archaeology,* edited by M. L. Fowler, pp. 43–48. Illinois Archaeological Survey Bulletin No. 7. University of Illinois, Urbana.

Wobst, H. Martin

1977 Stylistic Behavior and Information Exchange. In *For the Director: Research Essays in Honor of James B. Griffin,* edited by Charles E. Cleland, pp. 317–342. Anthropological Papers No. 61. Museum of Anthropology, University of Michigan, Ann Arbor.

Wolforth, Thomas J., and Cheryl A. Munson.

1994 Solar Alignments and Mississippian Construction. In *Archaeological Investigations at the Southwind Site, a Mississippian Community in Posey County, Indiana,* edited by Cheryl A. Munson, Chapter 16. Prepared for Indiana

Department of Natural Resources, Division of Historic Preservation and Archaeology, Indianapolis.

Wright, Henry T.

1984 Prestate Political Formation. In *On the Evolution of Complex Societies: Essays in Honor of Harry Hoijer,* edited by Timothy Earle, pp. 41–77. Undena, Malibu, California.

Yoffee, Norman

1993 Too Many Chiefs? (or, Safe Texts for the '90s). In *Archaeological Theory,* edited by Norman Yoffee and Andrew Sherratt, pp. 60–78. Cambridge University Press, Cambridge.

2005 *Myths of the Archaic State: Evolution of the Earliest Cities, States, and Civilizations.* Cambridge University Press, Cambridge.

Zeder, Melinda, and Susan Arter

1996 Meat Consumption and Bone Use in a Mississippian Village. In *Case Studies in Environmental Archaeology,* edited by Elizabeth J. Reitz, Lee A. Newsom, and Sylvia J. Scudder, pp. 319–337. Plenum Press, New York.

Index

Page numbers in italics refer to illustrations